Commercial Banking

Commercial Banking

Editor

Christopher Gan

MDPI • Basel • Beijing • Wuhan • Barcelona • Belgrade • Manchester • Tokyo • Cluj • Tianjin

Editor
Christopher Gan
Lincoln University
New Zealand

Editorial Office
MDPI
St. Alban-Anlage 66
4052 Basel, Switzerland

This is a reprint of articles from the Special Issue published online in the open access journal *Journal of Risk and Financial Management* (ISSN 1911-8074) (available at: https://www.mdpi.com/journal/jrfm/special_issues/commercial_banking).

For citation purposes, cite each article independently as indicated on the article page online and as indicated below:

LastName, A.A.; LastName, B.B.; LastName, C.C. Article Title. *Journal Name* **Year**, *Volume Number*, Page Range.

ISBN 978-3-0365-0940-2 (Hbk)
ISBN 978-3-0365-0941-9 (PDF)

© 2021 by the authors. Articles in this book are Open Access and distributed under the Creative Commons Attribution (CC BY) license, which allows users to download, copy and build upon published articles, as long as the author and publisher are properly credited, which ensures maximum dissemination and a wider impact of our publications.

The book as a whole is distributed by MDPI under the terms and conditions of the Creative Commons license CC BY-NC-ND.

Contents

About the Editor vii

Christopher Gan
Editorial for the Special Issue on Commercial Banking
Reprinted from: *Journal of Risk and Financial Management* **2020**, *13*, 111, doi:10.3390/jrfm13060111   1

Sichong Chen, Muhammad Imran Nazir, Shujahat Haider Hashmi and Ruqia Shaikh
Bank Competition, Foreign Bank Entry, and Risk-Taking Behavior: Cross Country Evidence
Reprinted from: *Journal of Risk and Financial Management* **2019**, *12*, 106, doi:10.3390/jrfm12030106   3

Seksak Jumreornvong, Chanakarn Chakreyavanich, Sirimon Treepongkaruna and Pornsit Jiraporn
Capital Adequacy, Deposit Insurance, and the Effect of Their Interaction on Bank Risk
Reprinted from: *Journal of Risk and Financial Management* **2018**, *11*, 79, doi:10.3390/jrfm11040079 .   29

Zhiheng Li, Shuangzhe Liu, Fanda Meng and Milind Sathye
Competition in the Indian Banking Sector: A Panel Data Approach
Reprinted from: *Journal of Risk and Financial Management* **2019**, *12*, 136, doi:10.3390/jrfm12030136   47

Zhenni Yang, Christopher Gan and Zhaohua Li
Role of Bank Regulation on Bank Performance: Evidence from Asia-Pacific Commercial Banks
Reprinted from: *Journal of Risk and Financial Management* **2019**, *12*, 131, doi:10.3390/jrfm12030131   63

Khanh Ngoc Nguyen
Revenue Diversification, Risk and Bank Performance of Vietnamese Commercial Banks
Reprinted from: *Journal of Risk and Financial Management* **2019**, *12*, 138, doi:10.3390/jrfm12030138   89

Quang T. T. Nguyen, Son T. B. Nguyen and Quang V. Nguyen
Can Higher Capital Discipline Bank Risk: Evidence from a Meta-Analysis
Reprinted from: *Journal of Risk and Financial Management* **2019**, *12*, 134, doi:10.3390/jrfm12030134   **111**

About the Editor

Christopher Gan is a Professor in Accounting and Finance in the Faculty of Agribusiness and Commerce, Lincoln University, New Zealand. He is recognized internationally for research leadership in banking, microfinance, stock markets and Asian financial economics. His approach is quantitative in nature, with an applied focus. He aims to expand the existing knowledge and develop recommendations for relevant agencies, government and businesses. He actively collaborates with academics from other universities (particularly from Asia) and inspires the next young generation of scholars through postgraduate supervision. He has an extensive publication record (with numerous students as co-authors) in well-ranked peer reviewed journals and is regularly cited by other researchers. In 2017, he instigated and currently leads the Lincoln University—Yunus Social Business Centre. The objectives of the Yunus Social Business Centre are to build awareness of social business, undertake training and education, provide mentoring, and support research on social business. It is the first Yunus Social Business Centre in New Zealand.

Editorial

Editorial for the Special Issue on Commercial Banking

Christopher Gan

Department of Financial and Business System, Faculty of Agribusiness and Commerce, P.O. Box 85084, Lincoln University, Lincoln 7647, Christchurch, New Zealand; Christopher.Gan@lincoln.ac.nz

Received: 27 May 2020; Accepted: 28 May 2020; Published: 1 June 2020

Abstract: The existence of financial intermediaries is arguably an artifact of information asymmetry. Beyond simple financial transactions, financial intermediation provides a mechanism for information transmission, which can reduce the degree of information asymmetry and consequently increase market efficiency. During the process of information transmission, the bank is able to provide unique services in the production and exchange of information. Therefore, banks have comparative advantages in information production, transmission, and utilisation. In credit provision, it is possible for lenders to make Type I and Type II errors. These types of errors are associated with whether banks decide to lend money to borrowers with low repayment capacity or risk missing out on potentially profitable lending. However, the recent US subprime loan crisis and previous financial crises (such as the Mexican, Argentinian, Chilean and Asian financial crises) show it is possible that banks can make both good and bad lending decisions. Does this mean that banks have lost their comparative advantages in leveraging information asymmetry? This Special Issue includes contribution in empirical methods in banking such risk and bank performance, capital regulation, bank competition and foreign bank entry, bank regulation on bank performance, and capital adequacy and deposit insurance.

Keywords: banks; risks; capital

The Special Issue in Commercial Banking has been successfully published in the *Journal of Risk and Financial Management* (JRFM). The Special Issue welcomes contribution in empirical methods in banking such as bank loans announcement, credit constraints, capital regulation and bank behaviour, bank regulation on bank performance, corporate governance in banking, maturity transformation risk in banking and bank's merger and acquisition.

With this in mind, the Special Issue features six papers that address several exciting topics of interest to our readers. The lead paper by Nguyen (2019) explore the relationship between revenue diversification, risk and bank performance using data from audited financial statements and annual reports of 26 commercial banks listed and unlisted in Vietnam during the period 2010–2018. Using the Generalized Method of Moment modeling techniques, the author's result shows that diversification negatively impacts profitability and the higher the diversification, the higher the risk of commercial banks.

Nguyen et al. (2019) investigate the effect of capital on bank risk employing a meta-analysis approach based on a wide range of empirical papers from 1990 to 2018. Their result shows negative effect of bank capital on bank risk, which implies the discipline role of bank capital, is more likely to be reported. However, the reported results are suffered from the publication bias due to the preference for significant estimates and favored results.

Using panel data for the period from 2005–2018, Li et al. (2019) evaluate the level of competition in the Indian banking sector overall as well as within the three groups of banks: foreign owned, state owned (public sector), and privately owned. They found that the overall competition in the Indian banking sector is strong, although there are differences by type of bank ownership. The Indian banking market continues to be characterized by monopolistic competition. The various policy measures taken by the Indian government in recent years appear to have helped boost competition. A policy suggestion would be to further liberalize the banking sector for foreign investment

Using the double bootstrap data envelopment analysis, Yang et al. (2019) measure bank efficiency and examine the relationship between regulation, supervision, and state ownership in commercial banks in the Asia-Pacific region for the period 2005 to 2014. Their results indicate that excluding off-balance sheet activities in efficiency estimations lead to underestimating of the pure technical efficiency, while overestimating the scale efficiency of banks in the Asia-Pacific region. Their bootstrap regression results suggest that bank regulation and supervision are positively related to bank technical efficiency, while state ownership is not significantly related to bank efficiency.

Chen et al. (2019) examine the interactive role of bank competition and foreign bank entry in explaining the risk-taking of banks over the globe. Using the pooled regression model and Two-stage Least Squares model (2SLS with Generalized Method of Moments GMM), they document that foreign bank entry decreases the risk-taking behavior of the banks to a certain level and exhibits an inverted U-shaped relation with financial stability. Furthermore, the joint effect of bank competition and foreign bank entry brings financial fragility because host banks tend to make risky investments due to undue competition induced by foreign bank entry. Their result supports the competition–fragility hypothesis when foreign bank entry goes beyond a certain threshold.

Finally, Jumreornvong et al. (2018) investigate how deposit insurance and capital adequacy affect bank risk for five developed and nine emerging markets over the period of 1992–2015. Although full coverage of deposit insurance induces moral hazard by banks, deposit insurance is still an effective tool, especially during the time of crisis. On the contrary, capital adequacy by itself does not effectively perform the monitoring role and leads to the asset substitution problem. Implementing the safety nets of both deposit insurance and capital adequacy together could be a sustainable financial architecture. An immediate-effect analysis reveals that the interplay between deposit insurance and capital adequacy is indispensable for banking system stability.

I hope you are delighted with the content of this Special Issue. *JRFM* is committed to providing you with stimulating and dynamic papers in future issues. I invite readers to suggest "themes" for special issues in *JRFM* future issues. We want *JRFM* to reflect your research interests and needs.

Funding: This research received no external funding.

Conflicts of Interest: The author declares no conflict of interest.

References

Chen, Sichong, Muhammad Imran Nazir, Shujahat Haider Hashmi, and Ruqia Shaikh. 2019. Bank Competition, Foreign Bank Entry, and Risk-Taking Behavior: Cross Country Evidence. *Journal of Risk and Financial Management* 12: 106. [CrossRef]

Jumreornvong, Seksak, Chanakarn Chakreyavanich, Sirimon Treepongkaruna, and Pornsit Jiraporn. 2018. Capital Adequacy, Deposit Insurance, and the Effect of Their Interaction on Bank Risk. *Journal of Risk and Financial Management* 11: 79. [CrossRef]

Li, Zhiheng, Shuangzhe Liu, Fanda Meng, and Milind Sathye. 2019. Competition in the Indian Banking Sector: A Panel Data Approach. *Journal of Risk and Financial Management* 12: 136. [CrossRef]

Nguyen, Khanh Ngoc. 2019. Revenue Diversification, Risk and Bank Performance of Vietnamese Commercial Banks. *Journal of Risk and Financial Management* 12: 138. [CrossRef]

Nguyen, Quang T. T., Son T. B. Nguyen, and Quang V. Nguyen. 2019. Can Higher Capital Discipline Bank Risk: Evidence from a Meta-Analysis. *Journal of Risk and Financial Management* 12: 134. [CrossRef]

Yang, Zhenni, Christopher Gan, and Zhaohua Li. 2019. Role of Bank Regulation on Bank Performance: Evidence from Asia-Pacific Commercial Banks. *Journal of Risk and Financial Management* 12: 131. [CrossRef]

© 2020 by the author. Licensee MDPI, Basel, Switzerland. This article is an open access article distributed under the terms and conditions of the Creative Commons Attribution (CC BY) license (http://creativecommons.org/licenses/by/4.0/).

Article

Bank Competition, Foreign Bank Entry, and Risk-Taking Behavior: Cross Country Evidence

Sichong Chen [1], Muhammad Imran Nazir [1,*], Shujahat Haider Hashmi [2] and Ruqia Shaikh [3]

[1] School of Finance, Zhongnan University of Economics and Law, Wuhan 430073, China
[2] School of Economics, Huazhong University of Science and Technology, Wuhan 430073, China
[3] School of Accounting, Zhongnan University of Economics and Law, Wuhan 430073, China
* Correspondence: imran.n13@outlook.com; Tel.: +86-13125195995

Received: 14 May 2019; Accepted: 14 June 2019; Published: 26 June 2019

Abstract: This unique study examines the interactive role of bank competition and foreign bank entry in explaining the risk-taking of banks over the globe. We used cross-country data for the banking sector from 2000 to 2016. Using the pooled regression model and Two-stage Least Squares model (2SLS with Generalized Method of Moments GMM), we document that foreign bank entry decreases the risk-taking behavior of the banks to a certain level and exhibits an inverted U-shaped relation with financial stability. Furthermore, the joint effect of bank competition and foreign bank entry brings financial fragility because host banks tend to make risky investments due to undue competition induced by foreign bank entry. We support the competition–fragility hypothesis when foreign bank entry goes beyond a certain threshold. Our results also suggest that restrictions on bank activities and capital regulation stringency reduce the level of the risk factor. We also applied various robustness tests, which further confirm our mainstream results. Our findings have policy implications for foreign investors and regulatory authorities.

Keywords: foreign bank entry; bank competition; H-statistics; pooled regression; dynamic panel models; risk-taking behavior

JEL Classification: D4; G21; C23; L1; E44

---

1. Introduction

International banks operate in foreign economies through local conglomerates and cross-border lending. They offer opportunities to stimulate economic growth as they bring in capital, proficiency, liquidity, and new innovative technologies, which can encourage higher competition and improved distribution of resources (Fischer 2015). International banks also have a role of risk sharing, which suggests that they help host economies stabilize their credit supply through an economic slump and that they shift funds back to the home economy when the circumstances gets worse. The role of risk sharing can also render domestic economies to greater instability from time to time, and as a result of the global financial crisis (GFC), researchers and policymakers have articulated concerns that credit policies pursued by lending economies can have adverse spillovers on emerging economies' position of financial stability (Rey 2013). With the formulation and implementation of financial liberalization and deregulation policies, different emerging economies have undergone substantial reforms in their banking sector since the 1990s, considered by the higher existence of foreign banks.

The transfer of bank capital across the border raises interesting questions about the central role played by foreign banks; particularly, permitting participation would introduce higher financial stability into the domestic banking market. The answer to this vital question is not only crucial for policymakers to better understand the benefits of financial globalization but also ensures better policy implications for regulatory authorities to maximize their rewards from the opening of their banking sector (Wu et al. 2017). Nowadays, the leading holding companies are organizations whose operations are distributed across the globe. Generally, such types of banks are headquartered in one of the leading developed economies, but they have extensive networks of branches by which they work abroad. The accomplishments of cross-border banking groups can generate trade-offs between benefits, with greater efficiency by better diversification and costs connected with financial instability. International diversification is also an indication of country-wise risks in a bank's portfolio (Fang et al. 2014).

The existence of foreign banks might be beneficial for the host countries' financial market in different ways. Firstly, foreign banks' entry tends to lessen the cost of financial intermediation and enhance its quality. Secondly, it enhances access to different financial services for firms and households. Thirdly, it increases the economic and financial performance of borrowers. All of these benefits result from an increase in the competition, technology, product innovation, and speeding up of internal restructuring (Kraft 2004). Foreign banks might have greater access to capital from abroad; they have more stable funding sources and patterns of lending than other banks. They also hold a geographically differentiated credit portfolio and would not be as affected during periods of pressure in domestic financial markets. Additionally, the international banks that are differentiated might easily captivate shocks occurring in domestic banking markets and might have a more stable source of funds. The extent of these benefits, therefore, depends on the features of the domestic market and the foreign banks themselves. In some situations, the benefits are enormous, whereas, in others, there are only marginal benefits (Polovina and Peasnell 2015).

The globalization in the banking industry has brought an incredible increase in foreign investment, generally due to a reduction in entry barriers and the lesser cost of financial intermediation. The positive effects of foreign investment include human resource development through improved higher education (Baskaran and Muchie 2008; East Asian Bureau of Economic Research, and China Center for International Economic Exchanges 2016), higher remunerations in the industry (Vijaya and Kaltani 2015), and stronger corporate governance practices accruing to better performance and financial stability (Spong and Sullivan 2007; Kim et al. 2010; Peng 2017). Foreign banks' entry in the banking industry across the globe is usually related to better performance and financial stability in the banking industry. The foreign banks' existence is supposed to increase the relative cost benefit in terms of production and the processing of information (Okuda and Rungsomboon 2006; Saif-Alyousfi et al. 2017). The positive association between financial stability and the existence of foreign banks in the banking industry is observed from more or less the level of the competitive environment (Yeyati and Micco 2007; Jeon et al. 2011). The banking sector serves as the primary channel by which financial fragility might be transferred to the other sectors in the economy by distracting the interbank lending market, by decreasing the credit availability, and by providing a better payment mechanism. The fear is that an increased level of bank competition might add to the financial system's fragility, which may cause regulators to concentrate on the strategic policies that preserve financial stability in the financial sector. Foreign banks' entry also brings advantage at the macro-economic level, particularly in enhancing profitability and also financial stability. Moreover, the existence of foreign banks heightens the growth rate and also the GDP of the host economies due to the new innovative plans and proficient distribution of resources (Shen et al. 2009; Wu et al. 2012; Ukaegbu and Oino 2014).

We used a balanced panel of 95 cross countries (developed and developing) over the period from 2000 to 2016 to examine the interactive role of bank competition and foreign banks entry on the risk-taking behavior across countries (Appendix B). We used different indicators to measure the risk-taking behavior (Z-score and non-performing loans to gross loans (NPG) ratio) and also the role of bank competition measured by H-statistics, which is a nonstructural element derived from the model (Bikker et al. 2012). Applying the pooled regression and two-stage least squares (2SLS) with generalized methods of moments (GMM) and using property rights and financial freedom as the instrumental variables, this study reveals that foreign banks' entry mitigates risk-taking behavior to a certain level and exhibits a bell-shaped relation with financial stability. The results also indicates that the interactive effect of the level of competition and foreign banks' entry deteriorates the financial stability of the banking sector across the globe. Our robustness tests further confirms these findings. Our results also suggest that some measures of bank regulations, such as restriction on bank activities and capital regulation stringency, reduces the level of the risk factor and enhances financial stability.

This study adds to the existing literature from different perspectives. Firstly, this is one of only a few cross-country studies that emphasizes banking sectors, in which the banking industries serve as the vital source of lending due to undeveloped financial markets. Secondly, to the best of our knowledge, this is the first study that investigates not only the interactive role of foreign bank entry and competition but also analyzes the inverted U-shaped effect of foreign banks' entry on risk-taking behavior. Thirdly, the sample of this study covers a period that comprehends the game-changing experience of the 2008 to 2009 global financial recession. Whereas the previous empirical studies have recognized the lending behavior of multinational financial institutions during the financial crisis, the existing literature emphasizes the effect of foreign banks' entry on domestic banks' performance and cost efficiency (De Haas and Van Lelyveld 2014; Dekle and Lee 2015). However, our research accounts for risk-taking behavior (Z-score), which is the inverse proxy for a banks' probability of failure. The higher value of the Z-score implies the lower level of risk and greater financial stability across the globe. Fourthly, we also included the NPG ratio as an alternative measure of financial stability and to check the robustness of results. By emphasizing the different behavior of banking sectors under different economic situations, we provide new evidence on the ongoing discussions concerning the risk-taking aspects of globalization of the bank industry. This study provides valuable insight into the ambiguous relationship between foreign banks' entry and risk-taking behavior by considering the interactive effect with bank competition, which has not been taken into account in previous studies. Finally, our analysis advances the empirical literature by applying the pooled regression model and dynamic panel estimation method to a wide range of economies as well as 2SLS with GMM estimations, which gives more rigorous handling for potential endogeneity problems.

The remainder of this paper is organized as follows: Section 2 explains the literature review related to bank completion, foreign banks' entry, and risk-taking behavior. Section 3 explains the data set, model specification, and econometric strategy. Section 4 describes the pooled regression, 2SLS estimation results, and robustness results, and Section 5 gives the conclusion and policy recommendations.

2. Literature Review

It is well recognized that foreign investors are inclined to be dynamically involved in monitoring and disciplining imbedded managers in emerging financial markets to overcome their informational disadvantage. Some studies propose a positive association between foreign ownership and domestic banks' operational efficiency. Levine (1997) summarized the advantage of the existence of foreign banks, including stimulation of the progress of a bank supervisory and legal structure, increased country's access to the international capital, adoption of new banking skills and technologies, and upgrading of the quality and availability of financial services. They also found that foreign banks' entry is beneficial to the operations of domestic banks (Claessens et al. 2001; Unite and Sullivan 2003; Ukaegbu and Oino 2014). Choi and Hasan (2005) also explained that the level of foreign banks' entry has a positive influence on the bank's risk and return.

Most empirical work has focused on aspects, such as the bank's operational cost, spread of net interest, level of the bank's profit, and credit growth (Claessens et al. 2001; Haber 2004; Gormley 2010; Claessens and Van Horen 2011, 2015). Claessens and Van Horen (2011) found that increased foreign banks' entry is related to the lesser profitability and higher overhead costs of the domestic banks. Gormley (2010) revealed the market-wide increase in the volume of bank loans of the host banks after the entry of foreign banks. Therefore, the extent and nature of the foreign banks' entry influence the other bank's risk-taking behavior, but the moderating role of bank competition has not been examined. Some empirical studies suggest that foreign banks' entry might reduce the local banks' risk factor and enhance financial stability by stimulating a spillover of new innovative ideas and better expertise from foreign banks to local banks, encouraging local banks to invest in new technology as well as human capital and enhance their proficiency in the long run (Edison et al. 2002; Lensink and Hermes 2004; Hassan et al. 2012; Kouretas and Tsoumas 2016).

The traditional theory reveals that the entry of foreign bank strengthens the level of competition in the banking industry, which enhances the allocative and productive proficiency of the hosts' banking industry (Vives 2011). There are also various challenging forces that might offset the beneficial influence of foreign banks' entry and expand the risk-taking behavior of local banks to disturb financial stability. Local banks might be undesirably affected by the shift of clients after the foreign banks' entry. On the one side, the entry of foreign banks might concentrate their credit and other services on well-informed customers, depriving the domestic banks of this market position and leaving only opaque organizations (Sengupta 2007; Ukaegbu and Oino 2014). Beck et al. (2018) argued that foreign banks' entry affects the availability of credit for small or opaque organizations. They suggest that larger firms may get benefits from the existence of a foreign bank(s), but small firms are not affected. On the other side, investors might transfer their savings out of domestic banks into foreign banks due to the better service quality and international status, causing the domestic banks to incur more costs to attract more traditional investors or alternative investors with different sources of funding. The consistently higher overheads of liabilities may lead the domestic banks to raise their lending costs, which might cause an adverse selection problem (Kleymenova et al. 2016). Therefore, domestic banks' fragility might escalate with the presence of foreign banks. This effect is perhaps more insightful in less developed economies, due to the limited flexibility of the domestic banks to amend their portfolio and diversify the risk factor, than banks in developed economies (Saleh 2015).

Competition might increase as foreign banks establish their business in domestic banking markets. The traditional theory reveals that a higher value of the franchise would limit the incentive to take undue risk (Claessens and Laeven 2004; Jeon et al. 2011). Therefore, if the entry of a foreign bank is related to higher competition levels, it can raise the franchise value due to the lower profitability, thus reducing the banking risk (Jiménez et al. 2013; Claessens and Van Horen 2014). Thus, the relationship between the franchise value and banks' risk-taking behavior needs to be further examined. The high franchise value permits banks to borrow more, and then higher leverage might offset the lesser incentive of risk-taking. The competition–stability view proposes that the level of competition might strengthen financial stability since more penetrating competition would lower the interest rate and lessen the borrower's default probability. If this effect offsets the competition–fragility influence, ceteris paribus, then domestic banks are expected to be related to greater financial stability when there is an increase in foreign bank(s) entry (Boyd and De Nicolo 2005). Claessens and Laeven (2004) applied the H-statistics model of banking sectors, based on the reduced-form revenue equation, and reported that entry is more competitive in banking sectors with a more significant presence of foreign bank(s). However, they explain that the lesser limitations on foreign bank(s) entry and fewer constraints on banking activities enhanced the level of competition. However, Yeyati and Micco (2007) proposed that the entry of a foreign bank would decrease the level of banking competition, along with a positive relationship between the foreign bank(s) entry and financial stability.

The competition–fragility hypothesis explains that higher level of competition between banks leads to an increased fragility. This point of view is also known as the 'charter value' view of the financial market, theoretically modelled by (Marcus 1984; Chan et al. 1986; Keeley 1990; Beck 2008). They comprehend banks when managing the risk of a portfolio. Beck (2008) revealed that banks have more incentives to take excessive risks in a more competitive environment, where there is more pressure on profits. Hence, the result is more fragile.

Furthermore, banks receive less information from their borrowers in a higher competitive environment, which decreases their incentives to monitor the borrowers. Vives (2011) explained that higher competition decreases financial stability through intensification of the coordination problem of investors and raising the incentives to take more risk and raise failure probabilities. In order to recover from financial fatalities, financial firms are more likely to finance riskier projects. Therefore, risk-taking behavior will weaken the financial stability of financial firms (Keeley 1990; Allen and Gale 2005).

Domestic banks might follow their foreign competitors in offering new innovative ideas and services to protect their market shares, which might enhance their overhead expenses and lead to higher risks if foreign banks own advantages on all of these services. Foreign banks' entry might constrain domestic banks to raise investment in high-end technologies and also employee training. Therefore, increased expenditure is transferred to higher overheads expenses, but the benefits take some time to emerge. Subsequent losses are likely to occur, at least in the short run. Although, the supply of new services, together with the training of employees and investment on new technology, might raise a domestic bank's efficiency and support their financial stability in the long run (Sufian and Habibullah 2010; Xu 2011). The existing empirical literature gives very limited empirical results on the interactive role of bank competition and foreign banks' entry on risk-taking behavior across the globe. Unite and Sullivan (2003) and Modén et al. (2008) found that the increase of foreign bank entries leads to an increase in the loan loss provision by domestic banks, whereas this relationship has not been observed in another study (Claessens et al. 2001). Degryse et al. (2012) observed that the entry of foreign banks undermines the trustworthiness of domestic banks. Therefore, Agoraki et al. (2011) and Bessler and Kurmann (2014) explained the mixed results, stating that the increased foreign bank presence is related with either a low or high risk factor, which ultimately influences the financial stability across the banking sector. However, the limited evidence has motivated this research to fill the gap in the empirical literature by examining the interactive role of bank competition and foreign bank entry on risk-taking behavior across the globe.

3. Data and Methodology

The objective of our research was to examine the effect of foreign bank entry on risk-taking behavior with the moderating role of bank competition across countries. The research sample was the banking industry in a cross-country analysis of 95 countries (developed and developing) from 2000 to 2016. To classify the countries, we used the categories of the World Bank classification. Data about the risk-taking indicators, foreign bank entry, bank-specific variables, industry-specific variables, and macro-economic variables were taken from the Global Financial Development Database, International Monetary fund, World Development Indicators, and Bank Focus. Finally, the period of the analysis, 2000–2016, revealed the data availability of some of the explanatory variables. Appendix A explains all the names of the countries that were used in this research.

The number of foreign bank assets has increased over time, which is also shown in Figure 1. All of these movements exhibit that the relative importance of foreign banks has increased extensively, from an average of 30.62% in 2000 to 40.69% in 2016. Figure 2 shows the indicators of financial stability; the first one is the Z-score and the other one is the NPG ratio. A higher value of the Z-score indicates a lower level of risk and improved financial stability. Both of the graphs show that the global financial crisis (GFC) episode played a crucial role in financial stability across the globe.

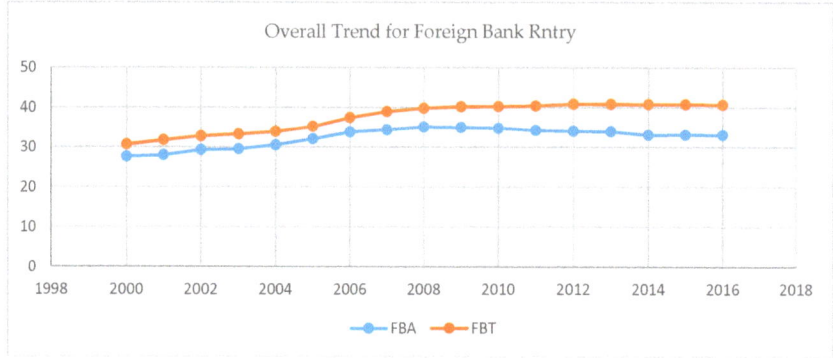

Figure 1. Overall trend of foreign bank entry across the globe. From 2000 to 2016, the banking system in different countries experienced essential transformations. The number of foreign banks and their assets has increased with time, which is also shown in Figures 1 and 2. All of these different trends mean that the relative importance of the foreign banks increased extensively, from some foreign banks of an average of 30.62% in 2000 to 40.69% in 2016 (Figure 2): Source: Author's calculation, World Bank Global Financial development database.

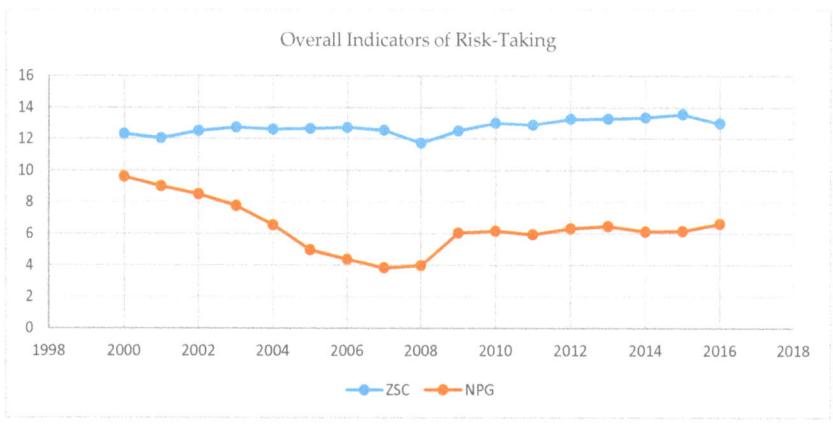

Figure 2. Overall level of financial stability across the globe. Across the globe the banking system is different experienced from 2000 to 2016. Both of the indicators are the risk-taking behavior (Z-score and non-performing loans to gross loans) Source: Author's calculation, World Bank, (GFDD).

3.1. Explanation of Variables

3.1.1. Measuring Foreign Bank Entry

We have measured foreign bank entry in two different ways. The first measure of foreign bank entry was related to the number of banks. For each host country, we determined the number of foreign-owned banks and divided this by the total number of banks in a particular country. The second measure of foreign bank entry was based on the bank's assets. For each host country, we determined the sum of foreign assets of foreign-owned banks and divided this by the total amount of bank assets in a country. These two measures are usually acknowledged as useful measures of foreign bank entry (Jeon et al. 2011; Molyneux et al. 2013; Yin et al. 2015).

3.1.2. Measuring Risk-Taking Behavior

We employed two different proxies to measure the risk-taking behavior across countries. These measures also indicates the stability position of the banks. The first one was the Z-score, which revealed the probability of banks' insolvency risk based on the amount of cushion the bank has to guard against the shocks to earnings. This Z-score was calculated as $Z = ((ROA + E/A)/\sigma (ROA))$, where the ROA is the return on the assets, E/A is the equity to asset ratio, and σ (ROA) is a measure of the standard deviation of the rate of return. A higher score indicates that the banks incur less risk and are more stable due to its inverse relationship with the probability of a bank's insolvency [48]. The second proxy was the NPL ratio (the ratio of non-performing loans to gross loans) to measure the banking risk. This risk is banking risk, and it results in an increased proportion of non-performing loans in the portfolio of the bank loan. The higher ratio shows a bank's greater inclination to keep a riskier loan portfolio, which also affects the bank's financial position (Allen et al. 2014; Luo et al. 2016; Baselga-Pascual et al. 2018).

3.1.3. Measuring the Bank Competition

To measure the bank competition, we used the H-statistics model, which is based on the econometric methodology of (Panzar and Rosse 1987). The Panzar and Rosse model is the first method issued on the new theory of industrial organization applied to the banks. This model attained the measurements of market power, as well the different competition conditions in the financial sector, by reviewing the influence of variations in the production elements prices over the revenues. This approach is based on the fact that the different banks employ different strategies based upon the prices, in response to variations in the input price of the market structure in which they function. This technique examines the transmission of changes in the input prices to bank revenue. It is generally used as a measure of competition, which is based on the new industrial organization empirical literature and based on the available bank-level data designating the level of bank competition. Additionally, it offers a quantitative assessment of the competitive condition of the market under market equilibrium and this technique has been applied by a number of empirical studies (Claessens and Laeven 2004; Yeyati and Micco 2007; Bikker et al. 2012; Apergis et al. 2016). The explanation of this model (H-statistics) is also very clear, which takes a value from $-\infty$ to $+1$, where a higher value of this model indicates greater competition in the financial market and vice versa. The method of Moch (2013) was followed in measuring the Panzar–Rosse H-statistics for each year, by the following reduced-form revenue equation, as indicated in Equation (1):

$$LnTRE_i = \alpha_0 + \beta_1 LnP_{1i} + \beta_2 LnP_{2i} + \beta_3 LnP_{3i} + \delta_1 LnY1_i + \delta_2 LnY2_i + \delta_3 LnY3_i + \varepsilon_i. \quad (1)$$

The dependent variable (TRE) is the total revenue over the total assets. According to the intermediation approach, we assumed that the banks use three different inputs, which are (I) deposits, (II) labor, and (III) capital. LnP_1 is the average cost of funds, LnP_2 is the average cost of labor, and LnP_3 is the average cost of capital. All of these input prices are followed by the explanatory variables, which reveal differences in the structure of cost, size, and risk. In the above equation, the right-hand side is a set of bank-specific variables that replicate differences in capitalization (Y1), liquidity (Y2), and product mix (Y3), and were used to allow for bank heterogeneity. All of these variables are the ratio of equity to total assets, the ratio of loans to total assets, and the ratio of other income to total assets, respectively, and these ratios are also expected to affect the bank revenue function form. The Panzar–Rosse H-statistics model is based on the reduced form revenue equation, by available bank-level data, variables to examine the market power for the product of price setting. The H-statistics is measured as a sum of the elasticity's of a bank's total revenue and input prices (intermediation approach), measured as $HSC = \beta_1 + \beta_2 + \beta_3$. A higher value shows that changes in inputs' prices increase revenue and market competition. In the situation of perfect competition, this value is equal to one; that is, the proportionate increase in the input price and total revenue is the same. In the monopoly condition, this value is zero or negative, which shows that an increase in input prices lowers the total bank revenue. In the monopolistic competition environment, the value of H-statistics is between zero and one. The following regression equation was used to examine whether the Panzar–Rose H statistics fulfilled the long-term equilibrium condition, as the presence of a disequilibrium condition might undermine the value of the H-statistic (Bikker and Haaf 2002; Moch 2013):

$$Ln(1 + ROA_i) = \alpha_0 + \beta_1 LnP_{1i} + \beta_2 LnP_{2i} + \beta_3 LnP_{3i} + \delta_1 LnY1_i + \delta_2 LnY2_i + \delta_3 LnY3_i + \varepsilon_i, \qquad (2)$$

where ROA is the bank's return on assets, in the condition of long-term equilibrium, $\beta_1 + \beta_2 + \beta_3 = 0$; it implies that input prices do not influence the banks' return on assets.

3.1.4. Control Variable

This study also employed different control variables that we drew from the empirical literature on bank competition, foreign bank entry, and the behavior of risk-taking (Beck et al. 2006; Agoraki et al. 2011; Karolyi and Taboada 2015). These control variables consisted of bank-specific variables, industry-specific variables, and macroeconomic variables. This study also considered country level governance and development, which have been shown to influence the risk-taking position across the globe. In terms of the bank-specific control variables, we used the five-bank concentration level (BC5) as a proxy for the big five banks in terms of the total assets and bank deposit to GDP ratio (BDG) to capture the effect of deposits and return on assets to capture the profitability of the banks (Houston et al. 2012; Karolyi and Taboada 2015).

In terms of the country level controls, we employed both industry level and macro-economic variables. The governance index is the average of six governance elements: Control of corruption, political stability, regulatory quality, voice and accountability, government effectiveness, and the rule of law. The value ranges from −2.5 to +2.5, with a higher value showing a greater governance index of a particular country, which also influences the financial stability. Additionally, to capture the extent of financial intermediation and stock market development, we employed the ratio of claims on the private sector to GDP for financial development (PCD) and the ratio of stock market capitalization to the GDP. Furthermore, to capture the effect of the stock market return, we employed the annual growth rate of the stock market index. As for macroeconomic variables, we employed the GDP growth rate as a proxy for deviations in economic activity and the inflation rate (INF) as a proxy for monetary instability, as inflation could influence risk-taking behavior. We also employed the current account and savings account to GDP (%) to examine the overall financial position of a particular county (Beck et al. 2006; Agoraki et al. 2011; Karolyi and Taboada 2015).

Moreover, there are other regulation factors in the regulatory and supervisory environments in each country that may affect risk-taking behavior. We used four banking regulation indices from the World Bank Database on "Bank Regulation and Supervision" (Barth et al. 2001, 2013). These bank regulations are explained in Appendix A. Restrictions on bank activities explain the extent to which banks face regulatory limitations on their activities. A higher score suggests that more regulations are placed on the scope of a banks' business operations; the index of capital regulatory stringency indicates more stringent regulation on banks of overall capital; the supervisory power index reveals the extent to which the country's supervisory agency has the influential authority to undertake actions and enhance the stability position; and the private monitoring index shows the degree to which banks are mandatorily required to release authentic information to the public (Karolyi and Taboada 2015).

3.2. Empirical Methodology

To examine the relationship between bank competition, foreign bank entry, and banking risk behavior across countries, two main concerns were considered before selecting a suitable econometric strategy. The first was the probable persistence of risk-taking behavior (Agoraki et al. 2011). The second as the potential endogeneity of risk-taking behavior (stability position) with foreign banks' entry and bank-specific and other variables (Delis et al. 2012). Therefore, because of these two reasons, we employed pooled regression models and dynamic panel models using the 2SLS approach with robust standard errors. Generally, we provided estimations of the general dynamic regression model:

$$Risk_{ijt} = \alpha_0 + \alpha_1 FORE_{it} + \alpha_2 COMP_{it} + \alpha_3 BANK_{it} + \alpha_4 BREG_{it} + \alpha_5 INDUSTRY_{it} + \alpha_6 MACRO_{it} + v_{it} + u_{it}. \quad (3)$$

In the above equation, RISK denotes the risk-taking behavior for bank i, in the j country at time t. It measures the Z-score and also checks the robustness of the alternative proxy, which is the NPL (ratio of non-performing loans to total loans). FORE denotes the foreign bank entry, which measures the two different proxies (foreign bank assets to total assets and the number of foreign banks to the total banks in a particular country). COMP shows the level of bank competition. It measures the Panzar–Rosse H-statistics model. The BREG shows different bank regulations, which also influences risk-taking behavior and enhances the stability position across the globe. BANK, INDUSTRY, and MACRO show the vectors of bank-specific (bank concentration, bank deposits, and return on assets), industry-specific (financial development, stock market development, governance index, stock market return), and macro-specific control variables (GDP growth, inflation, current and saving account to GDP%). The level of bank competition might also influence risk-taking behavior in the increased number of foreign banks over the period (Simpasa 2013; Wu et al. 2017). Therefore, we extended our dynamic model by including an interactive term of the foreign bank entry and level of competition using the above equation. This allowed us to examine the role of the level of competition in influencing the financial stability in the presence of foreign banks' entry for a cross country environment:

$$RISK_{ijt} = \alpha_0 + \alpha_1 FORE_{it} + \alpha_2 COMP_{it} + \alpha_3 COMP_{it} * FORE_{it} + \alpha_3 BANK_{it} + \alpha_4 BREG_{it} + \alpha_4 INDUSTRY_{it} + \alpha_5 MACRO_{it} + v_{it} + u_{it}. \quad (4)$$

In the above model, the dependent and independent variables are the same as those used for Equation (3), except the interaction term of competition and foreign bank entry ($COMP_{it} * FORE_{it}$), and were used to examine the interactive role of competition and foreign bank entry on risk-taking behavior across the globe.

3.3. Empirical Results and Discussion

The objective of this study was to understand the influence of foreign bank entry on banking risk behavior and also the moderating effect of bank competition across the globe. Table 1 shows the results of the descriptive statistics of the variables, which shows the level of bank competition, foreign bank entry, and country-specific data to understand the situation of bank characteristics and macro-economic conditions across the globe. Generally, the Z-score shows a bank's distance from insolvency. It means that a higher value of the Z-score implies greater financial stability. The average Z-score of all the banks was 12.67, and the standard deviation was 7.93. The Z-scores ranged between 1.11 and 39.34. These values show that the banks are, on average, financially stable. The average value of the non-performing loans to the gross loans was 6.37, with a standard deviation of 6.28. Berger et al. (2009) revealed that high capitalization might be used as a risk management plan to reduce credit risk and insolvency risk. Concerning foreign bank entry in terms of a total bank's assets, the average value of FBA was 32.47, and its standard deviation as 32.04, explaining a substantial heterogeneity for the existence of foreign banks across the globe. Regarding the number of foreign banks, FBT was found to be comparatively less diverse; the mean value was 37.53 and the standard deviation was 26.43. The average value of foreign bank entry in our sample was mainly influenced by some countries that own a large number of local banks but have a comparatively modest existence of foreign contestants. Concerning the competition level as measured by the Panzar–Rosse H-statistics (HSC), the average value was 0.5126, and its standards deviation was 0.2241, which ranged from 0.0200 to 0.9700. It explains the average monopolistic competition in the banking market across the countries.

Table 2 exhibits the correlation matrix between the main variables. The correlation between the Z-score and foreign bank entry measures was negative and statistically significant. It shows that the financial position of the banks is more stable in the existence of foreign bank's entry due to the risk factor being mitigated. The bank-specific variables and the other variables were not highly correlated with each other, showing that there is no problem of multicollinearity between the variables. Generally, foreign banks consider host countries' economic conditions as options to seize more of the market share, by a different set of available opportunities; the correlation between the existence of foreign banks and the GDP growth rate was found to be negative (Althammer and Haselmann 2011).

Table 1. Descriptive statistics.

Variable	Mean	Std. Dev.	Min	Max
ZSC	12.6755	7.9352	1.1100	39.3400
NPG	6.3728	6.2866	0.2500	31.0000
FBA	32.4731	32.0450	0.0000	99.0000
FBT	37.5362	26.4338	0.0000	95.0000
HSC	0.5126	0.2241	0.0200	0.9700
RBA	6.9853	1.7157	2.7000	12.0000
CRE	5.8194	1.2939	2.8300	9.0000
SPI	10.7864	2.0395	5.9800	14.0000
PMO	7.9398	1.2995	3.7700	11.0000
BC5	78.5313	16.1920	36.2700	100.0000
BDG	61.9320	51.6542	8.9300	331.3700
SMR	10.0817	26.6708	−44.1500	111.3400
ROA	1.1897	1.2278	−3.4800	5.4400
SMC	53.7691	57.7825	0.3300	356.5500
LGDP	25.4310	1.8285	20.9856	30.0289
LINF	4.4664	0.2756	3.4729	4.9822
LGPC	9.1812	1.3389	6.1317	11.4467
WGI	0.3468	0.8578	−1.1667	1.8667
CAG	−0.5778	9.0118	−26.2470	31.0675
GSG	23.7314	10.0284	4.0477	56.2200
PCD	60.0325	40.1317	6.6940	169.5500

Note: Std. Dev is the standard deviation; Min and Max shows the minimum and maximum value of all variables, respectively; ZSC shows a bank's Z-score; NPG is the ratio of non-performing loans to total gross loans; FBA is the foreign bank assets to total bank assets; FBT is the total number of foreign banks to total banks; RBA is the restriction on bank activities; CRE is the capital regulation; SPI is the supervisory power index; PMO is the private monitoring; BC5 is the five-bank asset concentration; BDG is the bank deposit to GDP (%); SMR is the stock market return; ROA is the return on assets; SMC shows the stock market capitalization to GDP (%); GDP is the log of GDP; LINF is the log of consumer price index; WGI denotes the world governance index; CAG is the current account (% of GDP); GSG shows the gross saving (% of GDP); and PCD is the private credit to GDP.

Table 2. Correlation matrix.

Variables	ZSC	NPG	FBA	FBT	HSC	RBA	CRE	SPI	PMO	BC5	BDG	SMR	ROA	SMC	LGDP	LINF	WGI	CAG	GSG	PCD
ZSC	1																			
NPG	-0.1338 *	1																		
FBA	-0.1251 *	-0.0279	1																	
FBT	-0.0719 *	-0.014	0.7816 *	1																
HSC	-0.0425 *	-0.0760 *	0.0192	0.0168	1															
RBA	-0.0549 *	0.1802 *	-0.1500 *	-0.1951 *	0.0473 *	1														
CRE	0.1219 *	0.1310 *	-0.1929 *	-0.1245 *	0.0699 *	0.0725 *	1													
SPI	0.0155	0.012	-0.0146	0.0317	0.0083	0.3493 *	0.2811 *	1												
PMO	0.2885 *	-0.0795 *	-0.2294 *	-0.1711 *	-0.0894 *	-0.1270 *	-0.0883 *	0.1487 *	1											
BC5	0.0979 *	-0.1319 *	0.0237	0.0139	-0.0650 *	-0.2564 *	-0.0885 *	-0.1671 *	0.1349 *	1										
BDG	0.2405 *	-0.1215 *	-0.0216	0.0821 *	0.0093	-0.2681 *	0.0588 *	0.047 *	0.1849 *	-0.0333	1									
SMR	-0.0335	-0.0757 *	-0.0106	-0.0416	0.0531 *	0.0735 *	0.0041	0.0461 *	-0.0311	-0.0417	-0.1288 *	1								
ROA	0.1335 *	-0.1958 *	0.1146 *	0.0729 *	-0.1437 *	0.0879 *	-0.0664 *	0.0266	-0.0897 *	0.001	-0.2408 *	0.2427 *	1							
SMC	0.2541 *	-0.3215 *	-0.1312 *	-0.0462 *	-0.029	-0.3175 *	0.0698 *	-0.0619 *	0.3392 *	0.1416 *	0.5548 *	-0.012	-0.0753 *	1						
LGDP	0.0478 *	-0.2061 *	-0.3754 *	-0.3293 *	0.2481 *	0.041 *	0.1220 *	0.0890 *	0.2441 *	-0.3012 *	0.1542 *	-0.0483 *	-0.2536 *	0.2898 *	1					
LINF	0.1188 *	-0.2457 *	0.0569 *	0.1358 *	0.1607 *	-0.0934 *	-0.0096	-0.025	0.1091 *	-0.0455 *	0.2474 *	-0.1603 *	-0.1545 *	0.1550 *	0.2814 *	1				
WGI	0.0567 *	-0.3374 *	0.0158	0.0144	0.1101 *	-0.3796 *	0.0115	0.1293 *	0.2303 *	0.2616 *	0.4823 *	-0.1263 *	-0.2538 *	0.4476 *	0.2839 *	0.2129 *	1			
CAG	0.0953 *	-0.0564 *	-0.2438 *	-0.2347 *	0.0514 *	-0.0207	0.015 *	0.0948 *	0.1506 *	0.1330 *	0.0703 *	0.0624 *	0.0028	0.3160 *	0.2112 *	-0.0269	0.0954 *	1		
GSG	0.1401 *	-0.1394 *	-0.2954 *	-0.2586 *	-0.028	0.0147	0.0654 *	0.1408 *	0.1712 *	0.1284 *	0.0122	0.0678 *	0.0577 *	0.2700 *	0.1916 *	0.0384	-0.0162	0.6302 *	1	
PCD	0.0781 *	-0.1694 *	-0.2460 *	-0.1443 *	0.0549 *	-0.2490 *	0.0524 *	-0.0750 *	0.2603 *	0.1661 *	0.6224 *	-0.1854 *	-0.3627 *	0.5025 *	0.3599 *	0.3195 *	0.6990 *	0.0687 *	0.0254	1

Note: ***, **, and * shows the coefficients are significant at the 1%, 5%, and 10% level of significance, respectively.

Tables 3 and 4 report the estimation results for different empirical models. Each model uses different dependent and independent variables, i.e., the NPG ratio and Z-score, respectively, and also different indicators of foreign bank entry, namely the FBA and FBT. A negative relationship was found between the foreign bank entry and the indicators of risk-taking in all the models. The first indicator of the foreign bank entry was the FBT; the results showed that a one unit increase in the entry of foreign banks decreases the risk factor by −0.0730 and −0.3010, and also enhances the stability position across the globe. The coefficient of HSC (bank competition) on the NPG ratio was negative and significant, and it was positive and significant on the Z-score. The result also denoted that the competition level (HSC) decreased bank risk in all models. It means that a higher level of bank competition means more lending opportunities, decreasing the profits, eroding the market power, and resulting in a deterioration of excessive bank risk-taking. These results are in line with the empirical work of previous studies (Berger et al. 2009; Rokhim and Susanto 2013). Therefore, a higher Z-score reflects the financial stability to a certain level and lesser risk-taking. It means that in general, the higher existence of foreign banks leads to the riskiness of domestic banks. The level of bank competition plays a vital role between the relation of foreign banks' entry and financial stability. The entry of foreign banks enhances the financial stability position and mitigates the risk factor. These results propose that an increased level of bank competition is compassionate for the financial stability across the globe, which is also consistent with the work of Boyd and De Nicolo (2005).

Tables 5 and 6 shows the result regarding the interactive role of bank competition and the foreign bank entry term, it had positive influence on financial stability; it means that this relationship enhances the risk factor and deteriorates the stability position. The results show that the level of competition is related to the riskier loans portfolios. The results are consistent across the different proxies of foreign bank entry and the interactive term for the foreign bank entry and level of competition (Wu et al. 2017). Our main argument is that even the market power in banking results in riskier loan portfolios. The Z-score is an inverse indicator for such overall risk. The higher value of the Z-score might come from either the higher earnings or more capital, and designates more financial stability, whereas higher inconsistency in earnings lowers the value of the Z-score and then increases the overall bank risk, which ultimately reduces the stability position across the globe. The results also lend support to the competition–fragility view that an increase in the level of competition is likely to reduce the franchise value of firms and encourage banks to increase their overall risk experience, which also influences the stability position. When financial institutions admire a higher franchise value that is derived from their level of competition, they are likely to command higher lending rates, thereby enhancing the riskiness of their loan portfolios (Boyd and De Nicolo 2005). Our results indicate that the interactive role of bank competition and foreign bank entry increases risk behavior and fragility. An excessive level of foreign bank entry in a less controlled environment brings more financial fragility to the local banking industry. Therefore, some researchers predict that a less competitive and more concentrated financial environment brings more stability because the higher level of profits provide a cushion against fragility and mitigate excessive risk taking behavior (Marcus 1984; Chan et al. 1986; Keeley 1990). On the other hand, when an excessive level of foreign bank entry stimulates the competitive environment of the banking industry, local banks are forced to take excessive risk and invest in risky asset portfolios due to the reduced level of profit and incentives (Beck 2008). Moreover, excessive competition induced by foreign bank entry pressures the local banks to reduce their incentives of proper loan screening, leading to a higher risk of fragility, as happened during the financial crisis of 2007 to 2008 (Šević 2002; Allen and Gale 2005; Boot and Greenbaum 2010). Thus, these models suggest that an excessive level of foreign bank entry, as occurred in the USA in the 1970s and 1980s and other developing countries, due to deregulation and a less restrictive environment may cause more fragility (Beck et al. 2005). The competition–fragility view is also further confirmed by our robustness tests, which identified an inverted U-shaped relation between foreign bank entry and financial stability. Our findings indicate that foreign bank entry initially improves the financial stability, but after a certain threshold, the entry induces fragility in the banking sector due to the excessive level of risk-taking behavior (Beck 2008).

We also found some impressive results about the stability position (banking risk) for other control variables. The coefficient of the five-bank asset concentration was negative and significant, which means that the big five bank asset ratio is also helpful for the stability position. The bank deposit to GDP (%) was positively related to the financial stability of the banks, and the results were statistically significant when using the alternative proxy for the robustness. The country-level governance index measures also exert a negative and significant effect on (Z-score) financial stability. Financial institutions located in countries where the authorities are accountable to investors enjoy a more level stability and also a mitigated risk factor. The return on assets was found to have a positive and significant effect on the (Z-score) financial stability. It also implies that a more concentrated system also influences the risk level. It suggests that a more concentrated system is inappropriate for banking systems across the globe. This concentrated system means that the banking industry only relies on some large banks. If there is a default case in one of the central banks, the whole system would have substantial effects. Moreover, the coefficient of the GDP growth rate was positive and significant in all the models, suggesting that less risk is incurred by banks when the economy is booming, and also the relationship with inflation was significant but negative. The results show the risk-taking channel of monetary policy; banks undertake more risk when banks adopt an expansionary monetary policy. These findings are consistent with the previous work of Anginer and Demirguc-Kunt (2014) and Wu et al. (2017).

Table 3. Bank competition, foreign bank entry, and bank risk-taking behavior (Z-Score).

Variables	Model 1	Model 2	Model 3	Model 4	Model 5	Model 6
FBT	−0.0073 ***	0.0049 ***	0.0311 ***			
	(0.0015)	(0.0018)	(0.0095)			
FBA				−0.0085 ***	−0.0003	−0.0343 ***
				(0.0012)	(0.0015)	(0.0072)
HSC	−0.3470 **	0.4260 ***	2.3450 ***	−0.4960 ***	0.1840 *	−1.8270 ***
	(0.1470)	(0.1130)	(0.6530)	(0.1140)	(0.0953)	(0.3550)
HSCT	0.0073 ***	−0.0065 ***	−0.0558 ***			
	(0.0028)	(0.0022)	(0.0151)			
HSCA				0.0128 ***	−0.0006	0.0522 ***
				(0.00231)	(0.0018)	(0.0109)
BAC5	0.00840 ***	−0.0054 ***	0.00732 ***	0.00878 ***	−0.0057 ***	0.0088 ***
	(0.0013)	(0.0009)	(0.0016)	(0.0012)	(0.0009)	(0.0014)
BDG	0.0042 ***	0.0011 *	0.0054 ***	0.0041 ***	0.0010 *	0.0039 ***
	(0.0004)	(0.0006)	(0.0004)	(0.0004)	(0.0006)	(0.0005)
SMR	−0.0009	−0.0003	−0.0007	−0.0010	−0.0003	−0.0014 **
	(0.0006)	(0.0003)	(0.0007)	(0.0006)	(0.0003)	(0.0006)
ROA	0.1350 ***	0.1320 ***	0.1250 ***	0.1440 ***	0.1330 ***	0.1750 ***
	(0.0155)	(0.0084)	(0.0225)	(0.0156)	(0.0084)	(0.0252)
SMC	0.0017 ***	0.0007 **	0.0005	0.0018 ***	0.0007 **	0.0030 ***
	(0.0004)	(0.0003)	(0.0006)	(0.0004)	(0.0003)	(0.0006)
LGDP	0.0920 ***	−0.0408	0.0929 ***	0.0945 ***	−0.0285	0.0555 **
	(0.0140)	(0.0275)	(0.0167)	(0.0140)	(0.0269)	(0.0243)
LINF	0.2650 ***	0.1440 ***	0.1320	0.2360 ***	0.1460 ***	0.3500 ***
	(0.0711)	(0.0475)	(0.0905)	(0.0708)	(0.0473)	(0.0823)
WGI	−0.0722 **	−0.0742	−0.0880 ***	−0.0937 ***	−0.0744	−0.0940 **
	(0.0291)	(0.0659)	(0.0337)	(0.0304)	(0.0655)	(0.0388)
CAG	−0.0022	0.0047 **	0.0015	−0.0010	0.0049 ***	−0.0023
	(0.0027)	(0.0018)	(0.0037)	(0.0027)	(0.0018)	(0.0029)
GSG	0.0032	0.0014	0.0101 **	0.0025	0.0012	−0.0044
	(0.0024)	(0.0019)	(0.0040)	(0.0024)	(0.0019)	(0.0032)
PCD	−0.0035 ***	−0.0019 ***	−0.0032 ***	−0.0030 ***	−0.0018 ***	−0.0030 ***
	(0.0007)	(0.0006)	(0.0008)	(0.0007)	(0.0006)	(0.0009)
Constant	−1.9180 ***	2.7263 ***	−3.0250 ***	−1.8840 ***	2.6270 ***	−0.4640
	(0.4470)	(−0.5600)	(0.6190)	(0.4500)	(0.5430)	(0.7750)

Table 3. Cont.

Variables	Model 1	Model 2	Model 3	Model 4	Model 5	Model 6
Adjusted R^2	0.2111	0.2385		0.2169	0.2334	
F-statistics	28.25	29.71		29.21	28.89	
Prob. value	0.0000	0.0000		0.0000	0.0000	
Mean VIF	1.75			1.81		
Wu–Hausman test			21.2251			17.0512
Prob. value			0.0000			0.0000
Hansen J-statistics			1.1382			0.908
Prob. value			0.286			0.3406

Note: This table exhibits OLS regression, pooled regression, and 2SLS with GMM results showing the effect of the interactive role of bank competition and foreign bank entry on risk-taking behavior across countries. The dependent variable is the log of ZSC for all models; FBA and FBT are both independent variables and an indicator of foreign bank entry; FBA is the foreign bank assets to total bank assets; FBT is the total number of foreign banks to total banks; HSC shows the H-statistics, which is a measurement of bank competition; HSCT and HSCA are both interactive terms for foreign bank entry and the level of competition to check the moderating effect on financial stability; BC5 is the five-bank asset concentration; BDG is the bank deposit to GDP (%); SMR is the stock market return; ROA is the return on assets; SMC shows the stock market capitalization to GDP (%); LGDP is the log of GDP; LINF is the log of the consumer price index; WGI denotes the world governance index; CAG is the current account (% of GDP); GSG shows the gross saving (% of GDP); and PCD is the private credit to GDP. The Hausman test of the fixed pooled model was selected and the small values of VIF denotes that the models are free from the problem of multicollinearity. The Wu–Hausman test shows the endogeneity, and the insignificant values of Hansen's J test confirm the instrumental variables are valid; the robust standard errors are reported in parentheses. ***, **, and * shows the coefficients are significant at the 1%, 5%, and 10% level of significance.

Table 4. Bank competition, foreign bank entry, and bank risk-taking behavior (NPG).

Variables	Model 1	Model 2	Model 3	Model 4	Model 5	Model 6
FBT	−0.0103	−0.0730 ***	−0.3010 ***			
	(0.0120)	(0.0275)	(0.0825)			
FBA				−0.0117	−0.0585 ***	−0.3860 ***
				(0.0103)	(0.0224)	(0.0863)
HSC	−3.0330 ***	−2.7110	−22.8400 ***	−2.2100 **	−3.4950 **	−22.0600 ***
	(1.1740)	(1.6740)	(5.8560)	(0.9140)	(1.4010)	(4.6700)
HSCT	0.0411 *	0.0661 **	0.5130 ***			
	(0.0227)	(0.0334)	(0.1350)			
HSCA				0.0287	0.0960 ***	0.6070 ***
				(0.0186)	(0.0271)	(0.1330)
BAC5	−0.0341 ***	0.0127	−0.0262 **	−0.0362 ***	0.0146	−0.0339 **
	(0.0104)	(0.0136)	(0.0126)	(0.0103)	(0.0136)	(0.0138)
BDG	−0.0012	−0.0096	−0.0090 *	2.29e−05	−0.0119	−0.0022
	(0.0037)	(0.0090)	(0.0046)	(0.0037)	(0.0090)	(0.0053)
SMR	−0.0153 ***	−0.0089 **	−0.0172 ***	−0.0157 ***	−0.0081 *	−0.0225 ***
	(0.0052)	(0.0044)	(0.0066)	(0.0053)	(0.0044)	(0.0073)
ROA	−1.4900 ***	−1.1820 ***	−1.3990 ***	−1.4740 ***	−1.1850 ***	−1.0170 ***
	(0.1240)	(0.1250)	(0.1780)	(0.1250)	(0.1250)	(0.2090)
SMC	−0.0192 ***	−0.0330 ***	−0.0094 **	−0.0189 ***	−0.0327 ***	−0.0021
	(0.0032)	(0.0055)	(0.0046)	(0.0032)	(0.0055)	(0.0069)
LGDP	−0.5430 ***	−2.3220 ***	−0.5650 ***	−0.6030 ***	−2.4940 ***	−1.1710 ***
	(0.1120)	(0.4070)	(0.1170)	(0.1130)	(0.3960)	(0.1980)
LINF	−4.5000 ***	−1.2180 *	−3.5240 ***	−4.3630 ***	−1.2710 *	−2.6820 ***
	(0.5680)	(0.7020)	(0.7930)	(0.5690)	(0.6960)	(0.9270)
WGI	−3.1660 ***	−1.8350 *	−3.0870 ***	−3.1560 ***	−2.2200 **	−3.1700 ***
	(0.2330)	(0.9760)	(0.2760)	(0.2440)	(0.9650)	(0.3430)
CAG	0.1520 ***	0.3210 ***	0.1230 ***	0.1510 ***	0.3190 ***	0.1340 ***
	(0.0219)	(0.0275)	(0.0301)	(0.0219)	(0.0275)	(0.0326)
GSG	−0.1380 ***	−0.1480 ***	−0.1960 ***	−0.1400 ***	−0.1440 ***	−0.2370 ***
	(0.0192)	(0.0293)	(0.0322)	(0.0193)	(0.0292)	(0.0363)
PCD	0.0323 ***	0.0645 ***	0.0317 ***	0.0321 ***	0.0655 ***	0.0328 ***
	(0.0057)	(0.0092)	(0.0070)	(0.0061)	(0.0093)	(0.0083)
Constant	49.8400 ***	77.4200 ***	58.5800 ***	50.7500 ***	81.3500 ***	71.3300 ***
	(3.5700)	(8.2940)	(4.9980)	(3.6140)	(7.9930)	(6.9260)

Table 4. Cont.

Variables	Model 1	Model 2	Model 3	Model 4	Model 5	Model 6
Adjusted R^2	0.3683	0.3390		0.3671	0.3417	
F-statistics	60.39	48.64		60.08	49.23	
Prob. value	0.0000	0.0000		0.0000	0.0000	
Mean VIF	1.75			1.81		
Wu–Hausman test			16.6254			35.4521
Prob. value			0.0000			0.0000
Hansen J-statistics			1.9429			0.172
Prob. value			0.1633			0.6783

Note: This table exhibits OLS regression, pooled regression, and 2SLS with GMM results showing the interactive role of bank competition and foreign bank entry on risk-taking behavior across the countries. The dependent variable is the NPG (ratio of non-performing loans to the gross loans). The FBA and FBT are both independent variables and an indicator for foreign bank entry, FBA is the foreign bank assets to total bank assets, FBT is the total number of foreign banks to total banks, HSC shows the H-statists as a measurement of bank competition, HSCT and HSCA are both an interactive term for foreign bank entry and level of competition to check the moderating effect on financial stability, BC5 is the five-bank asset concentration, BDG is the bank deposit to GDP (%), SMR is the stock market return, ROA is the return on assets, SMC shows the stock market capitalization to GDP (%), LGDP is the log of GDP, LINF is the log of consumer price index, WGI denotes the world governance index, CAG is the current account (% of GDP), GSG shows the gross saving (% of GDP), and PCD is the private credit to GDP. The Hausman test of the fixed pooled model was selected, and the small values of VIF denotes that the models are free from the problem of multicollinearity. The Wu–Hausman test shows the endogeneity, and the insignificant values of Hansen's J test confirm the instrumental variables are valid. The robust standard errors are reported in parentheses. ***, **, and * show that the coefficients are significant at the 1%, 5%, and 10% level of significance.

Table 5. Bank regulation, foreign bank entry, and bank risk-taking behavior (Z-Score).

Variables	Model 1	Model 2	Model 3	Model 4
FBA	−0.00113	−0.0387 ***		
	(0.00175)	(0.00729)		
FBT			0.0014	−0.0813 ***
			(0.0020)	(0.0226)
HSC	0.2000 *	−1.9930 ***	0.4320 ***	−5.2260 ***
	(0.1190)	(0.3570)	(0.1420)	(1.4840)
HSCA	−0.0005	0.0589 ***		
	(0.0023)	(0.0107)		
HSCT			−0.00635 **	0.1260 ***
			(0.00283)	(0.0359)
RBA	−0.0401	−0.1090 ***	−0.0344	−0.1720 ***
	(0.0455)	(0.0234)	(0.0455)	(0.0467)
CRE	0.0590	0.0247	0.0593	0.0883 ***
	(0.0515)	(0.0158)	(0.0514)	(0.0258)
SPI	−0.00528	0.0116	0.00163	0.0048
	(0.0367)	(0.0107)	(0.0371)	(0.0138)
PMO	0.1440 ***	0.0652 ***	0.142 **	0.0795 ***
	(0.0554)	(0.0204)	(0.0555)	(0.0242)
BAC5	−0.0051 ***	0.0079 ***	−0.0050 ***	0.0088 ***
	(0.0011)	(0.0017)	(0.0011)	(0.0022)
BDG	0.0016 **	0.0040 ***	0.0016 **	0.0025 ***
	(0.0007)	(0.0005)	(0.0007)	(0.0009)
SMR	−0.0003	−0.0014 *	−0.0004	−0.0011
	(0.0003)	(0.0007)	(0.0003)	(0.0009)
ROA	0.1570 ***	0.2040 ***	0.1580 ***	0.1940 ***
	(0.0108)	(0.0304)	(0.0108)	(0.0356)
SMC	0.00084 *	0.0022 ***	0.00082 *	0.0026 ***
	(0.0004)	(0.0007)	(0.0004)	(0.0009)
LGDP	−0.0127	0.0585 **	−0.0124	0.1060 ***
	(0.0295)	(0.0247)	(0.0296)	(0.0268)
LINF	0.1730 ***	0.4020 ***	0.1830 ***	0.5830 ***
	(0.0548)	(0.0888)	(0.0558)	(0.1420)
WGI	0.00638	−0.0633	0.0168	0.0490
	(0.0702)	(0.0548)	(0.0704)	(0.0810)

Table 5. Cont.

Variables	Model 1	Model 2	Model 3	Model 4
CAG	0.0048 **	−0.00164	0.0047 **	−0.0073 *
	(0.0023)	(0.0030)	(0.0023)	(0.0043)
GSG	0.0022	−0.0034	0.0020	−0.0081
	(0.0024)	(0.0031)	(0.0024)	(0.0054)
PCD	−0.0028 ***	−0.0029 ***	−0.0028 ***	−0.0039 ***
	(0.0007)	(0.0010)	(0.0007)	(0.0012)
LGPC	0.0013	−0.1030 **	0.0068	−0.1940 **
	(0.0564)	(0.0413)	(0.0564)	(0.0762)
Constant	0.8230	0.3140	0.5070	1.2630
	(0.870)	(1.093)	(0.857)	(1.601)
R^2	0.2078		0.211	
Wald Test	360.85	409.11	367.41	227.83
Prob. value	0.0000	0.0000	0.0000	0.0000
Wu–Hausman test		22.0305		23.3424
Prob. value		0.0000		0.0000
Hansen J-statistics		0.1951		1.7598
Prob. value		0.6587		0.1846

Note: This table exhibits pooled regression and 2SLS with GMM results showing the interactive role of bank competition and foreign bank entry on risk-taking behavior across countries with controlled banking regulations. The dependent variable is the log of ZSC for all models. The FBA and FBT are both independent variables and an indicator for foreign bank entry, FBA is the foreign bank assets to total bank assets, FBT is the total number of foreign banks to total banks, HSC shows the H-statistics as a measurement of bank competition, HSCT and HSCA are both interactive terms for foreign bank entry and level of competition to check the moderating effect on financial stability, RBA is the restriction on bank activities, CRE is the capital regulation, SPI is the supervisory power index, PMO is the private monitoring, BC5 is the five-bank asset concentration, BDG is the bank deposit to GDP (%), SMR is the stock market return, ROA is the return on assets, SMC shows the stock market capitalization to GDP (%), LGDP is the log of GDP, LINF is the log of consumer price index, WGI denotes the world governance index, CAG is the current account (% of GDP), GSG shows the gross saving (% of GDP), and PCD is the private credit to GDP. The Hausman test of the fixed pooled model was selected and the small values of VIF denotes that the models are free from the problem of multicollinearity. The Wu–Hausman test shows the endogeneity, and the insignificant values of Hansen's J test confirm the instrumental variables are valid. The robust standard errors are reported in parentheses. ***, **, and * shows the coefficients are significant at the 1%, 5%, and 10% level of significance.

Table 6. Bank regulation, foreign bank entry, and bank risk-taking behavior (Non-performing loans to gross loans NPG).

Variables	Model 1	Model 2	Model 3	Model 4
FBA	−0.0541 ***	−0.2970 ***		
	(0.0163)	(0.0706)		
FBT			−0.0483 **	−0.3650 ***
			(0.0191)	(0.1070)
HSC	−3.0550 **	−15.5400 ***	−2.3310	−25.0300 ***
	(1.2490)	(3.6070)	(1.5200)	(7.5350)
HSCA	0.0835 ***	0.4400 ***		
	(0.0245)	(0.1040)		
HSCT			0.0559 *	0.5830 ***
			(0.0301)	(0.1730)
RBA	−0.4170 *	−0.9520 ***	−0.3930	−0.8680 ***
	(0.2470)	(0.2230)	(0.2460)	(0.2390)
CRE	−0.1650	−0.4760 ***	−0.1280	−0.0511
	(0.2650)	(0.1370)	(0.2630)	(0.1330)
SPI	0.3160 *	0.4290 ***	0.3410 *	0.3140 ***
	(0.1910)	(0.0863)	(0.1950)	(0.0878)
PMO	0.2510	−0.0658	0.2610	0.0616
	(0.2940)	(0.1500)	(0.2940)	(0.1510)

Table 6. Cont.

Variables	Model 1	Model 2	Model 3	Model 4
BAC5	−0.00432	−0.0332 ***	−0.0053	−0.0235 *
	(0.0124)	(0.0120)	(0.0124)	(0.0125)
BDG	−0.00172	0.0003	−0.0007	−0.0072
	(0.0064)	(0.0044)	(0.0064)	(0.0050)
SMR	−0.0082 *	−0.0177 ***	−0.0086 *	−0.0163 **
	(0.0044)	(0.0064)	(0.0044)	(0.0066)
ROA	−1.2550 ***	−1.0940 ***	−1.2640 ***	−1.2650 ***
	(0.1220)	(0.1910)	(0.1220)	(0.1850)
SMC	−0.0297 ***	−0.0111 **	−0.0305 ***	−0.0137 ***
	(0.0047)	(0.0050)	(0.0047)	(0.0044)
LGDP	−0.7030 ***	−0.7440 ***	−0.6930 ***	−0.3470 ***
	(0.2190)	(0.1530)	(0.2160)	(0.1270)
LINF	−3.0080 ***	−2.5220 ***	−2.9180 ***	−2.7000 ***
	(0.5530)	(0.8430)	(0.5670)	(0.8580)
WGI	−1.4360 **	−1.1480 ***	−1.3050 **	−1.3050 ***
	(0.5950)	(0.4440)	(0.5970)	(0.4310)
CAG	0.3140 ***	0.1770 ***	0.3100 ***	0.1590 ***
	(0.0253)	(0.0307)	(0.0253)	(0.0317)
GSG	−0.1770 ***	−0.2170 ***	−0.1770 ***	−0.2130 ***
	(0.0256)	(0.0321)	(0.0257)	(0.0336)
PCD	0.0491 ***	0.0290 ***	0.0474 ***	0.0317 ***
	(0.0079)	(0.0073)	(0.0078)	(0.0072)
LGPC	−2.1440 ***	−2.2460 ***	−2.1450 ***	−2.0570 ***
	(0.4340)	(0.3830)	(0.4360)	(0.3870)
Constant	63.6200 ***	81.7700 ***	62.3100 ***	72.5200 ***
	(6.1640)	(8.2490)	(5.9260)	(7.2210)
R^2	0.3386		0.3356	
Wald Test	725.57	630.97	716.11	591.53
Prob. value	0.0000	0.0000	0.0000	0.0000
Wu–Hausman test		23.7720		17.8581
Prob. value		0.0000		0.0000
Hansen J-statistics		0.2137		3.1424
Prob. value		0.6439		0.0763

Note: This table exhibits pooled regression and 2SLS with GMM results showing the interactive role of bank competition and foreign bank entry on risk-taking across countries. The dependent variable is the NPG (ratio of non-performing loans to gross loans), FBA and FBT are both independent variables and an indicator for foreign bank entry, FBA is the foreign bank assets to total bank assets, FBT is the total number of foreign banks to total banks, HSC shows the H-statistics as a measurement of bank competition, HSCT and HSCA are both interactive terms for foreign bank entry and level of competition to check the moderating effect on financial stability, RBA is the restriction on bank activities, CRE is the capital regulation, SPI is the supervisory power index, PMO is the private monitoring, BC5 is the five-bank asset concentration, BDG is the bank deposit to GDP (%), SMR is the stock market return, ROA is the return on assets, SMC shows the stock market capitalization to GDP (%), LGDP is the log of GDP, LINF is the log of the consumer price index, WGI denotes the world governance index, CAG is the current account (% of GDP), GSG shows the gross saving (% of GDP), and PCD is the private credit to GDP. The Hausman test of the fixed pooled model was selected. The small values of VIF denote that the models are free from the problem of multicollinearity. The Wu–Hausman test shows the endogeneity, and the insignificant values of Hansen's J test confirm the instrumental variables are valid. The robust standard errors are reported in parentheses. ***, **, and * show the coefficients are significant at the 1%, 5%, and 10% level of significance.

4. Robustness Checks

To ensure the accuracy of the pooled regression models and dynamic estimation models, and to validate the findings of the interactive role of competition and foreign bank entry on risk-taking behavior across the globe, Tables 7 and 8 show some robustness checks on our main models. We ran our regressions using the alternative proxy of foreign bank entry with the other control variables. We also included the interactive dummy variable for developed countries to examine the effect of foreign bank entry on risk-taking behavior across countries. We also included the quadratic (squared) term in our regression models to examine the non-linear relationship between foreign bank entry and different indicators of risk-taking. The robustness checks confirmed the previous results. The robustness tests also confirmed that foreign bank entry decreases the level of risk and ultimately enhances financial stability to a certain level. The results also indicated that the interactive effect of the level of competition and foreign bank entry weakens the financial stability of the banking sector across countries. These results are more prevalent in emerging economies in which undeveloped financial systems depend heavily on banks to channel financial capitals into expansion projects, combined with the fact that the financial sector plays a vital role in boosting proficiency and economic development.

Table 7. Bank competition, foreign bank entry, and banking risk (2SLS results).

Variables	LZSC	LZSC	NPG	NPG
FBT	0.0567 **		−0.9330 **	
	(0.0245)		(0.3640)	
FBA		0.0305 ***		−0.4930 ***
		(0.0103)		(0.120)
HSC	3.8160 **	0.9830 **	−58.7700 ***	−21.8000 ***
	(1.6200)	(0.4340)	(22.5300)	(5.098)
HSCT	−0.0913 **		1.379 ***	
	(0.0380)		(0.5280)	
HSCA		−0.0322 **		0.618 ***
		(0.0125)		(0.148)
BAC5	0.0086 ***	0.0116 ***	−0.0471 **	−0.0633 ***
	(0.00179)	(0.0014)	(0.0215)	(0.0158)
BDG	0.0071 ***	0.0056 ***	−0.0481 **	−0.0159 **
	(0.0011)	(0.0005)	(0.0195)	(0.0068)
SMR	−0.0004	−0.0001	−0.0250 **	−0.0260 ***
	(0.0008)	(0.0007)	(0.0108)	(0.0080)
ROA	0.1140 ***	0.1080 ***	−1.2000 ***	−0.9990 ***
	(0.0268)	(0.0237)	(0.2940)	(0.2300)
SMC	−0.0003	−1.52 × 10^{-5}	0.0159	0.00363
	(0.0010)	(0.0007)	(0.0153)	(0.0080)
LGDP	0.1040 ***	0.2020 ***	−1.3140 ***	−1.8200 ***
	(0.0194)	(0.0302)	(0.3620)	(0.3360)
LINF	0.0830	0.0044	−0.2420	−1.6410
	(0.1250)	(0.1060)	(2.0050)	(1.0980)
WGI	0.0701	0.0128	−4.839 ***	−4.241 ***
	(0.0610)	(0.0412)	(0.845)	(0.454)
CAG	0.00188	−5.76e−05	0.0739	0.1370 ***
	(0.0043)	(0.0036)	(0.0554)	(0.0349)
GSG	0.0144 **	0.0127 ***	−0.2570 ***	−0.2650 ***
	(0.0063)	(0.0046)	(0.0657)	(0.0439)
PCD	−0.00626 ***	−0.00366 ***	0.0412 ***	0.0389 ***
	(0.0012)	(0.0008)	(0.0119)	(0.0088)
DD*FBT	−0.0109 ***		0.2070 **	
	(0.00364)		(0.0848)	
DD*FBA		−0.0136 ***		0.1380 ***
		(0.0032)		(0.0350)
Constant	−4.061 ***	−5.079 ***	88.82 ***	87.77 ***
	(1.027)	(0.9380)	(17.17)	(10.81)
Wald Test	210.99	352.20	208.82	401.81
Prob. value	0.0000	0.0000	0.0000	0.0000
Wu–Hausman test	11.7975	11.5997	26.3366	32.4296
Prob. value	0.0006	0.0000	0.0000	0.0000
Sargan Test	3.7527	0.0172	2.1604	0.486
Prob. value	0.0527	0.8954	0.1416	0.4857

Note: This table exhibits the 2SLS showing the interactive role of bank competition and foreign bank entry on the risk-taking behavior across countries. The dependent variables are the bank Z-score and NPG (ratio of non-performing loans to the gross loans), FBA and FBT are both independent variables and indicators of foreign bank entry, FBA is the foreign bank assets to total bank assets, FBT is the total number of foreign banks to total banks, HSC shows the H-statistics as a measurement of bank competition, HSCT and HSCA are both interactive terms for foreign bank entry and the level of competition to check the moderating effect on financial stability, BC5 is the five-bank asset concentration, BDG is the bank deposit to GDP (%), SMR is the stock market return, ROA is the return on assets, SMC shows the stock market capitalization to GDP (%), LGDP is the log of GDP, LINF is the log of the consumer price index, WGI denotes the world governance index, CAG is the current account (% of GDP), GSG shows the gross saving (% of GDP), and PCD is the private credit to GDP. DD*FBA and DD*FBT are both interactive terms used to examine foreign bank entry in developed economies. The significant value of the Wald test explains that the models are correctly specified, the Wu–Hausman test shows the endogeneity, the insignificant values of the Sargan test confirm the over-identifying restrictions, and the robust standard errors are reported in parentheses. ***, **, and * show the coefficients are significant at the 1%, 5%, and 10% level of significance.

Table 8. Bank competition, foreign bank entry, and banking risk (2SLS results).

Variables	LZSC	LZSC	NPG	NPG
FBT	0.0541 ***		−0.3890 ***	
	(0.0133)		(0.115)	
FBT^2	−0.0005 ***		0.0030 ***	
	(0.0001)		(0.0009)	
FBA		0.0823 ***		−0.6730 ***
		(0.0285)		(0.2440)
FBA^2		−0.0007 ***		0.0053 ***
		(0.0002)		(0.0019)
HSC	0.5220 *	0.3350	−10.03 ***	−8.8200 ***
	(0.2880)	(0.3170)	(2.320)	(2.6870)
HSCT	−0.0199 ***		0.2450 ***	
	(0.0072)		(0.0610)	
HSCA		−0.0199 *		0.2820 ***
		(0.0108)		(0.0923)
BAC5	0.0071 ***	0.0103 ***	−0.0265 **	−0.0469 ***
	(0.0014)	(0.0016)	(0.0118)	(0.0137)
BDG	0.0063 ***	0.0053 ***	−0.0142 **	−0.00904
	(0.0006)	(0.0006)	(0.0058)	(0.0060)
SMR	−0.0007	−0.0006	−0.0168 ***	−0.0185 **
	(0.0006)	(0.0008)	(0.00630)	(0.00749)
ROA	0.1200 ***	0.1260 ***	−1.396 ***	−1.334 ***
	(0.01940)	(0.0237)	(0.163)	(0.2010)
SMC	−0.0003	0.0004	−0.0065	−0.0084
	(0.0006)	(0.0007)	(0.0048)	(0.0056)
LGDP	0.0676 ***	0.1560 ***	−0.409 ***	−1.0610 ***
	(0.0162)	(0.0251)	(0.121)	(0.220)
LINF	0.2630 ***	0.1420	−4.378 ***	−3.62005 ***
	(0.0770)	(0.102)	(0.738)	(0.885)
WGI	0.0767 *	−0.0374	−3.9930 ***	−3.5408 ***
	(0.0423)	(0.0416)	(0.3960)	(0.361)
CAG	0.0057 *	−0.0066	0.1050 ***	0.1920 ***
	(0.0033)	(0.0048)	(0.0321)	(0.0369)
GSG	0.0121 ***	0.0281 ***	−0.1950 ***	−0.3270 ***
	(0.0037)	(0.0095)	(0.0323)	(0.0767)
PCD	−0.0054 ***	−0.0017	0.0432 ***	0.0232 ***
	(0.0008)	(0.0011)	(0.0078)	(0.0084)
Constant	−2.412 ***	−5.118 ***	53.58 ***	74.62 ***
	(0.5200)	(1.1500)	(4.3590)	(10.4100)
Wald Test	396.3	306.4	612.15	451.05
Prob. value	0.0000	0.0000	0.0000	0.0000
Wu–Hausman test	19.7545	15.1761	15.7237	13.4202
Prob. value	0.0000	0.0001	0.0001	0.0003
Sargan Test	0.2084	3.3309	3.6789	1.1793
Prob. value	0.648	0.068	0.0551	0.2775

Note: This table exhibits that the 2SLS showing the interactive role of bank competition and foreign bank entry on the risk-taking behavior across countries. The dependent variables are the bank Z-score and NPG (ratio of non-performing loans to the gross loans), FBA and FBT are both independent variables and indicators of foreign bank entry, FBA is the foreign bank assets to total bank assets, FBT is the total number of foreign banks to total banks. The FBA^2 and FBT^2 are both square terms of the independent variables to examine the non-linear relationship between foreign bank entry and risk-taking behavior (an inverted U-shape relationship). The HSC shows the H-statistics as a measurement of bank competition, HSCT and HSCA are both interactive terms of foreign bank entry and the level of competition to check the moderating effect on the stability position, BC5 is the five-bank asset concentration, BDG is the bank deposit to GDP (%), SMR is the stock market return, ROA is the return on assets, SMC shows the stock market capitalization to GDP (%), LGDP is the log of the GDP, LINF is the log of the consumer price index, WGI denotes the world governance index, CAG is the current account (% of GDP), GSG shows the gross saving (% of GDP), and PCD is the private credit to GDP. The significant value of the Wald test explains that the models are correctly specified. The Wu–Hausman test shows the endogeneity, and the insignificant values of the Sargan test confirm the over-identifying restrictions. The robust standard errors are reported in the parentheses. ***, **, and * shows the coefficients are significant at the 1%, 5%, and 10% level of significance.

5. Conclusions

Foreign bank entry brings both benefits and challenges to host economies. The recent instability in financial markets might make policymakers hesitant to relax liberalization policies on the activities and entry of foreign banks across the globe. This study examined the role of foreign bank entry and competition in the risk-taking behavior of banks across the globe. Our sample consisted of commercial banks from 95 countries (developed and developing countries) over the period of 2000 to 2016. This study used different indicators to measure risk-taking behavior (Z-score and NPG ratio) and the role of bank competition as measured by H-statistics, which is a nonstructural model. After applying the pooled regression and 2SLS with GMM and using the property rights and financial freedom as the instrumental variables, our results showed that the entry of foreign banks enhances the financial stability position and mitigates the risk factor to a certain level and the level of bank competition plays an extensive role between foreign bank entry and risk-taking behavior. This study revealed that foreign banks have an inverted U-shaped relation with risk-taking behavior; this implies that foreign bank entry decreases the level of risk-taking behavior before to a certain extent and then brings financial fragility to the host country because of excessive competition, which may cause local banks to undertake risky investments. Thus, our findings support the competition–fragility hypothesis, which was also confirmed by the interactive role of the competition level and foreign bank entry. The findings of our study also suggest that some measures of bank regulation significantly reduce risk-taking behavior across countries. In particular, we found that restriction on bank activities and capital regulation stringency reduces the level of risk. This result was the same as those of the robustness tests.

The results of this research have important policy implications for bank managers, regulators, and policy-makers. There are both pessimistic and optimistic sides for the existence of foreign banks across countries. Despite providing a steady source of credit in host economies, the entry of foreign banks might lead to an enhancement of domestic banks' risk, proposing a reasonable trade-off between the susceptibility of credit quality in domestic banks and the stability of credit quantity from foreign banks. Therefore, when planning optimal policies of financial liberalization, policymakers need to be attentive to the possible detrimental influence of foreign banks' eminence on the financial stability in host countries. Moreover, financial authorities must also be conscious that the business expansion of local banks might enhance their risk, therefore influencing the stability of domestic banks disparagingly. After all, this research proposes that the adaptation of a Basel III framework by countries enhances the risk management capability and brings restraints to the market, and would be favorable for the region to enhance the financial stability.

In addition, this study reveals that the entry of foreign banks is an overall blessing in underdeveloped markets to a reasonable level, although it has the potential for risk. Given the probable harms brought by banking instability during the global financial crisis (GFC), the other direction for further study is to examine the foreign bank penetration on risk-taking behavior, bank efficiency, and, in particular, how to achieve the optimal level of performance when foreign ownership and different banking regulations are taken into consideration. All of these extensions will remain a priority for researchers in future.

Author Contributions: All the authors have contributed equally to the paper.

Funding: This research received no external funding.

Conflicts of Interest: The authors declare no conflict of interest.

Appendix A

Table A1. Definition of variables, data sources, and acronyms.

Variables	Acronyms	Definition
Foreign Bank Entry	FBT	The number of foreign banks to the total banks (%).
	FBA	Foreign bank assets to the total bank assets (%). This proxy has been used by Molyneux et al. (2013) and Yin et al. (2015). Source: WB, GFDD
Z-score	ZSC	It captures the probability of the defaulting of a country's commercial banking system. This proxy has been used by Wu et al. (2017) Source: GFDD, WB
Non-performing loans to gross loans	NPG	This is the ratio of non-performing loans to the total gross loans; This proxy has taken from Allen et al. (2014), Source: GFDD, WB
Restriction on Bank Activities	RBA	The index of restriction on bank activities. The higher score suggests that more regulations on the scope of the bank's business operation. The data obtained from (Barth et al. 2013)
Capital regulation Stringency	CRE	The index of capital regulatory stringency. The index ranges from 2 to 12, with a higher score indicating more stringent regulation on banks' overall capital. The data obtained from (Barth et al. 2013)
Supervisory Power index	SPI	The index of supervisory power. The score ranges from 0 to 14; the higher score suggests that when the supervisory agencies are authorized more oversight power. The data obtained from (Dong et al. 2011; Barth et al. 2013)
Private monitoring	PMO	The index of the private monitor strength. The index ranges from 0 to 12, and the higher value denotes a more private monitoring force. The data obtained from (Dong et al. 2011; Barth et al. 2013)
Bank Concentration	BC5	This is the large five banks ratio in terms of total assets to the total assets of the banking industry. This proxy has been used by Karolyi and Taboada (2015), Source: WB, GFDD
Bank Deposits	BDG	BDG is the bank deposit to GDP (%). This proxy has been used by Houston et al. (2012) and Karolyi and Taboada (2015), Source: World Bank Global Financial development database
Return on Assets	ROA	The bank's net income to the total assets. This proxy has taken from (Houston et al. 2012), Source: GFDD, WB
Financial Development	PCD	Private credit by deposits money banks to GDP (%). This proxy has been used by (Luo et al. 2016). Source: Global market information database
Stock market development	SMC	SMC is the stock market capitalization to GDP (%). This proxy has been used by (Luo et al. 2016), Source: Global market information database
Governance index	WGI	The average of six governance elements. Each of the indices arrays from −2.5 to 2.5, with the higher values showing better governance. This proxy has been used by (Luo et al. 2016). Source: GFDD, WB
Stock market return	SMR	The stock market return is the growth rate of an annual stock market index. This proxy has been used by (Karolyi and Taboada 2015), Source: World Bank Global Financial development database.
GDP growth	GDP	Annual GDP growth rate, This proxy has taken from (Noman et al. 2018). Source: IMF
Inflation	INF	Inflation rate (annual % change of Average consumer price index). This proxy has taken from (Noman et al. 2018). Source: IMF
Current account/GDP %	CAG	The current account divided by GDP (%). This proxy has taken from (Houston et al. 2012), Source: IMF
Saving/GDP %	GSG	The gross savings of both the public and the private sectors divided by GDP (%). This proxy has taken from (Karolyi and Taboada 2015), Source: IMF
Population	POP	Log population (millions). Source: IMF
Financial Freedom	FIF	This index that takes value from 0–100 showing the level of regulatory restrictions on the financial freedom of the firms. This variable is used as the instrumental variables and has been used by (Noman et al. 2018), Source: HFD
Property Rights	PRR	This index takes a value from 0–100, showing the level to which the laws protect private property right. This variable is used as the instrumental variables and has been used by (Noman et al. 2018), Source: HFD

Note: IMF shows the International Monetary Fund, GFDD is the Global Financial Development Database, WBI is the World Development Indicators. HFD is the Heritage Foundation database.

Appendix B

Table A2. List of countries.

Sr. No	Country	Region	Classification
1	Algeria	Middle East and North Africa	Upper middle income
2	Antigua and Barbuda	Latin America and Caribbean	High income
3	Argentina	Latin America and Caribbean	High income
4	Armenia	Europe and Central Asia	Upper middle income
5	Australia	East Asia and Pacific	High income
6	Austria	Europe and Central Asia	High income
7	Azerbaijan	Europe and Central Asia	Upper middle income
8	Bahrain	Middle East and North Africa	High income
9	Bangladesh	South Asia	Lower middle income
10	Belgium	Europe and Central Asia	High income
11	Benin	Sub-Saharan Africa	Low income
12	Bosnia and Herzegovina	Europe and Central Asia	Upper middle income
13	Brazil	Latin America and Caribbean	Upper middle income
14	Bulgaria	Europe and Central Asia	Upper middle income
15	Canada	North America	High income
16	Chile	Latin America and Caribbean	High income
17	China	East Asia and Pacific	Upper middle income
18	Colombia	Latin America and Caribbean	Upper middle income
19	Croatia	Europe and Central Asia	High income
20	Cyprus	Europe and Central Asia	High income
21	Czech Republic	Europe and Central Asia	High income
22	Denmark	Europe and Central Asia	High income
23	Dominican Republic	Latin America and Caribbean	Upper middle income
24	Ecuador	Latin America and Caribbean	Upper middle income
25	Egypt, Arab Rep.	Middle East and North Africa	Lower middle income
26	El Salvador	Latin America and Caribbean	Lower middle income
27	Estonia	Europe and Central Asia	High income
28	Finland	Europe and Central Asia	High income
29	France	Europe and Central Asia	High income
30	Germany	Europe and Central Asia	High income
31	Ghana	Sub-Saharan Africa	Lower middle income
32	Greece	Europe and Central Asia	High income
33	Guatemala	Latin America and Caribbean	Upper middle income
34	Hong Kong SAR, China	East Asia and Pacific	High income
35	Hungary	Europe and Central Asia	High income
36	Iceland	Europe and Central Asia	High income
37	India	South Asia	Lower middle income
38	Indonesia	East Asia and Pacific	Lower middle income
39	Ireland	Europe and Central Asia	High income
40	Israel	Middle East and North Africa	High income
41	Italy	Europe and Central Asia	High income
42	Japan	East Asia and Pacific	High income
43	Jordan	Middle East and North Africa	Upper middle income
44	Kazakhstan	Europe and Central Asia	Upper middle income
45	Kenya	Sub-Saharan Africa	Lower middle income
46	Kuwait	Middle East and North Africa	High income
47	Lebanon	Middle East and North Africa	Upper middle income
48	Lithuania	Europe and Central Asia	High income
49	Luxembourg	Europe and Central Asia	High income
50	Malaysia	East Asia and Pacific	Upper middle income
51	Malta	Middle East and North Africa	High income
52	Mauritius	Sub-Saharan Africa	Upper middle income
53	Mexico	Latin America and Caribbean	Upper middle income
54	Moldova	Europe and Central Asia	Lower middle income
55	Morocco	Middle East and North Africa	Lower middle income
56	Mozambique	Sub-Saharan Africa	Low income
57	Namibia	Sub-Saharan Africa	Upper middle income
58	Netherlands	Europe and Central Asia	High income
59	New Zealand	East Asia and Pacific	High income
60	Nicaragua	Latin America and Caribbean	Lower middle income
61	Nigeria	Sub-Saharan Africa	Low income
62	Norway	Europe and Central Asia	High income
63	Oman	Middle East and North Africa	High income
64	Pakistan	South Asia	Lower middle income
65	Peru	Latin America and Caribbean	Upper middle income

Table A2. *Cont.*

Sr. No	Country	Region	Classification
66	Philippines	East Asia and Pacific	Lower middle income
67	Poland	Europe and Central Asia	High income
68	Portugal	Europe and Central Asia	High income
69	Qatar	Middle East and North Africa	High income
70	Romania	Europe and Central Asia	Upper middle income
71	Russian Federation	Europe and Central Asia	Upper middle income
72	Saudi Arabia	Middle East and North Africa	High income
73	Serbia	Europe and Central Asia	Upper middle income
74	Singapore	East Asia and Pacific	High income
75	Slovak Republic	Europe and Central Asia	High income
76	Slovenia	Europe and Central Asia	High income
77	South Africa	Sub-Saharan Africa	Upper middle income
78	Spain	Europe and Central Asia	High income
79	Sri Lanka	South Asia	Lower middle income
80	Sweden	Europe and Central Asia	High income
81	Switzerland	Europe and Central Asia	High income
82	Taiwan, China	East Asia and Pacific	High income
83	Thailand	East Asia and Pacific	Upper middle income
84	Trinidad and Tobago	Latin America and Caribbean	High income
85	Tunisia	Middle East and North Africa	Lower middle income
86	Turkey	Europe and Central Asia	Upper middle income
87	Uganda	Sub-Saharan Africa	Low income
88	Ukraine	Europe and Central Asia	Lower middle income
89	United Arab Emirates	Europe and Central Asia	Lower middle income
90	United Kingdom	Europe and Central Asia	High income
91	United States	North America	High income
92	Uruguay	Latin America and Caribbean	High income
93	Venezuela, RB	Latin America and Caribbean	Upper middle income
94	Vietnam	East Asia and Pacific	Lower middle income
95	Zambia	Sub-Saharan Africa	Lower middle income

Source. International Monetary Fund.

References

Agoraki, Maria-Eleni K., Manthos D. Delis, and Fotios Pasiouras. 2011. Regulations, competition and bank risk-taking in transition countries. *Journal of Financial Stability* 7: 38–48. [CrossRef]

Allen, Franklin, and Douglas Gale. 2005. Competition and Financial Stability. *Journal of Money, Credit, and Banking* 36: 453–80. [CrossRef]

Allen, Franklin, Elena Carletti, and Douglas Gale. 2014. Money, financial stability and efficiency. *Journal of Economic Theory* 149: 100–27. [CrossRef]

Althammer, Wilhelm, and Rainer Haselmann. 2011. Explaining foreign bank entrance in emerging markets. *Journal of Comparative Economics* 39: 486–98. [CrossRef]

Anginer, Deniz, and Asli Demirguc-Kunt. 2014. Has the global banking system become more fragile over time? *Journal of Financial Stability* 13: 202–13. [CrossRef]

Apergis, Nicholas, Irene Fafaliou, and Michael L. Polemis. 2016. New evidence on assessing the level of competition in the European Union banking sector: A panel data approach. *International Business Review* 25: 395–407. [CrossRef]

Barth, James R., Gerard Caprio, and Ross Levine. 2001. The Regulation and Supervision of Banks Around the World. Forum American Bar Association, (April). Available online: www.worldbank.org/research/projectslbank_regulation.htm (accessed on 13 May 2019).

Barth, James R., Chen Lin, Yue Ma, Jesús Seade, and Frank M. Song. 2013. Do bank regulation, supervision and monitoring enhance or impede bank efficiency? *Journal of Banking and Finance* 37: 2879–92. [CrossRef]

Baselga-Pascual, Laura, Olga del Orden-Olasagasti, and Antonio Trujillo-Ponce. 2018. Toward a more resilient financial system: Should banks be diversified? *Sustainability (Switzerland)* 10: 1903. [CrossRef]

Baskaran, Angathevar, and Mammo Muchie. 2008. *Foreign Direct Investment and Internationalization of RandD: The Case of BRICS Economics*. Development, Innovation and International Political Economy Research. p. 36. Available online: https://eprints.mdx.ac.uk/4200/1/Baskaran_-_Mammo_DIIPER_Working_paper_2008-7.pdf (accessed on 3 May 2019).

Beck, Thorsten. 2008. *Bank Competition And Financial Stability: Friends or Foes?* Washington, DC: The World Bank. [CrossRef]

Beck, Thorsten, Asli Demirgüç-Kunt, and Ross Levin. 2005. *Bank Concentration and Fragility: Impact and Mechanics*. NBER Working Paper Series; Chicago: University of Chicago Press, Available online: http://www.nber.org/papers/w11500 (accessed on 9 May 2019).

Beck, Thorsten, Aslı Demirgüç-Kunt, and Ross Levine. 2006. Bank supervision and corruption in lending. *Journal of Monetary Economics* 53: 2131–63. [CrossRef]

Beck, Thorsten, Hans Degryse, Ralph De Haas, and Neeltje Van Horen. 2018. When arm's length is too far: Relationship banking over the credit cycle. *Journal of Financial Economics* 127: 174–96. [CrossRef]

Berger, Allen N., Leora F. Klapper, and Rima Turk-Ariss. 2009. Bank competition and financial stability. *Journal of Financial Services Research* 35: 99–118. [CrossRef]

Bessler, Wolfgang, and Philipp Kurmann. 2014. Bank risk factors and changing risk exposures: Capital market evidence before and during the financial crisis. *Journal of Financial Stability* 13: 151–66. [CrossRef]

Bikker, Jacob A., and Katharina Haaf. 2002. Measures of Competition and Concentration in the BankingIndustry: A Review of the Literature. *Economic and Financial Modelling* 9: 53–98.

Bikker, Jacob A., Sherrill Shaffer, and Laura Spierdijk. 2012. Assessing competition with the panzar-rosse model: The role of scale, costs, and equilibrium. *Review of Economics and Statistics* 94: 1025–44. [CrossRef]

Boot, Arnoud, and Stuart Greenbaum. 2010. Bank regulation, reputation and rents: theory and policy implications. In *Capital Markets and Financial Intermediation*. Cambridge: Cambridge University Press, pp. 262–85. [CrossRef]

Boyd, John H., and Gianni De Nicolo. 2005. The Theory of Bank Risk Taking Revisited. *Journal of Finance* 60: 1329–43. [CrossRef]

Chan, Yuk-Shee, Stuart I. Greenbaum, and Anjan V. Thakor. 1986. Information reusability, competition and bank asset quality. *Journal of Banking and Finance* 10: 243–53. [CrossRef]

Choi, Sungho, and Iftekhar Hasan. 2005. Ownership, governance, and bank performance: Korean experience. *Financial Markets, Institutions and Instruments* 14: 215–42. [CrossRef]

Claessens, Stijn, and Luc Laeven. 2004. What Drives Bank Competition? Some International Evidence. *Journal of Money, Credit, and Banking* 36: 563–83. [CrossRef]

Claessens, Stijn, and Neeltje Van Horen. 2011. *Foreign Banks: Trends, Impact and Financial Stability*. Washington, DC: International Monetary Fund. [CrossRef]

Claessens, Stijn, and Neeltje Van Horen. 2014. Foreign banks: Trends and impact. *Journal of Money, Credit and Banking* 46: 295–326. [CrossRef]

Claessens, Stijn, and Neeltje Van Horen. 2015. The Impact of the Global Financial Crisis on Banking Globalization. *IMF Economic Review* 63: 868–918. [CrossRef]

Claessens, Stijn, Aslı Demirgüç-Kunt, and Harry Huizinga. 2001. How does foreign entry affect domestic banking markets? *Journal of Banking and Finance* 25: 891–911. [CrossRef]

De Haas, Ralph, and Iman Van Lelyveld. 2014. Multinational banks and the global financial crisis: Weathering the perfect storm? *Journal of Money, Credit and Banking* 46: 333–64. [CrossRef]

Degryse, Hans, Olena Havrylchyk, Emilia Jurzyk, and Sylwester Kozak. 2012. Foreign bank entry, credit allocation and lending rates in emerging markets: Empirical evidence from Poland. *Journal of Banking and Finance* 36: 2949–59. [CrossRef]

Dekle, Robert, and Mihye Lee. 2015. Do foreign bank affiliates cut their lending more than the domestic banks in a financial crisis? *Journal of International Money and Finance* 50: 16–32. [CrossRef]

Delis, Manthos D., Kien C. Tran, and Efthymios G. Tsionas. 2012. Quantifying and explaining parameter heterogeneity in the capital regulation-bank risk nexus. *Journal of Financial Stability* 8: 57–68. [CrossRef]

Dong, Hui, Frank M. Song, and Libin Tao. 2011. Regulatory Arbitrage: Evidence from Bank Cross-Border MandAs. *SSRN Electronic Journal*. [CrossRef]

East Asian Bureau of Economic Research, and China Center for International Economic Exchanges. 2016. Investment, human capital and labour movement. In *Partnership for Change*. ANU Press, pp. 109–36. Available online: http://www.jstor.org/stable/j.ctt1rqc94n.12 (accessed on 3 May 2019).

Edison, Hali J., Ross Levine, Luca Ricci, and Torsten Sløk. 2002. International financial integration and economic growth. *Journal of International Money and Finance* 21: 749–76. [CrossRef]

Fang, Yiwei, Iftekhar Hasan, and Katherin Marton. 2014. Institutional development and bank stability: Evidence from transition countries. *Journal of Banking and Finance* 39: 160–76. [CrossRef]

Fischer, Stanley. 2015. The Federal Reserve and the Global Economy. *IMF Economic Review* 63: 8–21. [CrossRef]

Gormley, Todd A. 2010. The impact of foreign bank entry in emerging markets: Evidence from India. *Journal of Financial Intermediation* 19: 26–51. [CrossRef]

Haber, Stephen. 2004. Comment on "How Foreign Participation and Market Concentration Impact Bank Spreads: Evidence from Latin America" by Maria Soledad Martinez Peria and Ashoka Mody. *Journal of Money, Credit and Banking* 36: 539–42. [CrossRef]

Hassan, M. Kabir, Benito Sanchez, Geoffrey M. Ngene, and Ali Ashraf. 2012. Financial Liberalization and Foreign Bank Entry on the Domestic Banking Performance in MENA Countries. *African Development Review* 24: 195–207. [CrossRef]

Houston, Joel F., Chen Lin, and Yue Ma. 2012. Regulatory Arbitrage and International Bank Flows. *Journal of Finance* 67: 1845–95. [CrossRef]

Jeon, Bang Nam, María Pía Olivero, and Ji Wu. 2011. Do foreign banks increase competition? Evidence from emerging Asian and Latin American banking markets. *Journal of Banking and Finance* 35: 856–75. [CrossRef]

Jiménez, Gabriel, Jose A. Lopez, and Jesús Saurina. 2013. How does competition affect bank risk-taking? *Journal of Financial Stability* 9: 185–95. [CrossRef]

Karolyi, G. Andrew, and Alvaro G. Taboada. 2015. Regulatory Arbitrage and Cross-Border Bank Acquisitions. *Journal of Finance* 70: 2395–450. [CrossRef]

Keeley, Michael C. 1990. Deposit insurance, risk, and market power in banking. *American Economic Review* 80: 1183–200.

Kim, In Joon, Jiyeon Eppler-Kim, Wi Saeng Kim, and Suk Joon Byun. 2010. Foreign investors and corporate governance in Korea. *Pacific Basin Finance Journal* 18: 390–402. [CrossRef]

Kleymenova, Anya, Andrew K. Rose, and Tomasz Wieladek. 2016. Does Government Intervention Affect Banking Globalization? *Journal of the Japanese and International Economies* 40: 43–58. [CrossRef]

Kouretas, Georgios P., and Chris Tsoumas. 2016. Foreign bank presence and business regulations. *Journal of Financial Stability* 24: 104–16. [CrossRef]

Kraft, Evan. 2004. Foreign Banks in Croatia: Reasons for Entry, Performance and Impacts. *Journal of Emerging Market Finance* 3: 153–74. [CrossRef]

Lensink, Robert, and Niels Hermes. 2004. The short-term effects of foreign bank entry on domestic bank behavior: Does economic development matter? *Journal of Banking and Finance* 28: 553–68. [CrossRef]

Levine, Ross. 1997. American Economic Association Financial Development and Economic Growth: Views and Agenda Financial Development and Economic Growth: Views and Agenda. *Source Journal of Economic Literature Journal of Economic Literature* 35: 688–726.

Luo, Yun, Sailesh Tanna, and Glauco De Vita. 2016. Financial openness, risk and bank efficiency: Cross-country evidence. *Journal of Financial Stability* 24: 132–48. [CrossRef]

Marcus, Alan J. 1984. Deregulation and bank financial policy. *Journal of Banking and Finance* 8: 557–65. [CrossRef]

Moch, Nils. 2013. Competition in fragmented markets: New evidence from the German banking industry in the light of the subprime crisis. *Journal of Banking and Finance* 37: 2908–19. [CrossRef]

Modén, Karl-Markus, Pehr-Johan Norbäck, and Lars Persson. 2008. Efficiency and ownership structure: The case of Poland. *World Economy* 31: 437–60. [CrossRef]

Molyneux, Philip, Linh H. Nguyen, and Ru Xie. 2013. Foreign bank entry in South East Asia. *International Review of Financial Analysis* 30: 26–35. [CrossRef]

Noman, Abu Hanifa Md, Chan Sok Gee, and Che Ruhana Isa. 2018. Does bank regulation matter on the relationship between competition and financial stability? Evidence from Southeast Asian countries. *Pacific Basin Finance Journal* 48: 144–61. [CrossRef]

Okuda, Hidenobu, and Suvadee Rungsomboon. 2006. Comparative cost study of foreign and Thai domestic banks in 1990–2002: Its policy implications for a desirable banking industry structure. *Journal of Asian Economics* 17: 714–37. [CrossRef]

Panzar, John C., and James N. Rosse. 1987. Testing for "Monopoly" Equilibrium. *Journal of Industrial Economics* 35: 443–56. [CrossRef]

Peng, Xu. 2017. *Foreign Institutional Ownership and Risk Taking*. REIT Discussion Paper Series; Tokyo: Research Institute of Economy, Trade and Industry, pp. 1–33.

Polovina, Nereida, and Ken Peasnell. 2015. The effect of foreign management and board membership on the performance of foreign acquired turkish banks. *International Journal of Managerial Finance* 11: 359–87. [CrossRef]

Rey, Hélène. 2013. *Dilemma not Trilemma: The Global Financial Cycle and Monetary Policy Independence*. Cambridge: National Bureau of Economic Research. [CrossRef]

Rokhim, Rofikoh, and Anindya Pradipta Susanto. 2013. The increase of foreign ownership and its impact on the performance, competition and risk in the Indonesian banking industry. *Asian Journal of Business and Accounting* 6: 139–55. [CrossRef]

Saif-Alyousfi, Abdulazeez Y. H., Asish Saha, and Rohani Md-Rus. 2017. Profitability of Saudi Commercial Banks: A comparative evaluation between domestic and foreign banks using CAMEL parameters. *International Journal of Economics and Financial Issues* 7: 477–84.

Saleh, Mohamad Sofuan Mohamad. 2015. The impact of foreign banks entry on domestic banks' profitability in a transition economy. Paper presented at 2nd International Conference on Management and Muamalah, Selangor, Malaysia, November 16–17; pp. 300–10.

Sengupta, Rajdeep. 2007. Foreign entry and bank competition. *Journal of Financial Economics* 84: 502–28. [CrossRef]

Šević, Zeljko. 2002. Comparing Financial Systems. Franklin Allen and Douglas Gale, The MIT Press, Cambridge, MA. *International Journal of Finance and Economics* 6: 269–70. [CrossRef]

Shen, Chung-Hua, Chin-Hwa Lu, and Meng-Wen Wu. 2009. Impact of foreign bank entry on the performance of chinese banks. *China and World Economy* 17: 102–21. [CrossRef]

Simpasa, Anthony M. 2013. Increased foreign bank presence, privatisation and competition in the Zambian banking sector. *Managerial Finance* 39: 787–808. [CrossRef]

Spong, Kenneth, and Richard J. Sullivan. 2007. Corporate Governance and Bank Performance. In *Corporate Governance in Banking: A Global Perspective*. Cheltenham: Edward Elgar Publishing. [CrossRef]

Sufian, Fadzlan, and Muzafar Shah Habibullah. 2010. Does Foreign Banks Entry Fosters Bank Efficiency? Empirical Evidence from Malaysia. *Inzinerine Ekonomika-Engineering Economics* 21: 464–74.

Ukaegbu, Ben, and Isaiah Oino. 2014. The impact of foreign bank entry on domestic banking in a developing country the Kenyan perspective. *Banks and Bank Systems* 9: 28–35.

Unite, Angelo A., and Michael J. Sullivan. 2003. The effect of foreign entry and ownership structure on the Philippine domestic banking market. *Journal of Banking and Finance* 27: 2323–45. [CrossRef]

Vijaya, Ramya M., and Linda Kaltani. 2015. Foreign direct investment and wages:a bargaining power approach. *Journal of World-Systems Research* 13: 83–95. [CrossRef]

Vives, Xavier. 2011. Competition policy in banking. *Oxford Review of Economic Policy* 27: 479–97. [CrossRef]

Wu, Ji, Bang Nam Jeon, and Alina C. Luca. 2012. Foreign Bank Penetration, Resource Allocation and Economic Growth: Evidence from Emerging Economies. *Journal of Economic Integration* 25: 167–93. [CrossRef]

Wu, Ji, Minghua Chen, Bang Nam Jeon, and Rui Wang. 2017. Does foreign bank penetration affect the risk of domestic banks? Evidence from emerging economies. *Journal of Financial Stability* 31: 45–61. [CrossRef]

Xu, Ying. 2011. Towards a more accurate measure of foreign bank entry and its impact on domestic banking performance: The case of China. *Journal of Banking and Finance* 35: 886–901. [CrossRef]

Yeyati, Eduardo Levy, and Alejandro Micco. 2007. Concentration and foreign penetration in Latin American banking sectors: Impact on competition and risk. *Journal of Banking and Finance* 31: 1633–47. [CrossRef]

Yin, Yingkai, Yahua Zhang, Xiaotian Tina Zhang, and Fang Hu. 2015. Does Foreign Bank Entry Make Chinese Banks Stronger? *Global Economic Review* 44: 269–85. [CrossRef]

© 2019 by the authors. Licensee MDPI, Basel, Switzerland. This article is an open access article distributed under the terms and conditions of the Creative Commons Attribution (CC BY) license (http://creativecommons.org/licenses/by/4.0/).

Article

Capital Adequacy, Deposit Insurance, and the Effect of Their Interaction on Bank Risk

Seksak Jumreornvong [1,*], Chanakarn Chakreyavanich [2], Sirimon Treepongkaruna [3] and Pornsit Jiraporn [4]

1. Department of Finance, Thammasat Business School, Thammasat University, Bangkok 10200, Thailand
2. Kasikorn Bank, Bangkok 10200, Thailand; chanakarn_ch@hotmail.com
3. Accounting and Finance, Business School, University of Western Australia, Perth, WA 6009, Australia; sirimon.treepongkaruna@uwa.edu.au
4. Great Valley School of Graduate Professional Studies, Pennsylvania State University, Malvern, PA 19355, USA; pjiraporn@gmail.com
* Correspondence: disaksek@gmail.com

Received: 20 September 2018; Accepted: 15 November 2018; Published: 19 November 2018

Abstract: This paper investigates how deposit insurance and capital adequacy affect bank risk for five developed and nine emerging markets over the period of 1992–2015. Although full coverage of deposit insurance induces moral hazard by banks, deposit insurance is still an effective tool, especially during the time of crisis. On the contrary, capital adequacy by itself does not effectively perform the monitoring role and leads to the asset substitution problem. Implementing the safety nets of both deposit insurance and capital adequacy together could be a sustainable financial architecture. Immediate-effect analysis reveals that the interplay between deposit insurance and capital adequacy is indispensable for banking system stability.

Keywords: deposit insurance; capital adequacy; bank risk

JEL Classification: G21; G28

1. Introduction

Banking crises have a long history, spreading over a hundred years from the 18th century until the latest one in December 2016, which was triggered by the resignation of the Italian prime minister upon a failed referendum to amend their constitution to give the government more power. A banking crisis usually has an adverse effect on the overall economy. The Great Depression in 1930s and the Global Financial Crisis (GFC) in 2008 are two most prominent examples of banking crises. The great depression in the 1930s was caused by the loss of confidence in financial institutions and the widespread insolvency of debtors, resulting in bank panic and bank runs, while the 2008 GFC was triggered by the liquidity shortfall in the US banking system, caused by subprime lending and resulting in many bank runs, and also a loss of confidence in the financial system. These examples highlight the importance of maintaining public confidence and financial system stability.

One of the major roles played by banks is to accept deposits from their clients. Bank deposits are basic and common instruments that people use to park their funds. Individuals usually perceive bank deposits as the least risky investments, due to the deposit guarantee that is made by their governments. As noted above, the failure of the banking system could lead to potentially disastrous events such as financial crises and recessions. As such, to protect bank depositors, many countries have set up financial safety nets such as deposit insurance, bank regulation and supervision, central bank lender-of-last resort facilities, and bank insolvency resolution procedures. To ensure that banks are prudently managed, and in order to promote public confidence and financial system stability, most countries set up bank regulations and supervisions by establishing rules stating that financial institutions must hold enough capital to safeguard the banking system. The capital requirement, also known as the regulatory capital or capital adequacy, is the amount of capital that a bank must hold to meet the regulatory requirement. In essence, regulators set capital adequacy to protect the banks themselves, and their customers, as well as the government, who would be liable for the cost of deposits in the case of a bank run.

A deposit insurance scheme is another popular tool that is adopted by authorities in many countries to promote public confidence and to stabilize the financial system. Typically, two types of guarantee (e.g., implicit and explicit deposit insurances) are used; however, the guarantee level differs among countries. Some countries that do not have explicit deposit insurance usually implement some implicit forms of insurance by giving a higher priority to depositors over other claimants of insolvent banks in the solvency proceeding, while some countries implement more advanced forms of implicit deposit insurance, such as implicit coverage where relevant authorities are always responsible, albeit partially, in case of bank failure. As noted by Demirgüç-Kunt and Kane (2002), the use of a deposit insurance scheme is controversial, as it could lead to moral hazard problems and excessive risk-taking by banks.

Although the unintended consequences of deposit insurance are widely debated in the literature, few empirical studies have explicitly tested the relation between deposit insurance and bank risk. For example, Davis and Obasi (2009) examine the link between deposit insurance and bank risk for 914 banks in 64 countries using the International Monetary Fund financial soundness indicators, and they find that deposit insurance mainly affects bank risk through its relationship with profitability and asset quality. Recently, Anginer et al. (2013) studied the relation between deposit insurance and bank risk before and after the GFC, and documented that generous financial safety nets increase bank risk in the pre-GFC period, but not during the GFC period. They concluded that deposit insurance schemes lead to the moral hazard problem during normal times, but they provide stability during the crisis period.

In a seminal paper by Calem and Rob (1999), they document a U-shaped relationship between capital and risk-taking. As a bank's capital increases, it first takes less risk, then more risk. Their argument is as follows: "a deposit insurance premium surcharge on undercapitalized banks induces them to take more risk. An increased capital requirement, whether flat or risk-based, tends to induce more risk-taking by ex-ante well-capitalized banks that comply with the new standard". Further, Blum (1999) notes that capital adequacy rules may increase the bank's riskiness.

This paper fills the gap in the literature by investigating the interplay between deposit insurance and capital adequacy on bank risk. Specifically, we aim to answer the following research questions. First, does deposit insurance affect bank risk? Second, is there a relation between bank risk and capital adequacy? Third, what is the interplay effect between changes in the level of deposit insurance and capital adequacy on bank risk? Finally, how does the financial crisis affect these relations? By addressing these research questions, we contribute to the existing debate on the moral hazard generated by the tools used by regulators to maintain the stability of the financial system.

Overall, we find that deposit insurance induces moral hazard in the normal period. Further, during the time of crisis, implementing only deposit insurance does not reduce bank risk. When considering only capital adequacy, we find that it does not properly perform its monitoring function during the normal period. However, during a time of stress, capital adequacy helps to monitor the system. When considering the interaction between deposit insurance and capital adequacy during the normal period, we find that reduction in deposit insurance is not harmful. Nevertheless, deposit insurance may be necessary, since it creates confidence among depositors, attracts small depositors to invest money in banks, and hence, alleviates the adverse selection problem. The interaction between deposit insurance and capital adequacy during the stressful period indicates the asset substitution problem. That is why banks gamble even more during the crisis period. This raises the question of whether we need blanket deposit insurance during a time of stress, as it does increase moral hazards by banks even more.

The remainder of this paper is organized as follows. Section 2 reviews the related literature. Section 3 describes the data and the methods. Section 4 presents the empirical results. Section 5 concludes.

2. Literature Review

To promote a healthy financial system and avoid bank run, regulators provide financial safety nets such as deposit insurance, bank regulation and supervision, a central bank lender of last resort facilities, and bank insolvency resolution procedures. Among these tools, this paper focuses on capital adequacy and deposit insurance, and the interaction between the two.

2.1. Capital Adequacy and Bank Risk

As noted by Demirgüç-Kunt and Kane (2002), a deposit insurance scheme could lead to moral hazard problems, as banks have incentives to take excessive risk. As such, regulators need to establish some regulations to alleviate this moral hazard problem. Kim and Santomero (1988) argue that bank capital regulation is a way to curb excessive risk-taking by banks. Further, Calem and Rob (1999) examine the effect of capital adequacy and risk taking in the banking industry from 1984 to 1993, and find that the relation between capital and risk-taking is U-shaped. That is, when a bank first increases its capital, risk is lowered. However, as the level of capital keeps rising, the risk increases. Similarly, Blum (1999) notes that capital adequacy rules may increase the bank's riskiness. More recently, Lin et al. (2005) examine the relation between bank failure and capital adequacy in the banking industry in Taiwan from 1993–2000, and find a significant positive relation between the two. Hao and Zheng (2015) show that competition in the banking industry can reduce risk taking activities by banks. Therefore, with competition, banks with low capital engage in lower risk in lending.

Shrieves and Dahl (1992) and Altunbas et al. (2007) document a positive association between changes in bank capital and risk-taking. Some prior studies suggest that higher regulatory capital requirements result in lower bank risk-taking. For instance, Keeley and Furlong (1990) report that higher regulatory capital requirements reduce the moral hazard problem generated by deposit insurance, and as a result, they weaken incentives for banks to take on higher risk. Similarly, several empirical studies such as Jacques and Nigro (1997) for American banks, Ediz et al. (1998) for British banks, Konishi and Yasuda (2004) for Japanese banks, and Maji and De (2015) for Chinese banks, report an inverse association between bank capital and risk-taking.

Recently, Ashraf et al. (2016) investigate the effect of risk-based capital requirements on bank risk-taking behavior, using a panel data set of Pakistani banks. They find that commercial banks reduce asset portfolio risk in response to stringent risk-based capital requirements. Ashraf et al. (2017) study the effect of trade openness on bank risk-taking behavior using a sample of 291 banks from 37 emerging markets. The results suggest that higher trade openness diminishes bank risk-taking. Ashraf (2018) document that higher trade openness promotes bank development by raising the volume and decreasing the cost and risk of bank credit.

2.2. Deposit Insurance and Bank Risk

A bank run happens when depositors withdraw their deposits simultaneously, due to concerns over the bank's solvency. Panic withdrawals by depositors during a bank run could destabilize the banking system. Therefore, the government introduces deposit insurance to protect depositors, banks, and the financial system. Illiquidity is often known as the prime cause of a bank run. Diamond and Rajan (2005) document the contagious nature of bank failures by arguing that bank failures can squeeze the common pool of liquidity, leading to the exacerbation of aggregate liquidity shortages, and eventually a contagion of bank failures and a total collapse of the system. They further suggest that it is difficult to determine what causes a banking crisis, as liquidity and solvency problems interact and cause each other. Levy-Yeyati et al. (2010) examine bank runs in Argentina and Uruguay over the period of 2000–2002 and find that macroeconomic risk is also a key factor for a bank run.

Given that a bank run can lead to a meltdown of the system, it is important for the government to intervene and to provide a safety net to the system. Diamond and Dybvig (1983) propose a deposit insurance system to promote stability for the banking system. Existing studies on the effect of deposit insurance on bank risk-taking and the potential for banking sector fragility are mixed. For example, Wheelock and Wilson (1995) and Alston et al. (1994) find no relationship between historical US bank failure rates and deposit insurance. Karel and McClatchey (1999) also find no evidence that the adoption of deposit insurance increases the risk-taking of US credit unions. On the other hand, Grossman (1992), Wheelock (1992), and Thies and Gerlowski (1989) document a positive and significant relationship between deposit insurance and bank risk. Similarly, Demirgüç-Kunt and Detragiache (2002) find recent evidence of a positive relation between deposit insurance and the probability of a banking crisis in a sample of 61 countries over the period 1980–1997.

More recently, Acharya and Mora (2015) empirically study the onset of the 2007–2009 crisis and find that deposit inflows into banks weakened—this increased banks' loan-to-deposit shortfalls. As this problem worsened, banks needed to attract deposits by offering higher rates, but the resulting private funding was insufficient to cover the shortfalls and, as a result, they reduced new credit. Obviously, banks weather this crisis through the government's support. Angkinand (2009) investigates how deposit insurance systems and the ownership of banks affect the degree of market discipline on banks' risk-taking, and document a U-shaped relationship between explicit deposit insurance coverage; she also finds that banks' risk-taking is influenced by country-specific institutional factors, including bank ownership. Anginer et al. (2013) study how deposit insurance affects bank risk during the recent crisis, and suggest that deposit insurance works well during a crisis, but it leads to moral hazard during normal times.

Further, some studies empirically explore the impact of deposit insurance coverage. Demirgüç-Kunt and Detragiache (2002) find that a greater coverage of deposit insurance leads to more bank risk. Imai (2006) provides evidence that changing from a blanket deposit insurance to limited coverage results in less risk-taking in the banking industry in Japan. Schotter and Yorulmazer (2009) also report that partial insurance reduces bank risk. However, Madiès (2006) does not support such findings.

Shy et al. (2014) compare three systems of deposit insurance: no deposit insurance, unlimited deposit insurance, and limited deposit insurance. They show that limited deposit insurance coverage softens the bank competition for deposits, and this leads to a loss in total welfare, compared with unlimited or no deposit insurance. Limited deposit coverage induces some depositors to transfer money between banks, in order to improve their insurance coverage. Therefore, they conclude that limited deposit insurance will soften the lending rate competition, and that banks can target specific borrowers with less competition. This implies that limited deposit insurance leads to higher bank risk.

2.3. The Interplay

Cooper and Ross (1988) extend the Diamond–Dybvig model to theoretically analyze the effect of deposit insurance in the presence of capital adequacy requirements. They theoretically show that regardless of whether the deposit insurance is full or partial, banks will take excessively risky projects. Thus, capital requirements are needed in order to overcome the adverse incentive problem from deposit insurance. In their model, the combination of these two regulatory policies can generate the first-best allocation. Manz (2009) concludes that capital adequacy regulation is not a substitute for deposit insurance. An insight from Manz's model is that blanket deposit insurance can be detrimental, and an optimal level of deposit insurance and its interaction with capital regulation can be beneficial in risk reduction.[1]

---

[1] In the literature, capital adequacy regulation and deposit insurance can be viewed either as substitutes or complements. To the extent that they are substitutes, when one mechanism exists, the other is less likely to be adopted. According to Manz (2009), however, these two mechanisms can be complements and therefore they can co-exist and be beneficial.

3. Data and Methodology

3.1. Data

As shown in Table 1, our sample includes 2129 banks from five developed and nine emerging countries from 1992 to 2015. The key variables of interest in this paper are deposit insurance and capital adequacy. Transition dates for deposit insurance are from various sources as follows. The data for Australia, Germany, and Denmark are sourced from Demirgüç-Kunt et al. (2014). The others are collected from the research paper of the International Association of Deposit Insurers (IADI) from 2005 and 2012. Based on the transition dates reported in Table 1, we define the limited guarantee of deposit insurance dummy variable (LDI) as 0 for full deposit insurance and 1 otherwise.

Table 1. Deposit Insurance Reduction Dates.

Country	Deposit Insurance Reduction Date	No. of Firm-Year Observations	No. of Firm Observations	Sample Period
Developed Markets				
Australia	1 February 2012	261	31	2005–2015
Germany	1 January 2011	25,577	1446	1992–2015
Denmark	30 September 2010	974	70	1992–2015
Ireland	1 October 2008	166	17	2000–2015
Japan	1 April 2005	2681	179	1992–2014
Sweden	1 July 1996	997	81	1995–2015
Emerging Markets				
Ecuador	1 January 2002	217	14	2000–2015
Indonesia	1 March 2007	1090	78	1992–2015
South Korea	1 January 2001	146	22	1993–2015
Mexico	1 January 2003	773	60	1992–2015
Malaysia	1 January 2011	322	67	1995–2015
Nicaragua	1 July 2003	73	5	1992–2014
Thailand	11 August 2012	399	27	1993–2015
Turkey	1 July 2004	343	32	1999–2015

This table reports the date when each country in our samples reduces its deposit insurance. Data are collected from various sources as follows: For Australia, Germany, and Denmark, data are sourced from Demirgüç-Kunt et al. (2014). The others are sourced from research paper of International Association of Deposit Insurers (IADI, IADI).

Bank characteristics are sourced from Bankscope. For bank capital adequacy, which is another key variable of interest, we follow Demirgüç-Kunt et al. (2013), and we define capital adequacy (CAR) as the risk-adjusted regulatory capital ratio, calculated according to Basel rules (the sum of Tier I and Tier II capital, divided by the risk-adjusted assets and off-balance sheet exposures).

To measure bank risk, we used two accounting based measures as follows. First, we followed Laeven and Levine (2009) and computed the z-score, a common measure of bank risk in the banking literature, as the summation of the current bank return on assets (ROA), which is the net income divided by the total assets and the bank's equity-to-assets ratio, scaled by the standard deviation of the return on assets over the full sample period. The lower z-score indicates a higher bank risk. Following Laeven and Levine (2009), we use the natural logarithm of the z-score in our analysis due to the highly-skewed distribution of the z-score (as reported in Table 2 below). Another accounting-based measure of bank risk adopted in this paper is the earnings volatility, which is the standard deviation of the ratio of earnings before tax and loan loss provision to the average assets from year t to $t-5$.

In addition, we include various bank- and country-level control variables as follows. For the bank-level control variables, for each bank and each year, we include provisions (loan loss provisions divided by total assets), bank size (natural logarithm of total assets), deposit representation (deposits of each bank divided by total deposit of each country), leverage (equities divided by total assets), revenue growth (total revenue (EBIT) over the past year), and loan proportion (net loans divided by total assets).[2]

Table 2. Descriptive Statistics.

Variables	Full Sample			Developed Markets			Emerging Markets		
	N	μ	σ	N	μ	σ	N	μ	σ
Log(Z-Score)	33,908	1.5935	0.7247	30,610	1.5257	0.6850	3298	2.2228	0.7781
Earning volatility	24,662	0.0040	0.0093	22,586	0.0029	0.0038	2076	0.0162	0.0265
CAR	15,902	0.1709	0.1258	13,457	0.1634	0.1027	2445	0.2124	0.2070
LDI	34,019	0.3288	0.4698	30,656	0.2924	0.4549	3363	0.6604	0.4736
LLP	33,420	0.1516	0.3696	30,217	0.1461	0.3059	3203	0.2040	0.7345
Log(Asset)	34,019	13.8614	1.8863	30,656	13.7873	1.8322	3363	14.5365	2.2106
Deposit	34,019	0.0003	0.0026	30,656	0.0001	0.0018	3363	0.0018	0.0060
Equity/Total Assets	34,019	0.0732	0.0647	30,656	0.0658	0.0397	3363	0.1413	0.1509
Revenue growth	31,826	0.0489	2.2553	28,784	0.0484	1.2121	3042	0.0540	6.2708
Loan	33,995	0.5946	0.1477	30,655	0.5993	0.1377	3340	0.5515	0.2143
Log(GDP Per Capita)	33,687	10.2873	0.7229	30,530	10.4875	0.2482	3157	8.3510	0.9188
Trade/GDP	34,019	0.6628	0.2350	30,656	0.6573	0.2089	3363	0.7126	0.3975
Log(Population)	34,019	18.0976	0.6992	30,656	18.0760	0.6666	3363	18.2946	0.9232
Stock Market Cap/GDP	34,019	0.4414	0.2264	30,656	0.4426	0.1990	3363	0.4310	0.3968
GDP Growth Volatility	31,808	6.5860	8.4382	28,731	5.8939	6.2583	3077	13.0492	18.0054

This table reports the descriptive statistics of all variables included in this study for the full sample, the developed and the emerging markets. Log(Z-Score) is the natural logarithm of the average return on assets (ROA) plus the equity–asset ratio, divided by the standard deviation of ROA. Earning volatility is the average standard deviation of the ratio of total earnings before taxes and loan loss provisions to the average total assets over the past five years. CAR is the Capital Adequacy Ratio: Tier I capital plus Tier II capital, divided by the risk-weighted assets. LDI is a dummy variable, being 1 for limited deposit insurance and 0 otherwise. LLP is the loan loss provision divided by the net interest revenue. Log(Asset) is the natural logarithm of total assets. Deposit represent is the percentage of the bank's deposits to the total deposits in each country. Equity/Total Assets is the ratio of equity to total assets. Revenue growth represents the growth in total revenues (EBIT) of the bank over the past year. Loan measures the net loans to the total assets. Log(GDP Per Capita) is the natural logarithm of the gross domestic product divided by midyear population. Trade/GDP is the sum of the exports and imports of goods and services measured as a share of the gross domestic product. Log(Population) is the natural logarithm of the total population of each country. Stock Market capitalization/GDP is the ratio of stock market capitalization to GDP. GDP Growth Volatility measures the variance of GDP growth for the previous five years. Firm-level data are collected from Bankscope, while country-level data are sourced from World Bank. N represents the number of observations, while μ and σ are the mean and standard deviation, respectively. The sample period for each country is as stated in Table 1.

To deal with potential omitted variables, we also control for a number of country-level variables, as both bank risk and deposit insurance can be affected by the economic conditions in a country. We draw these measures of economic development from the World Bank's World Development Indicator (WDI) database. We use the natural logarithm of GDP per capita as the proxy for the economic development of a country, the variance of the GDP growth rate for economic stability, the natural logarithm of the population for country size, and imports plus exports of goods and service divided by GDP for global integration (see Karolyi et al. 2012) and finally, the stock market capitalization divided by the GDP (Beck et al. (2010) for differences in financial development). Finally, to capture the effect of the global financial crisis (GFC), we also include the GFC dummy variable, taking a value of 1 for the years of 2007 to 2009, and zero otherwise.

Table 2 reports the summary statistics of all the variables included in this study for the full sample, both the developed and emerging markets. The two proxies for bank risk appear to measure different aspects of bank risk, as we find contrasting results for the developed and emerging markets. That is, for the Log(Z-score) variable, we find higher means and volatility in the emerging markets than those in the developed markets. The higher mean of Log(Z-score) implies a lower bank risk in the emerging markets, and longer distant to default (less likely to be bankrupt). However, for the earnings' volatility

---

[2] Revenue growth is the total revenue in the current year minus the total revue in the previous year, all divided by the total revenue in the previous year.

variable, we find that, on average, banks in the emerging markets experience higher earnings volatility, indicating a higher bank risk in the emerging markets. It should be noted that higher earnings volatility in the emerging markets, nonetheless, reflects unstable revenue growth, rather than a more direct measure of the probability of default.

Almost all bank-level variables, except for the ratio of net loans to total assets, have higher means in the emerging markets than in the developed markets. This implies that banks in the emerging markets are larger in size, have higher loan loss provisions, higher percentage of the bank's deposits to total deposits, higher equity-to-total assets ratio, and higher revenue growth, than banks in the developed markets. For the country control variables, we find that emerging markets have smaller stock markets and lower GDP, but higher GDP growth volatility, trades, and population. Further, dispersions of all independent variables in the emerging markets are larger than those in the developed markets.

3.2. Empirical Modelling

To investigate the relationship between deposit insurance and bank risk, we estimate the following panel regression model:

$$Risk_{ijt} = \beta_0 + \beta_1 LDI_{ijt} + \beta_2 GFC + \beta_3 \times GFC \times LDI_{ijt} \\ + \sum_{k=1}^{N} \beta_k Control_{ijkt} + \sum_{z=1}^{N} \beta_z Country_{izt} + \varepsilon_{ijt} \tag{1}$$

where $Risk_{ijt}$ is bank risk measured by the log of the z-score at the end of year t. $\beta_1, \beta_2, \beta_3$ are the coefficients to be estimated. LDI_{ijt} is the type of deposit insurance, 0 for blanket deposit insurance and 1 for limited deposit insurance. GFC stands for global financial crisis, and it equals 1 for the years of the global financial crisis (2007–2009), and 0 otherwise.

We include a number of control variables that are consistent with prior studies (Laeven and Levine 2009; Ashraf et al. 2016; and Ashraf et al. 2017; Ashraf 2018). $Control_{ijkt}$ is a matrix of bank-level control variables, which include LLP (loan loss provision), log(assets), Deposit (the percentage of the bank's deposits to total deposits in each country), Equity (equity to total assets), Revenue Growth (growth in EBIT of the bank over the past year) and Loan (net loan to total assets), and $\sum_{k=1}^{N} \beta_k$ are their coefficients to be estimated. $Country_{izt}$ is a matrix of country-level control variables, which includes log(GDP per capita), Trade/GDP (the sum of exports and imports of goods and services divided by GDP), log(population), stock market capitalization/GDP, and GDP growth volatility (the variance of GDP growth for the previous five years).[3] $Risk_{ijt}$ is also measured by the earning volatility as an alternative to bank risk. $GFC \times LDI_{ijt}$ is the interaction term that represents the impact of type of deposit insurance and its role on bank risk during the global financial crisis. Finally, ε_{ijt} is a disturbance term.

In testing the relationship between bank risk and capital adequacy, we estimate the following panel regression model:

$$Risk_{ijt} = \beta_0 + \beta_1 CAR_{ijt} + \beta_2 GFC + \beta_3 \times GFC \times CAR_{ijt} \\ + \sum_{k=1}^{N} \beta_k Control_{ijkt} + \sum_{z=1}^{N} \beta_z Country_{izt} + \varepsilon_{ijt} \tag{2}$$

where CAR_{ijt} is the Capital Adequacy Ratio, computed as Tier I capital plus Tier II capital, divided by the risk-weighted assets. $GFC \times CAR_{ijt}$ is the interaction term, which represents the impact of the

---

[3] Ashraf et al. (2017), using a sample of 291 banks from 37 emerging countries, report that stronger trade openness diminishes bank risk-taking. Trade openness provides diversification opportunities to banks in lending activities, which decreases the overall bank risk. In addition, Ashraf (2018) finds that higher trade openness promotes bank development by increasing the volume and decreasing the cost and risk of bank credit.

Capital Adequacy Ratio and its role on bank risk during the global financial crisis. The others are the same as in (1).

Next, to investigate the interplay between deposition insurance and capital adequacy on bank risk, we fit the following panel regression models:

$$Risk_{ijt} = \beta_0 + \beta_1 LDI_{ijt} + \beta_2 CAR_{ijt} + \beta_3 GFC + \beta_4 CAR_{ijt} \times LDI_{ijt} + \beta_5 \times GFC \\ \times CAR_{ijt} + \sum_{k=1}^{N} \beta_k Control_{ijkt} + \sum_{z=1}^{N} \beta_z Country_{izt} + \varepsilon_{ijt} \quad (3)$$

$$Risk_{ijt} = \beta_0 + \beta_1 LDI_{ijt} + \beta_2 CAR_{ijt} + \beta_3 GFC + \beta_4 CAR_{ijt} \times LDI_{ijt} + \beta_5 \times GFC \\ \times CAR_{ijt} + \beta_6 \times LDI_{ijt} \times GFC \times CAR_{ijt} \\ + \sum_{k=1}^{N} \beta_k Control_{ijkt} + \sum_{z=1}^{N} \beta_z Country_{izt} + \varepsilon_{ijt} \quad (4)$$

The variables in (3) and (4) are the same as in (1) and (2). Additionally, $CAR_{ijt} \times LDI_{ijt}$ is the interaction term, which represents the interplay between the Capital Adequacy Ratio and the type of deposit insurance and their interplaying effect on bank risk. $GFC \times CAR_{ijt} \times LDI_{ijt}$ is the interaction term, which represents the impact on bank risk of both Capital Adequacy Ratio and type of deposit insurance and their interplaying role during the global financial crisis.

We divide the whole sample into two sub samples, one for the developed markets and the other for the emerging markets and repeat the testing for Models 1 to 4.

4. Empirical Results

4.1. Deposit Insurance, Capital Adequacy, and Bank Risk

Table 3 reports the panel regression results for Models 1 to 5, where, using the log of z-score, we investigate the relation between overall deposit insurance, capital adequacy, and bank risk. Model 1 focuses on bank risk when deposit insurance is the only tool that is adopted by the authorities. As shown in Model 1, we find a positive and significant relation between the log of the z-score and limited deposit insurance, a negative and significant relation between the log of the z-score and the GFC dummy, and between the log of the z-score and the interaction term of LDI and GFC. Taken together, we argue that (i) a reduction in the deposit insurance, or limited deposit insurance, reduces bank risk; (ii) bank risk increases during the GFC period; and (iii) a reduction in insurance or limited deposit insurance intensifies bank risk during the GFC period. When deposit insurance is the only tool that is adopted by the authorities, our findings are evidence of the moral hazard problem during the normal time, while a panic-driven period may warrant the need for blanket deposit insurance, as documented by Anginer et al. (2013). Further, we find evidence that is consistent with Demirgüç-Kunt and Kane (2002), who argues that deposit insurance could lead to the moral hazard problem, and that limited coverage is an important way to mitigate such excess risk-taking by banks.

The coefficients of the control variables are generally consistent with the expectations, and with the results from prior research. For instance, larger banks with more total assets experience lower risk. Banks with larger deposits experience less risk. Banks in more wealthy countries (higher GDP per capita) sustain lower risk. Banks in countries with more GDP volatility exhibit higher risk.

Table 3. Effect of deposit insurance and capital adequacy on bank risk.

Model	(1)	(2)	(3)	(4)
LDI	0.174 ***		0.293 ***	0.314 ***
	(0.00924)		(0.0504)	(0.0504)
CAR		−0.300 *	0.0861	−0.0438
		(0.154)	(0.344)	(0.325)
PREM				
GFC	−0.494 ***	−0.642 ***	−0.592 ***	−0.686 ***
	(0.00596)	(0.0388)	(0.0379)	(0.0583)
LDI × CAR			−0.593 *	−0.415
			(0.311)	(0.307)
LDI × GFC	−0.170 ***			0.0523
	(0.0173)			(0.0764)
CAR × GFC		0.0973	0.136	1.139 ***
		(0.253)	(0.252)	(0.379)
LDI × CAR × GFC				−1.349 ***
				(0.519)
LLP	−0.147 ***	−0.197 ***	−0.175 ***	−0.176 ***
	(0.0201)	(0.0263)	(0.0263)	(0.0263)
Log(Assets)	−0.0384 ***	−0.0329 ***	−0.0337 ***	−0.0319 ***
	(0.00401)	(0.00487)	(0.00491)	(0.00471)
Deposit	5.381 **	5.862 **	5.891 ***	5.912 ***
	(2.647)	(2.381)	(2.230)	(2.229)
Equity/Total Assets	6.193 ***	6.755 ***	6.699 ***	6.711 ***
	(0.372)	(0.610)	(0.585)	(0.581)
Revenue growth	0.00119	0.00175	0.00151	0.00162
	(0.00199)	(0.00252)	(0.00253)	(0.00253)
Loan	0.238 ***	0.110 *	0.101	0.116 *
	(0.0386)	(0.0626)	(0.0649)	(0.0626)
Log(GDP Per Capita)	0.138 ***	0.470 ***	0.212 ***	0.148 **
	(0.0270)	(0.0522)	(0.0625)	(0.0646)
Trade/GDP	1.157 ***	0.238 ***	−0.234 **	−0.268 **
	(0.0445)	(0.0850)	(0.111)	(0.112)
Log(Population)	1.485 ***	−0.817 **	−0.122	−0.0967
	(0.246)	(0.336)	(0.354)	(0.352)
Stock Market Cap/GDP	−0.446 ***	0.253 ***	0.142 ***	0.128 ***
	(0.0304)	(0.0297)	(0.0319)	(0.0325)
GDP Growth Volatility	−0.000944	0.00155 **	8.97×10^{-5}	-3.08×10^{-5}
	(0.000591)	(0.000693)	(0.000776)	(0.000777)
Constant	−24.85 ***	10.25 **	1.489	1.735
	(3.972)	(5.215)	(5.449)	(5.391)
Country dummies	Yes	Yes	Yes	Yes
Year dummies	No	No	No	No
Observations	30,025	14,709	14,709	14,709
R-squared	0.590	0.714	0.724	0.726

The sample consists of 2129 banks from 14 countries. The dependent variable is the log of the z-score, computed as the natural logarithm of the bank's return on assets, plus the capital asset ratio divided by the standard deviation of asset returns. The LDI is set to 0 for blanket deposit insurance, and 1 for limited deposit insurance. CAR is the Capital Adequacy Ratio computed as Tier I capital plus Tier II capital, divided by risk-weighted assets. GFC is 1 for the years of the global financial crisis (2007–2009), and 0 otherwise. LLP is the loan loss provision divided by the net interest revenue. Log(Assets) is the natural logarithm of the total assets. Deposit Representation is the percentage of the bank's deposits to the total deposits in each country. Equity is equity-to-total assets. Revenue growth is the growth in total revenues (EBIT) of the bank over the past year. Loan is the net loans to total assets. Log(GDP Per Capita) is the natural logarithm of GDP divided by the midyear population. Trade/GDP is the sum of exports and imports of goods and services, measured as a share of the GDP. Population is the total population of each country. Stock Market capitalization/GDP is the stock market capitalization divided by GDP. GDP growth volatility is the variance of GDP growth for the previous five years. Panels A and B report full sample and subsamples, respectively. The p-values shown in Panel B are based on the Chi-square tests for the equality of coefficients on interaction terms in two subsamples with developed and emerging countries. Robust standard errors are in parentheses. *** $p < 0.01$, ** $p < 0.05$, * $p < 0.1$.

Model 2 considers the effect of capital adequacy on bank risk using the log of the z-score, when capital adequacy is the only tool that is adopted by the authorities. We find a negative and statistically significant relation between CAR and the log of z-score, and between the GFC dummy variable and the log of z-score. Taking these together, we argue that (i) a higher capital adequacy induces a higher bank risk, (ii) bank risk increases during the GFC period, (iii) during the GFC period, higher capital adequacy has no impacts on bank risk. This evidence suggests that capital adequacy does not perform an effective monitoring role. Our findings confirm a positive relation between capital adequacy and bank risk, as documented by Calem and Rob (1999), Blum (1999), and Lin et al. (2005). Hao and Zheng (2015) also show that, with the competition in the banking industry represented by the number of interstate branches, there is a positive relationship between capital adequacy and bank risk. Moreover, Zhang et al. (2015) find that all three regulations, Tier I leverage ratio, Tier I Capital ratio, and Tier I risked-based capital ratio are very important for controlling bank risk, especially in the post-crisis period. Bornemann et al. (2014) also conclude that capital reserves, within the financial accounting framework, are effective in controlling bank risk.

We argue that this positive relation between capital adequacy and bank risk implies that capital adequacy alone may not be an effective tool for monitoring bank risk, as it leads to the asset substitution problem. The asset substitution problem refers to an agency conflict where shareholders prompt the firm to take riskier investments, which in turn causes an adverse effect on the bondholder. Higher capital or equity exacerbates such an agency problem. Generally, the asset substitution problem becomes more severe during a stressful period. In our case, with a high level of capital adequacy, banks act on shareholders' (owners of the banks) interests by taking on more risky loans to increase the bank's profit, resulting in an adverse effect to depositors with limited deposit insurance. This implication for the asset substitution problem is in line with Blum (1999), who shows that, in a dynamic framework under the binding capital requirements of bank, the additional value of banks will be created with an additional unit of equity. The reason for this is that raising equity is excessively costly. The only way to compensate for such a cost is to engage in risk-taking activities.

Model 3 considers the effect of both deposit insurance and capital adequacy on bank risk, when both tools are adopted by the authorities. Overall, we find largely consistent results as in Model 1. The bank risk is heightened during the GFC period and a reduction in deposit insurance reduces bank risk. Similar to Model 2, capital adequacy has no relation with bank risk. However, the combined effect of both a reduction in the deposit insurance and the use of capital adequacy intensifies bank risk.

Model 4 considers the influence of the GFC on the effect of both deposit insurance and capital adequacy on bank risk, when both tools are adopted by the authorities. We find a positive and statistically significant relation between LDI and the log of the z-score, and also between the log of the z-score and the interaction term between capital adequacy and the GFC dummy variable. We find a negative and statistically significant relation between the GFC dummy and the log of z-score, and between the log of the z-score and the interaction term among LDI, capital adequacy, and the GFC dummy variable. These findings imply that bank risk heightens during the GFC period, but that an increase in capital adequacy during that period reduces bank risk. As such, capital adequacy appears to perform its monitoring role well during the GFC period. On the contrary, a reduction in deposit insurance, together with an increase in capital adequacy during the GFC period, intensifies bank risk. The combination of capital adequacy and limited deposit insurance heightens the asset substitution problem during the time of turmoil. Further, this is also consistent with the findings from Model 1 stating that during the stressful time, there might be a need for blanket insurance.

Furthermore, we partition the sample into the developed versus the emerging markets (results not shown, but available upon request). We find stronger results in the developed markets. When deposit insurance is the only tool that is adopted by the authorities, we find that for both the developed and the emerging markets, a reduction in deposit insurance reduces bank risk during the normal time. This is evidence of the moral hazard problem due to deposit insurance during the normal time, but not during the stressful period (Anginer et al. 2013). When capital adequacy is the only tool that is used by regulators, we find no relation between capital adequacy and bank risk in the emerging markets, but capital adequacy increases bank risk in the developed markets. This implies that capital adequacy may not be effectively used or enforced in the emerging markets. (Calem and Rob 1999; Blum 1999; Lin et al. 2005; Hao and Zheng 2015). The combined tools show an adverse effect during the normal time for the developed markets. However, the combined tools do not show any significant impact during the stressful time in either the developed or emerging markets. During the global financial crisis, a reduction in deposit insurance and an increase in capital adequacy does not significantly affect bank risk.

Table 4 reports the results when earnings volatility is used as a proxy for bank risk. We find that limited insurance coverage reduces risk significantly. This result supports the argument that the moral hazard problem is associated with the use of blanket deposit insurance. However, this relationship is not significant in the emerging markets. An increase in capital adequacy significantly reduces bank risk, as shown in Models 3 and 4. Interestingly, when these two regulatory tools are simultaneously used, limited deposit insurance and increased capital adequacy ratio significantly intensifies bank risk.

Table 4. Effect of deposit insurance and capital adequacy on bank risk—earning volatility.

	(1)	(2)	(3)	(4)
LDI	−0.000908 ***		−0.00502 ***	−0.00440 ***
	(0.000244)		(0.00140)	(0.00154)
CAR		−0.00465	−0.0218 **	−0.0235 **
		(0.00388)	(0.00855)	(0.00925)
GFC	0.00142 ***	0.000966	0.00112	2.89×10^{-6}
	(0.000252)	(0.00106)	(0.00106)	(0.00113)
LDI × CAR			0.0238 ***	0.0261 ***
			(0.00848)	(0.00953)
LDI × GFC	−0.00238 ***			-7.55×10^{-5}
	(0.000696)			(0.00177)
CAR × GFC		0.000967	−0.00140	0.0139 *
		(0.00692)	(0.00718)	(0.00732)
LLP	0.000578	2.04×10^{-5}	9.01×10^{-5}	0.000109
	(0.000563)	(0.000552)	(0.000532)	(0.000534)
Log(Assets)	−0.000470 ***	−0.000393 ***	−0.000390 ***	−0.000366 ***
	(8.00×10^{-5})	(8.86×10^{-5})	(8.24×10^{-5})	(8.07×10^{-5})
Deposit	−0.0625 *	−0.0728 **	−0.0566	−0.0585
	(0.0378)	(0.0358)	(0.0374)	(0.0378)
Equity/Total Assets	0.0286 **	0.0270 *	0.0321 **	0.0331 **
	(0.0127)	(0.0154)	(0.0149)	(0.0150)
Revenue growth	2.43×10^{-5}	2.81×10^{-5}	3.01×10^{-5}	3.27×10^{-5}
	(5.11×10^{-5})	(6.05×10^{-5})	(5.99×10^{-5})	(5.92×10^{-5})
Loan	−0.00305 ***	−0.00335 ***	−0.00327 ***	−0.00299 **
	(0.00106)	(0.00124)	(0.00122)	(0.00122)
Log(GDP Per Capita)	−0.00864 ***	−0.0105 ***	−0.00876 ***	−0.0100 ***
	(0.00174)	(0.00186)	(0.00180)	(0.00201)
Trade/GDP	0.00394 *	0.00389	0.00744 **	0.00667 *
	(0.00225)	(0.00319)	(0.00352)	(0.00343)
Log(Population)	−0.0112	−0.0225 *	−0.0320 **	−0.0318 **
	(0.0186)	(0.0134)	(0.0134)	(0.0134)
Stock Market Cap/GDP	−0.00173 ***	−0.00358 ***	−0.00285 ***	−0.00308 ***
	(0.000509)	(0.000882)	(0.000953)	(0.000968)
GDP Growth Volatility	0.000204 ***	0.000182 ***	0.000191 ***	0.000185 ***
	(3.95×10^{-5})	(3.90×10^{-5})	(3.94×10^{-5})	(3.86×10^{-5})

Table 4. Cont.

	(1)	(2)	(3)	(4)
Constant	0.298	0.511 **	0.653 ***	0.663 ***
	(0.305)	(0.218)	(0.218)	(0.217)
Country dummies	Yes	Yes	Yes	Yes
Year dummies	No	No	No	No
Observations	24,069	12,411	12,411	12,411
R-squared	0.298	0.339	0.353	0.357

The sample consists of 2129 banks from 14 countries. The dependent variable is the earning volatility, computed as the standard deviation of the bank's earnings over the past five years. LDI is set to 0 for blanket deposit insurance, and 1 for limited deposit insurance. CAR is the Capital Adequacy Ratio computed as Tier I capital plus Tier II capital, divided by the risk-weighted assets. GFC is set to 1 for years of the global financial crisis (2007–2009) and 0 otherwise. PREM is set to 0 for countries that use a fixed premium, and 1 for a risk-adjusted premium of deposit insurance. LLP is the loan loss provision divided by the net interest revenue. Log(Assets) is the natural logarithm of total assets. Deposit Represent is the percentage of the bank's deposits to the total deposits in each country. Equity is the equity to total assets. Revenue growth is the growth in total revenues (EBIT) of the bank over the past year. Loan is the net loans to total assets. Log(GDP Per Capita) is the natural logarithm of GDP divided by the midyear population. Trade/GDP is the sum of exports and imports of goods and services, measured as a share of GDP. Population is the total population of each country. Stock Market capitalization/GDP is the stock market capitalization divided by the GDP. GDP growth volatility is the variance of GDP growth for the previous five years. Panels A and B report full samples and subsamples, respectively. The *p*-values shown in Panel B are based on the Chi-square tests for the equality of coefficients on the interaction terms in two subsamples with developed and emerging countries.

4.2. The Immediate Effect of Deposit Insurance Reduction on Capital Adequacy and Bank Risk

In this section, we further investigate in Tables 5 and 6 how the timing of deposit insurance reduction, together with capital adequacy, affects bank risk. Table 5 uses the log of the z-score as the proxy for bank risk. Model 5 indicates that blanket insurance, limited insurance, and capital adequacy, each used by itself, are not an effective tool in bank risk reduction. Consistent with the findings in Table 3, we also find that the GFC period intensifies bank risk. However, when deposit insurance (blanket or limited) is used together with capital adequacy, these tools become effective, as evidenced by the bank risk reduction. Further, findings from Model 5 also highlight that blanket insurance during the GFC period lowers bank risk. This warrants blanket insurance during the stressful time. The findings from Model 6 are largely consistent with those from Model 5, with additional evidence supporting the benefit of blanket insurance and capital adequacy during GFC. Overall, we find that deposit insurance (blanket or limited) by itself leads to the moral hazard problem, while capital adequacy by itself does not perform the monitoring role well (Demirgüç-Kunt and Kane 2002; Davis and Obasi 2009; Schotter and Yorulmazer 2009). However, when capital adequacy and deposit insurance are both adopted, capital adequacy does the monitoring job well, and it alleviates the moral hazard problem of the deposit insurance scheme (Cooper and Ross 2002). Finally, during the stressful period, with capital adequacy serving as a monitoring tool, it may be beneficial to implement blanket deposit insurance rather than a reduction in deposit insurance (Madiès 2006).

Partitioning the sample into the developed versus emerging markets, we again find stronger results in the developed markets. The results from the developed markets are consistent with those that are reported for the full sample. Table 6 uses earnings volatility as the proxy for bank risk. The results from this table are in line with those in Table 5. Overall, the evidence on the immediate effect supports our main findings, as reported in Appendix A.

Table 5. The immediate effect of reduction in deposit insurance, capital adequacy and bank risk.

Model	(5)	(5a) Developed	(5b) Emerging	(6)	(6a) Developed	(6b) Emerging
Pre	−0.326 ***	−0.543 ***	0.118 *	−0.298 ***	−0.564 ***	0.125 *
	(0.0542)	(0.0799)	(0.0659)	(0.0525)	(0.0704)	(0.0672)
During	−0.0781 *	−0.116 **	0.0709	−0.0902 **	−0.114 **	0.106
	(0.0416)	(0.0453)	(0.0778)	(0.0449)	(0.0445)	(0.120)
CAR	−0.551 ***	−0.670 ***	−0.110	−0.497 ***	−0.677 ***	−0.0740
	(0.189)	(0.163)	(0.202)	(0.175)	(0.161)	(0.212)
GFC	−0.677 ***	−0.587 ***	−0.596 ***	−0.613 ***	−0.619 ***	−0.577 ***
	(0.0337)	(0.0587)	(0.0493)	(0.0509)	(0.119)	(0.0556)
CAR × Pre	0.651 **	2.096 ***	0.236	0.471	2.234 ***	0.193
	(0.330)	(0.438)	(0.221)	(0.320)	(0.385)	(0.230)
p-value for Chi-Square			0.5991			0.9940
CAR × During	1.009 ***	1.327 ***	0.386	1.090 ***	1.315 ***	0.197
	(0.249)	(0.263)	(0.247)	(0.271)	(0.259)	(0.566)
p-value for Chi-Square			0.0134			0.0008
Pre × GFC	0.152 ***	0.160 ***	0.0373	−0.0743	0.237 *	−0.0864
	(0.0239)	(0.0471)	(0.0512)	(0.0804)	(0.129)	(0.145)
p-value for Chi-Square			0.0005			0.0347
During × GFC	−0.110 *	−0.630 ***	0.0147	−0.0847	−1.118 ***	−0.0525
	(0.0669)	(0.206)	(0.0647)	(0.116)	(0.311)	(0.128)
p-value for Chi-Square			0.0021			0.0025
CAR × GFC	0.0915	−0.596	0.125	−0.311	−0.363	0.0325
	(0.255)	(0.607)	(0.234)	(0.369)	(1.073)	(0.266)
p-value for Chi-Square						
Pre × CAR × GFC				1.460 ***	−0.532	0.653
				(0.553)	(1.109)	(0.766)
p-value for Chi-Square						0.0116
During × CAR × GFC				−0.0672	3.575 *	0.322
				(0.496)	(1.867)	(0.626)
p-value for Chi-Square						−
LLP	−0.170 ***	−0.149 ***	−0.142 *	−0.171 ***	−0.149 ***	−0.143 *
	(0.0262)	(0.0202)	(0.0750)	(0.0262)	(0.0201)	(0.0751)
Log(Assets)	−0.0322 ***	−0.0257 ***	0.00876	−0.0307 ***	−0.0259 ***	0.00895
	(0.00489)	(0.00512)	(0.0103)	(0.00470)	(0.00505)	(0.0103)
Deposit	5.972 ***	8.172 ***	1.400	5.946 ***	8.248 ***	1.430
	(2.232)	(3.002)	(2.072)	(2.224)	(3.021)	(2.079)
Equity/Total Assets	6.722 ***	9.795 ***	4.712 ***	6.733 ***	9.790 ***	4.694 ***
	(0.582)	(0.996)	(0.491)	(0.578)	(1.000)	(0.497)
Revenue growth	0.00164	0.00439 ***	−0.00138	0.00162	0.00439 ***	−0.00138
	(0.00258)	(0.00166)	(0.00220)	(0.00256)	(0.00166)	(0.00220)
Loan	0.110 *	0.118 ***	0.248 **	0.124 *	0.121 ***	0.254 **
	(0.0657)	(0.0456)	(0.120)	(0.0633)	(0.0457)	(0.121)
Log(GDP Per Capita)	0.191 ***	0.576 ***	0.144 *	0.185 ***	0.571 ***	0.141 *
	(0.0648)	(0.115)	(0.0837)	(0.0655)	(0.116)	(0.0839)
Trade/GDP	−0.245 **	−1.054 ***	−0.221	−0.244 **	−1.057 ***	−0.225
	(0.110)	(0.182)	(0.194)	(0.110)	(0.181)	(0.195)
Log(Population)	−0.281	1.199 **	0.924 **	−0.311	1.224 **	0.933 **
	(0.358)	(0.584)	(0.421)	(0.356)	(0.582)	(0.422)
Stock Market Cap/GDP	0.171 ***	0.257 ***	0.307 **	0.177 ***	0.251 ***	0.307 **
	(0.0342)	(0.0525)	(0.133)	(0.0347)	(0.0522)	(0.133)
GDP Growth Volatility	−0.000424	−0.000145	−0.00293 **	−0.000330	−0.000254	−0.00291 **
	(0.000777)	(0.000925)	(0.00115)	(0.000773)	(0.000888)	(0.00116)
Constant	4.624	−24.66 ***	−14.77 **	5.165	−25.03 ***	−14.91 **
	(5.477)	(8.874)	(6.403)	(5.428)	(8.844)	(6.418)

Table 5. Cont.

Model	(5)	(5a) Developed	(5b) Emerging	(6)	(6a) Developed	(6b) Emerging
Country Dummies	Yes	Yes	Yes	Yes	Yes	Yes
Observations	14,709	12,704	2005	14,709	12,704	2005
R-squared	0.727	0.757	0.687	0.728	0.757	0.687

The sample consists of 2129 banks from 14 countries. Dependent variable is log of z-score, computed as the natural logarithm of the bank's return on assets plus the capital asset ratio divided by the standard deviation of asset returns. Pre is set to 1 for the year preceding the year of transition to limited deposit insurance, and zero otherwise. During is set to 1 for the year of transition to limited deposit insurance and zero otherwise. CAR is the Capital Adequacy Ratio computed as Tier I capital plus Tier I capital, divided by the risk-weighted assets. GFC is 1 for years of global financial crisis (2007–2009), and 0 otherwise. LLP is the loan loss provision divided by the net interest revenue. Log(Assets) is the natural logarithm of the total assets. Deposit Represent is the percentage of the bank's deposits to total deposits in each country. Equity is the equity to total assets. Revenue growth is the growth in total revenues (EBIT) of the bank over the past year. Loan is net loans to total assets. Log(GDP Per Capita) is the natural logarithm of GDP divided by the midyear population. Trade/GDP is the sum of exports and imports of goods and services, measured as a share of GDP. Population is the total population of each country. Stock Market capitalization/GDP is the stock market capitalization divided by GDP. GDP growth volatility is the variance of GDP growth for the previous five years. Country dummies are included. The p-values shown in the table are based on the Chi-square tests for the equality of coefficients on interaction terms in two subsamples with developed and emerging countries. Robust standard errors in parentheses. *** $p < 0.01$, ** $p < 0.05$, * $p < 0.1$

Table 6. The immediate effect of reduction in deposit insurance, capital adequacy, and bank risk—earning volatility.

Model	(5)	(5a) Developed	(5b) Emerging	(6)	(6a) Developed	(6b) Emerging
Pre	0.00403 ***	0.00170	0.00891 **	0.00447 ***	0.00226	0.00887 **
	(0.00142)	(0.00113)	(0.00406)	(0.00161)	(0.00138)	(0.00415)
During	0.00132	0.00164 *	0.00323	0.00273 ***	0.00172 *	0.0113
	(0.00137)	(0.000872)	(0.00547)	(0.000943)	(0.000906)	(0.00855)
CAR	0.00240	−0.000358	0.0189	0.00317	−0.000262	0.0187
	(0.00465)	(0.00255)	(0.0191)	(0.00502)	(0.00263)	(0.0197)
GFC	−0.000938	0.00111	−0.00163	0.000427	0.00227 *	−0.00157
	(0.000985)	(0.000672)	(0.00338)	(0.00126)	(0.00136)	(0.00359)
CAR × Pre	−0.0243 ***	−0.00322	−0.0416 **	−0.0269 ***	−0.00663	−0.0415 **
	(0.00860)	(0.00541)	(0.0182)	(0.00974)	(0.00692)	(0.0188)
p-value for Chi-Square			0.0011			0.9029
CAR × During	−0.00938	−0.00683	0.00726	−0.0178 ***	−0.00714	−0.0473
	(0.00835)	(0.00526)	(0.0262)	(0.00567)	(0.00539)	(0.0463)
p-value for Chi-Square			0.7906			—
Pre × GFC	0.00317 ***	−2.93 × 10^{-6}	0.00302	−0.000415	−0.00222	0.00592
	(0.000765)	(0.000590)	(0.00233)	(0.00177)	(0.00158)	(0.00495)
p-value for Chi-Square			0.1952			0.0459
During × GFC	−0.000326	0.000743	−0.00194	−0.00754 *	0.000129	−0.0112
	(0.00278)	(0.00243)	(0.00326)	(0.00419)	(0.00399)	(0.00906)
p-value for Chi-Square			—			—
CAR × GFC	−0.000698	−0.00306	−0.0155	−0.00948	−0.0120	−0.0158
	(0.00687)	(0.00424)	(0.0183)	(0.00898)	(0.00930)	(0.0194)
p-value for Chi-Square						
Pre × CAR × GFC				0.0231 *	0.0159	−0.0179
				(0.0123)	(0.00999)	(0.0251)
p-value for Chi-Square						0.1307
During × CAR × GFC				0.0364	0.00373	0.0590
				(0.0285)	(0.0264)	(0.0542)
p-value for Chi-Square						
LLP	7.67 × 10^{-5}	0.000388 ***	−0.000728	7.42 × 10^{-5}	0.000375 ***	−0.000809
	(0.000540)	(0.000125)	(0.00136)	(0.000541)	(0.000124)	(0.00138)
Log(Assets)	−0.000391 ***	−0.000136 ***	−0.00226 ***	−0.000374 ***	−0.000131 ***	−0.00226 ***
	(8.16 × 10^{-5})	(4.86 × 10^{-5})	(0.000856)	(8.02 × 10^{-5})	(4.93 × 10^{-5})	(0.000861)
Deposit	−0.0567	−0.0179	0.0825	−0.0572	−0.0194	0.0829
	(0.0378)	(0.0279)	(0.118)	(0.0377)	(0.0273)	(0.119)
Equity/Total Assets	0.0323 **	0.0350 **	0.0219	0.0332 **	0.0353 **	0.0224
	(0.0148)	(0.0147)	(0.0227)	(0.0150)	(0.0148)	(0.0228)

Table 6. Cont.

Model	(5)	(5a) Developed	(5b) Emerging	(6)	(6a) Developed	(6b) Emerging
Revenue growth	3.32×10^{-5}	-9.59×10^{-5}	8.33×10^{-5}	3.39×10^{-5}	-9.86×10^{-5}	8.38×10^{-5}
	(5.93×10^{-5})	(0.000122)	(7.89×10^{-5})	(5.93×10^{-5})	(0.000124)	(7.91×10^{-5})
Loan	−0.00326 ***	−0.00196 **	−0.00489	−0.00321 **	−0.00202 **	−0.00493
	(0.00124)	(0.000830)	(0.00638)	(0.00125)	(0.000856)	(0.00638)
Log(GDP Per Capita)	−0.0101 ***	−0.000455	−0.00426	−0.0100 ***	−0.000171	−0.00430
	(0.00214)	(0.00268)	(0.00347)	(0.00213)	(0.00270)	(0.00347)
Trade/GDP	0.00657 *	−0.00147	−0.0128	0.00639 *	−0.00149	−0.0129
	(0.00337)	(0.00237)	(0.00849)	(0.00336)	(0.00237)	(0.00855)
Log(Population)	−0.0297 **	−0.0249 **	−0.0432	−0.0313 **	−0.0260 **	−0.0434
	(0.0144)	(0.0114)	(0.0264)	(0.0142)	(0.0115)	(0.0264)
Stock Market Cap/GDP	−0.00337 ***	−0.000684	−0.00706	−0.00346 ***	−0.000495	−0.00696
	(0.00107)	(0.00149)	(0.00515)	(0.00106)	(0.00151)	(0.00517)
GDP Growth Volatility	0.000187 ***	2.69×10^{-5} **	0.000327 ***	0.000187 ***	2.94×10^{-5} **	0.000327 ***
	(3.88×10^{-5})	(1.25×10^{-5})	(8.44×10^{-5})	(3.88×10^{-5})	(1.35×10^{-5})	(8.45×10^{-5})
Constant	0.626 ***	0.432 ***	0.792 *	0.651 ***	0.448 ***	0.795 *
	(0.231)	(0.167)	(0.417)	(0.229)	(0.168)	(0.417)
Country Dummies	Yes	Yes	Yes	Yes	Yes	Yes
Observations	12,411	10,987	1424	12,411	10,987	1424
R-squared	0.356	0.238	0.267	0.358	0.239	0.267

The sample consists of 2129 banks from 14 countries. The dependent variable is earning volatility, computed as the standard deviation of the bank's earnings over the past five years. Pre is set to 1 for the year preceding the year of transition to limited deposit insurance, and zero otherwise. During is set to 1 for the year of transition to limited deposit insurance, and zero otherwise. CAR is the Capital Adequacy Ratio computed, as Tier I capital plus Tier II capital, divided by risk weighted assets. GFC is 1 for the years of global financial crisis (2007–2009), and 0 otherwise. LLP is the loan loss provision divided by the net interest revenue. Log(Assets) is the natural logarithm of the total assets. Deposit Represent is the percentage of the bank's deposits to total deposits in each country. Equity is the equity to total assets. Revenue growth is the growth in total revenues (EBIT) of the bank over the past year. Loan is net loans to total assets. Log(GDP Per Capita) is the natural logarithm of the GDP divided by the midyear population. Trade/GDP is the sum of exports and imports of goods and services, measured as a share of GDP. Population is the total population of each country. Stock Market capitalization/GDP is stock market capitalization divided by GDP. GDP growth volatility is the variance of GDP growth for the previous five years. Country dummies are included. The p-values shown in the table are based on the Chi-square tests for the equality of coefficients on interaction terms in two subsamples, with developed and emerging countries. Robust standard errors are in parentheses. *** $p < 0.01$, ** $p < 0.05$, * $p < 0.1$.

5. Conclusions

Given the recent fragility of the financial market, due to its exposure to various risks, it is important to thoroughly investigate the effectiveness of regulatory tools in curbing potential disastrous events. Our paper focuses on how regulatory tools (deposit insurance and capital adequacy) impact bank risks. To test the effectiveness of these regulatory tools in risk reduction, we conduct empirical tests for countries that introduce limited deposit insurance policies, and test its interaction with capital adequacy requirements. We further investigate how the timing of deposit insurance reduction, together with capital adequacy affects bank risk. Overall, we find that these tools used separately are not effective in curbing bank risk. In particular, capital adequacy leads to the asset substitution problem, while blanket insurance could lead to the moral hazard problem. However, the interplay between these two regulatory tools demonstrate their abilities to reduce bank risk.

Author Contributions: Conceptualization, S.J.; Methodology, S.J.; Software, S.J.; Validation, S.J.; Formal Analysis, S.J. and C.C.; Investigation, S.J. and C.C.; Resources, S.J.; Data Curation, S.J. and C.C.; Writing—Original Draft Preparation, S.J., C.C., and S.T.; Writing—Review & Editing, S.J., C.C., S.T., and P.J.; Visualization, S.J., C.C., S.T., and P.J.; Supervision, S.J.; Project Administration, S.J.; Funding Acquisition, S.J.

Funding: This research was funded by Thammasat Business School, Thammasat University.

Conflicts of Interest: The authors declare no conflict of interest.

Appendix A

Table A1. Variable Definitions.

Variable	Definition	Source/Note
Z-Score	The average return on assets (ROA) plus equity–asset ratio, divided by the standard deviation of ROA	Bankscope
CAR	Capital Adequacy Ratio: Tier I capital plus Tier II capital, divided by risk-weighted assets	Bankscope
LDI	Set to 0 for blanket deposit insurance, and 1 for limited deposit insurance	Dummy variable
GFC	Set to 1 for the years of global financial crisis (2007–2009), and 0 otherwise.	Dummy variable
pre	Set to 1 for years before transition date, and 0 otherwise	Dummy variable
during	Set to 1 for year of transition date, and 0 otherwise	Dummy variable
post	Set to 1 for years after transition date, and 0 otherwise	Dummy variable
LLP	Loan loss provision divided by the net interest revenue	Bankscope
Log(Assets)	Natural logarithm of the total assets	Bankscope
Deposit	The percentage of the bank's deposits to total deposits in each country	Bankscope
Equity/Total Assets	Equity to total assets	Bankscope
Revenue growth	Growth in total revenues (EBIT) of the bank over the past year	Bankscope
Loan	Net loans to total assets	Bankscope
GDP per capita	GDP per capita is the gross domestic product divided by the midyear population.	World Bank
Trade/GDP	Trade is the sum of exports and imports of goods and services measured as a share of the gross domestic product.	World Bank
Population	Total population of each country	World Bank
Stock Market capitalization/GDP	Stock market capitalization divided by GDP	World Bank
GDP growth volatility	The variance of GDP growth for the previous five years	World Bank

References

Acharya, Viral V., and Nada Mora. 2015. A crisis of banks as liquidity providers. *The Journal of Finance* 70: 1–43. [CrossRef]

Alston, Lee J., Wayne A. Grove, and David C. Wheelock. 1994. Why Do Banks Fail? Evidence from the 1920s. *Explorations in Economic History* 31: 409–31. [CrossRef]

Altunbas, Yener, Santiago Carbo, Edward P. M. Gardener, and Philip Molyneux. 2007. Examining the relationships between capital, risk, and efficiency in European banking. *European Financial Management* 13: 49–70. [CrossRef]

Anginer, Deniz, Asli Demirgüç-Kunt, and Min Zhu. 2013. How does deposit insurance affect bank risk? Evidence from the recent crisis. *Journal of Banking and Finance* 48: 312–21. [CrossRef]

Angkinand, Apanard. 2009. Banking regulation and the output cast of banking crises. *Journal of International Financial Markets. Institutions and Money* 19: 240–57. [CrossRef]

Ashraf, Badar Nadeem. 2018. Do trade and financial openness matter for financial development? Bank-level evidence from emerging market economies. *Research in International Business and Finance* 44: 434–58. [CrossRef]

Ashraf, Badar Nadeem, Sidra Arshad, and Yuancheng Hu. 2016. Capital regulation and bank risk-taking behavior: Evidence from Pakistan. *International Journal of Financial Studies* 4: 16. [CrossRef]

Ashraf, Badar Nadeem, Sidra Arshad, and Liang Yan. 2017. Trade openness and bank risk-taking behavior: Evidence from emerging economics. *Journal of Risk and Financial Management* 10: 15. [CrossRef]

Beck, Thorsten, Aslı Demirgüç-Kunt, and Ross Levine. 2010. Financial institutions and marketsacross countries and over time: the updated financial development andstructure database. *World Bank Economic Review* 24: 77–92. [CrossRef]

Blum, Jürg. 1999. Do capital adequacy requirements reduce risks in banking? *Journal of Banking and Finance* 23: 755–71. [CrossRef]

Bornemann, Sven, Susanne Homölle, Carsten Hubensack, Thomas Kick, and Andreas Pfingsten. 2014. Visible Revserves in Banks—Determinants of Initial Creation, Usage and Contribution to Bank Stability. *Journal of Business Finance & Accounting* 41: 507–44.

Calem, Paul, and Rafael Rob. 1999. The Impact of Capital-Based Regulation on Bank Risk-Taking. *Journal of Financial Intermediation* 8: 317–52. [CrossRef]

Cooper, Russell, and Thomas W. Ross. 2002. Bank Runs: Deposit Insurance and Capital Requirement. *International Economic Review* 43: 55–72. [CrossRef]

Davis, E. Philip, and Ugochi Obasi. 2009. *Deposit Insurance Systems and Bank Risk*. Working Paper No. 09-26. London: Brunel University West London.

Demirgüç-Kunt, Asli, and Edward J. Kane. 2002. Deposit Insurance Around the Globe: Where Does It Work? *Journal of Economic Perspectives* 16: 175–95. [CrossRef]

Demirgüç-Kunt, Asli, and Enrica Detragiache. 2002. Does deposit insurance increase banking system stability? An empirical investigation. *Journal of Monetary Economics* 49: 1373–406. [CrossRef]

Demirgüç-Kunt, Asli, Enrica Detragiache, and Ouarda Merrouche. 2013. Bank Capital: Lessons from the Financial Crisis. *Journal of Money, Credit and Banking* 45: 1147–64. [CrossRef]

Demirgüç-Kunt, A., Edward Kane, and Luc Laeven. 2014. *Deposit Insurance Database*. IMF Working Paper. Washington: IMF.

Diamond, Douglas W., and Philip H. Dybvig. 1983. Bank runs, deposit insurance and liquidity. *Journal of Political Economy* 91: 401–19. [CrossRef]

Diamond, Douglas W., and Raghuram G. Rajan. 2005. Liquidity shortages and banking crises. *The Journal of Finance* 60: 615–47. [CrossRef]

Ediz, Tolga, Ian Michael, and William Perraudin. 1998. The impact of capital requirements on UK bank behavior. *Federal Reserve Bank of New York Economic Policy Review* 4: 15–22.

Grossman, Richard S. 1992. Deposit Insurance Regulation, and Moral Hazard in the Thrift Industry: Evidence from the 1930s. *American Economic Review* 82: 800–21.

Hao, Jia, and Kuncheng Zheng. 2015. Bank Equity Capital and Risk-Taking Behavior: The Effect of Competition. SSRN. Available online: https://ssrn.com/abstract=2552206 (accessed on 14 November 2018).

Imai, Masami. 2006. Market Discipline and Deposit Insurance Reform in Japan. *Journal of Banking and Finance* 30: 3433–52. [CrossRef]

International Association of Deposit Insurers (IADI). 2005. *Transitioning from a Blanket Guarantee to a Limited Coverage System*. Basel: IADI.

International Association of Deposit Insurers (IADI). 2012. *Transitioning from a Blanket Guarantee or Extended Coverage to a Limited Coverage System*. Basel: IADI.

Jacques, Kevin, and Peter Nigro. 1997. Risk-based capital, portfolio risk, and bank capital: A simultaneous equations approach. *Journal of Economics and Business* 49: 533–47. [CrossRef]

Karel, Gordon V., and Christine A. McClatchey. 1999. Deposit insurance and risk-taking behaviour in the credit union industry. *Journal of Banking and Finanace* 23: 105–34. [CrossRef]

Karolyi, G. Andrew, Kuan-Hui Lee, and Mathijs A. Van Dijk. 2012. Understanding commonality inliquidity around the world. *Journal of Financial Economics* 105: 82–112. [CrossRef]

Keeley, Michael C., and Frederick Furlong. 1990. A re-examination of mean-variance analysis of bank capital regulation. *Journal of Banking and Finance* 14: 69–84. [CrossRef]

Kim, Daesik, and Anthony M. Santomero. 1988. Risk in banking and capital regulation. *The Journal of Finance* 43: 1219–33. [CrossRef]

Konishi, Masaru, and Yukihiro Yasuda. 2004. Factor affecting bank risk-taking: Evidence from Japan. *Journal of Banking and Finance* 28: 215–32. [CrossRef]

Laeven, Luc, and Ross Levine. 2009. Bank governance, regulation, and risk taking. *Journal of Finance and Econonics* 93: 259–75. [CrossRef]

Levy-Yeyati, Eduardo, Maria Soledad Martinez Peria, and Sergio L. Schmukler. 2010. Deposit behavior under macroeconomic risk: evidence from bank runs in emerging economies. *Journal of Money, Credit and Banking* 42: 585–614. [CrossRef]

Lin, Shu Ling, Jack HW Penm, Shang-Chi Gong, and Ching-Shan Chang. 2005. Risk-based capital adequacy in assessing on insolvency-risk and financial performances in Taiwan's banking industry. *Research in International Business and Finance* 19: 111–53. [CrossRef]

Madiès, Philippe. 2006. An Experimental Exploration of Self-Fulfilling Banking Panics: Their Occurrence, Persistence, and Prevention. *The Journal of Business* 79: 1831–66. [CrossRef]

Maji, Santi Gopal, and Utpal Kumar De. 2015. Regulatory capital and risk of Indian banks: A simultaneous equation approach. *Journal of Financial Economic Policy* 7: 140–56. [CrossRef]

Manz, Michael. 2009. *The Optimal Level of Deposit Insurance Coverage*. Wirking Paper No. 09-6. Boston: Federal Reserve Ban of Boston.

Schotter, Andrew, and Tanju Yorulmazer. 2009. On the Dynamics and Severity of Bank Runs: An Experimental Study. *Journal of Finanical Intermediation* 18: 217–41. [CrossRef]

Shrieves, Ronald E., and Drew Dahl. 1992. The relationship between risk and capital in commercial banks. *Journal of Banking and Finance* 16: 439–57. [CrossRef]

Shy, Oz, Rune Stenbacka, and Vladimir Yankov. 2014. *Limited Deposit Insurance Coverage and Bank Competition*; Finance and Economics Discussion Series 2014-99; Washington: Board of Governors of the Federal Reserve System.

Thies, Clifford F., and Daniel A. Gerlowski. 1989. Deposit Insurance: A History of Failure. *Cato Journal* 8: 677–93.

Wheelock, David C. 1992. Deposit Insurance and Bank Failures: New Evidence from the 1920s. *Economic Inquiry* 30: 530–43. [CrossRef]

Wheelock, David C., and Paul W. Wilson. 1995. Explaining Bank Failures: Deposit Insurance, Regulation, and Efficiency. *Review of Economics and Statistics* 77: 689–700. [CrossRef]

Zhang, Zhichao, Xie Li, Xiangyun Lu, and Zhuang Zhang. 2015. Deterrnants of Financial Distress in Large Financial Institutions: Evidence from U.S. Bank Holding Companies. *Contemporary Economic Policy* 34: 250–67. [CrossRef]

© 2018 by the authors. Licensee MDPI, Basel, Switzerland. This article is an open access article distributed under the terms and conditions of the Creative Commons Attribution (CC BY) license (http://creativecommons.org/licenses/by/4.0/).

Article

Competition in the Indian Banking Sector: A Panel Data Approach

Zhiheng Li [1], Shuangzhe Liu [1], Fanda Meng [1] and Milind Sathye [2,*]

1 Faculty of Science & Technology, University of Canberra, Canberra, ACT 2617, Australia
2 Faculty of Business, Government and Law, University of Canberra, Canberra, ACT 2617, Australia
* Correspondence: Milind.Sathye@canberra.edu.au; Tel.: +61-2-6201-5489

Received: 5 July 2019; Accepted: 17 August 2019; Published: 22 August 2019

Abstract: The paper aims to assess the level of competition in the Indian banking sector overall as well as within the three groups of banks: foreign owned, state owned (public sector), and privately owned. We use panel data for the period from 2005–2018. We found that the overall competition in the Indian banking sector is strong, although there are differences by type of bank ownership. The Indian banking market continues to be characterized by monopolistic competition. The various policy measures taken by the Indian government in recent years appear to have helped boost competition. A policy suggestion would be to further liberalize the banking sector for foreign investment.

Keywords: competition; Indian banking sector; panel data

1. Introduction

This paper aims to assess the competitive conditions in the Indian banking sector overall and within the three sets of banks: state-owned, foreign-owned and privately-owned. The research is motivated by the following: First, though there is a vast literature on banking competition in the US and Europe, India, the 6th largest economy in the world (IBEF 2019a), has received limited attention. Second, we use the most recent panel data for the years 2005–2018 to study competition in the Indian banking sector and analyze the competition by bank ownership type. Third, given the importance of India in the world economy and the size of its banking sector, and the liberalized foreign investment policy, several international banks are contemplating entry in India's banking sector. While competition is generally considered to be robust, issues like market dominance of public sector banks, consumer reluctance to switch, and a high proportion of un-provided non-performing assets continue to be a drag on the banking system. Finally, we extend the methodology proposed by Apergis et al. (2016) and apply it to the Indian banking sector.

The context of India is important because the banking sector continues to play an important role in the Indian economy and contributes around 3% of India's GDP growth (Debnath and Shankar 2008). Second, several reforms were initiated by the Modi government to restore the health of the banking institutions. These included the introduction of Insolvency and Bankruptcy Code 2016 and recapitalization of public sector banks[1]. Whether these measures initiated by the Modi government after it came to power in 2014, improved competitive conditions in the Indian banking sector is an issue that has not been examined so far. We fill this gap.

The Indian commercial banking sector consists of 27 public sector banks, 21 private sector banks, and 49 foreign banks. There are also 56 regional rural banks, 1562 urban cooperative banks, and 94,384

---

[1] As noted by Mohapatra and Jha (2018), the Modi government infused Rs 66.90 billion in the public sector banks during 2014–2015 and Rs 250 billion each in the years 2015–2016 and 2016–2017. It further intended to infuse Rs 880 billion in 2017–2018.

rural cooperative banks. The total loans extended by commercial banks alone amounted to Rs 93,751.17 billion (US$1299.39 billion), and deposits amounted to Rs 120,818.92 billion (US$1866.22 billion) by the end of first quarter of 2019, while the assets of public sector banks alone were US$1557.04 billion in 2018 (IBEF 2019b).

We make following important contributions to the literature:

(a) We compare the competitive conditions among the public, private, and foreign banks, which has not been attempted in prior studies on Indian banking except by Prasad and Ghosh (2007);
(b) We use panel data analysis similar to Apergis et al. (2016) to bring additional insights not found in prior studies;
(c) We confirm the findings of prior studies on competition in Indian banking, using a different methodology and latest available data.

Besides these contributions to the literature, the study could also help inform policy and strategic managerial decisions, especially for banks considering to enter or expand in the flourishing Indian banking market.

The paper is organized as follows. Section 2 presents the literature review. The methodology is presented in Section 3. Section 4 presents the results and discussion, and Section 5 concludes.

2. Theory and Literature Review

The theory of contestable markets (Baumol 1982) provides the theoretical rationale for competition studies. The theory posits that in a contestable market there are no entry or exit barriers. Consequently, the market reaches stability and equilibrium, whatever be the structure—monopoly, oligopoly or duopoly—provided the market outcome is sustainable.

In the literature, competition is measured by either the structural (non-formal) approach or the non-structural (formal) approach. The structure-conduct-performance (SCP) paradigm is used as the framework in the structural approach. It posits that concentration of market power can lead to lower deposit rates and higher lending rates thereby enabling banks to earn monopolistic profits. The Herfindahl–Hirschman index (HHI) is used to examine the relationship between concentration and market power. To obtain HHI, either the deposits or total assets or total loans for each bank are squared and thereafter summed up. The three or five-firm concentration ratio is calculated which depicts the state of market concentration.

The alternative efficient structure hypothesis (ESH) posits that it is not market power that brings higher profits but the efficiency gains that follow market concentration. In the non-structural approach, generally two methods have been used: Bresnahan (1982) model and the Panzar and Rosse (1987) model. Bresnahan (1982) and Lau (1982) used aggregate industry data and a parameter to proxy market power and estimated a simultaneous equation model. Researchers such as Shaffer (1993) and Bikker and Haaf (2002) have used this model.

The Panzar and Rosse (1987) model examines how the changes in factor input prices affect the revenue of a bank. As the model uses bank-specific data, it captures unique bank characteristics. Many studies have used the Panzar and Rosse H statistic to assess the competitive conditions in the banking market in US, Europe, and other countries. These studies (for example, Berg and Kim 1998; Bikker and Groeneveld 2000; Shaffer 2002; Bikker and Haaf 2002; Beck et al. 2006), generally found that banks operated in a monopolistic competition. When a multi-country study was conducted by Gutiérrez de Rozas (2007), it was found that US Banks were more competitive compared to the European banks. Claessens and Laeven (2004) computed H statistic for the years 1994–2001 for 50 countries—both developed and developing—and found that monopolistic competition prevailed in the banking markets of these countries. Bikker and Spierdijk (2008) similarly found monopolistic competition in the banking market of EU countries. Fosu (2013) in the context of a sub-regional study of banking competition in Africa found that the banking markets could be described by monopolistic competition. Barros and Mendes (2016) found that in Angola, the banking market was monopolistic.

Similarly, Anginer et al. (2012) used data for 63 countries over 1997–2009 and found a positive relationship between competition and systemic stability. The majority of the other studies on banking competition also suggest that generally the market is characterized by monopolistic competition (Apergis et al. 2016). In such a market, as suggested by the theory of monopolistic competition, firms have little to no control over the market price and, as such, compete on the basis of product differentiation. Consequently, to improve profitability and to compete in the market, managers have to resort to strategies like mergers, acquisitions, improving operational cost efficiency, asset and liabilities diversification, and increasing non-interest revenue (Andrieș and Căpraru 2014). There are many other notable studies on competition in banking (for example, Yüksel et al. 2016, 2018; Dinçer and Yüksel 2018; Dinçer et al. 2019).

Studies on competition in Indian banking are limited. Prasad and Ghosh (2005) computed the Panzar and Rosse H-statistic of Indian banks using data of 64 commercial banks for the period 1997–2004 and found that the Indian banking market demonstrated a monopolistic competition. Prasad and Ghosh (2007) used annual data of scheduled commercial banks for the period 1996–2004 and again confirmed the results of their earlier study. Mishra (2011) studied 75 banks classified by ownership—public, private, and foreign—over a period of 1997–2008 using two panel data sets—each of 6 years. They found that the Indian banking sector is characterized by monopolistic competition and that liberalization has helped improve its efficiency, productivity and stability. Mishra and Sahoo (2012) studied 59 Indian banks for the years 1999–2000 to 2008–2009 and found a multi-directional and dynamic relationship in the Indian banking sector. Ansari (2012) found that the Indian loan market was monopolistic and that public sector banks and private sector banks were more competitive than foreign banks. Dutta (2013) analyzed the degree of competition in the Indian banking sector for the period 1997–1998 to 2004–2005 and found that the competitive environment improved following banking reforms and that competition has become more severe. Apergis (2015) in a study of 21 emerging market economies, that included India, found that these markets were characterized by monopolistic competition. Rakshit and Bardhan (2019) measured the competitive conditions in India using a sample of 70 commercial banks over the period 1996–2016. It was found that public sector banks experienced a relatively higher degree of competition compared to private and foreign banks. Like other emerging markets, Sinha and Sharma (2016) found that the Indian banking market is characterized by monopolistic competition. Arrawatia et al. (2019) studied banking competition in India for the period 1996–2016 using the learner index approach and confirmed the monopolistic competitive conditions.

The present study improves on prior studies in the following ways:

(a) We use more recent data, that is, for the years, 2005–2018;
(b) We examine the competitive conditions faced by ownership group of banks;
(c) We use the Panzar and Rosse (1987) model as extended by Apergis et al. (2016) and apply it to the Indian context and provide new insights not available hitherto in the literature.

3. Data and Method

In this section, the data and method have been described.

3.1. Data

The required data was obtained from the Reserve Bank of India website where yearly data is available for the years 2005–2018. The banks for which data was missing on some of the variables were dropped from the analysis. Some banks merged during the period, and new banks entered the Indian banking market. Consequently, it is unbalanced panel data. The total observations used for the analysis were 784.

3.2. Method

The Panzar and Rosse H statistic is typically used in the literature to test the theory of competitive conditions in the market. To determine the market structure, a four-step methodology is followed; that is, a log-linear form regression is estimated, and factor input elasticities are calculated; these are summed up to give the H statistic, and then the criteria as indicated below is used to determine the competitiveness of the market. The elasticities are calculated by estimating a reduced form revenue equation involving a vector of input prices and other control variables. The reduced form revenue equation of the Panzar and Rosse (1987) variety is written as below:

$$\ln GR = a + \sum_{i=1}^{n} B_i \ln \omega_i + \sum_{i=1}^{n} \gamma_i \ln CF_i + \varepsilon$$

where GR refers to gross revenue, ω_i refers to the ith input factor, and CF refers to firm-specific control factors. The equation for computing H statistic is as below:

$$H = \sum_{i=1}^{k} B_i$$

where $k = 3$ refers to the three factor input elasticities.

Panzar and Rosse (1987) show that when H is negative the market is monopolistic. If it is 1, the market is perfectly competitive and in long-run equilibrium, and when the H lies between 0 and 1, it is considered to be monopolistically competitive market.

Apergis et al. (2016), however, point out that the method is not useful for comparing the competition between large and small banks or between banks by ownership type—foreign vs. domestic, for example. Furthermore, as Bikker and Spierdijk (2008) and Bikker et al. (2012) show, the use of both scaled and unscaled price or revenue function in modelling, as most prior studies have done, can lead to unreliable estimation of the H statistic. To overcome these limitations of prior studies, Apergis et al. (2016) used both scaled and unscaled price and revenue equations to estimate H statistic in the context of European banking.

Following from Molyneux et al. (1994), Bikker and Haaf (2002), Bikker and Spierdijk (2008), Anginer et al. (2012), and Apergis et al. (2016), we estimate five reduced-form revenue equations as below:

$$\ln(P_{it}) = a + \beta_1 \ln(FUND_{it}) + \beta_2 \ln(WAGE_{it}) + \beta_3 \ln(CAP_{it}) \\ + \gamma_1 \ln(LEV_{it}) + \gamma_2 \ln(RISK_{it}) + \gamma_3 \ln(SIZE_{it}) + \epsilon_{it} \quad (1)$$

$$\ln(ROA_{it}) = a + \beta_1 \ln(FUND_{it}) + \beta_2 \ln(WAGE_{it}) + \beta_3 \ln(CAP_{it}) \\ + \gamma_1 \ln(LEV_{it}) + \gamma_2 \ln(RISK_{it}) + \gamma_3 \ln(SIZE_{it}) + \epsilon_{it} \quad (2)$$

$$\ln(Z_{it}) = a + \beta_1 \ln(FUND_{it}) + \beta_2 \ln(WAGE_{it}) + \beta_3 \ln(CAP_{it}) \\ + \gamma_1 \ln(LEV_{it}) + \gamma_2 \ln(RISK_{it}) + \gamma_3 \ln(SIZE_{it}) + \epsilon_{it} \quad (3)$$

Since Bikker et al. (2012) point out that scaled revenue and price functions as above are likely to over-estimate banking competition, we estimate H indices generated by following unscaled models as a check of robustness.

$$\ln(GIR_{it}) = a + \beta_1 \ln(FUND_{it}) + \beta_2 \ln(WAGE_{it}) + \beta_3 \ln(CAP_{it}) \\ + \gamma_1 \ln(LEV_{it}) + \gamma_2 \ln(RISK_{it}) + \gamma_3 \ln(SIZE_{it}) + \epsilon_{it} \quad (4)$$

$$\ln(TR_{it}) = a + \beta_1 \ln(FUND_{it}) + \beta_2 \ln(WAGE_{it}) + \beta_3 \ln(CAP_{it}) \\ + \gamma_1 \ln(LEV_{it}) + \gamma_2 \ln(RISK_{it}) + \gamma_3 \ln(SIZE_{it}) + \epsilon_{it} \quad (5)$$

In the above equations, a and ϵ_{it} are the intercept and the error term respectively. The other variables and their measures are tabulated below in Table 1.

Table 1. Variables and their measurements.

Variable	Description
P_{it}	Ratio of gross interest revenue to total assets for bank i at time t, which is a proxy for loan prices
$FUND_{it}$	Ratio of interest expenses to total deposits and money market funds for bank i at time t, which is a proxy for average funding cost
$WAGE_{it}$	Ratio of personnel expenses to total assets for bank i at time t, which is a proxy for wage rate
CAP_{it}	Ratio of operating and administrative expenses to total assets for bank i at time t, which is a proxy for the price for physical capital employed
LEV_{it}	Ratio of equity to total assets for bank i at time t, which is a proxy for the leverage
$RISK_{it}$	Ratio of net loans to total assets for bank i at time t, which is a proxy for the credit risk
$SIZE_{it}$	Total assets
ROA_{it}	Represents pre-tax return on assets
Z_{it}	Ratio of total revenue to total assets for bank i at time t
GIR_{it}	Gross interest revenue
TR_{it}	Total revenue

The sum of three elasticities yields the H statistic in Equations (1) and (3) above.

The data for all variables is annual and the variables are in their natural logarithms. The data are reported in Indian currency (Rupees). Conversion into US dollars or other foreign currency is required in a multi-country study.

Summary statistics of the variables included in the model are presented in Tables A1 and A2 in the Appendix A. As can be seen from the standard deviation of the variables, the data do not depict any major variation from the mean. Similarly, the values of skewness and kurtosis suggest that the data are not normally distributed.

The level of competition has been assessed using fixed effects panel GLS estimator, and robustness has been tested by OLS estimator advocated by Pedroni (2000).

4. Results and Discussion

We present and discuss the results of our study in this section.

4.1. Stationarity Test

The results of unit root test are presented in Table A3. The results do not support the presence of unit root. Consequently, the levels data were used for estimation purposes.

4.2. Estimation

We present the results of estimation of the five models as indicated earlier in Table A4. The profit, ROA, and Z columns refer to scaled regression results, while GIR and TR are unscaled regression results representing Equations (1) to (3) and (4) and (5), respectively.

Table A4 presents the results of OLS, fixed effects, and random effects regressions for all banks as well as separately for the foreign banks group, public sector banks groups, and private-sector banks group. As the tables are large, these have been presented in the Appendix A.

As can be seen from the tables, the CAP variable has a smaller (co-efficient) value than FUND and WAGE variables in Equation (1) (profit equation). It is indicative of the fact that excess physical capital (such as the number of branches) does not result in abnormal revenue. In the ROA test and in the Z test, the CAP variable has a larger value than FUND and WAGE variables whichever regression method—OLS, fixed effects, or random effects—is used. It signifies that return on assets is impacted by input prices. The robustness of models 1 to 3 has been checked by Equations (4) and (5)—the GIR and TR columns in Table A4. The high R squared values in OLS of these equations indicate high collinearity.

Table A4 also shows the values of VIF. It can be seen that the values are much below 10. VIF values above 10 are indicative of multi-collinearity (Hair et al. 2006).

The H index (which is the sum of elasticities in Equations (1) to (3)) is presented in Table A5 (see the Appendix A).

From Table A5, it can be seen that the H statistic for all banks in India for all the years of the study stood at 0.47, which indicates that monopolistic competition prevailed. For the public sector banks group, private-sector banks group, and the foreign banks group, the H statistic was 0.50, 0.65, and 0.46, respectively, which suggests that private sector banks groups were more competitive as compared to the other two groups, and the foreign banks group was the least competitive amongst the three groups. The empirical results of this study are similar to those of prior studies (such as Claessens and Laeven 2004; Casu and Girardone 2006; Gutiérrez de Rozas 2007; Prasad and Ghosh 2007; Ansari 2012; Dutta 2013) and provide evidence of monopolistic competition.

Prasad and Ghosh (2007) analyzed scheduled commercial banks data for the period 1996–2004, and found that the H statistic was 0.20 for public sector banks. In our study, the value stands at 0.50 which indicates increased competition in the public sector banks group. Similarly, for the foreign banks and private bank groups, these authors reported H statistic of 0.45 and 0.55, respectively. We found the H statistic for these group to be 0.46 and 0.65, respectively, indicating increased competition in all the three groups. Zhao et al. (2010) who examined the Indian lending market found that during 1998–2004 (study years) competition was stronger. Ansari (2012) using data for the period 1996–2011 found that the concentration in public sector banks and private sector banks was lower than in foreign banks. Our results are similar.

The competitive conditions in the Indian banking market are different from those in other developing countries. In Ghana, for example, banking is highly concentrated (Adjei-Frimpong et al. 2016). Studies in Africa and Angola by Fosu (2013) and Barros and Mendes (2016), respectively, found that the African banking market demonstrated monopolistic competition while the Angolan banking market was monopolistic.

The Government of India has initiated a program of merger of public sector banks to form four major banks in that sector to enable them to be internationally competitive. Accordingly, three major public sector banks, viz., Dena Bank, Vijaya Bank, and Bank of Baroda were merged in 2018. The merger will become effective from 1 April 2019. More mergers are on the cards as the government wants to create large banks that could compete globally. The mergers are unlikely to adversely impact competition in the sector as a whole. The Indian banking sector is, however, sagged with some major problems such as bad loans, cyber threats, and bank frauds, observed the Financial Stability Report of the Reserve Bank of India (RBI). The Report found that the average bad loans of public sector banks constituted 75% of their net worth and were squeezing banks' profitability and capital positions, endangering the health of the banking system.

5. Conclusions

Typically, the three firm or five firm concentration index or the HHI are used to assess competition in the banking market. However, these ratios and indices may not be appropriate to assess competition, given the information asymmetries in corporate borrowing, switching costs in retail lending, and network externalities in payment systems (Apergis et al. 2016).

The present study aimed to assess the competition in the Indian banking sector overall and within the three bank groups by ownership, that is, state-owned, foreign-owned, and privately-owned. Unbalanced panel data for the period 2005–2018 available at the Reserve Bank of India website was used. Panzar and Rosse H statistic was computed. Following from Apergis et al. (2016), we empirically estimated the level of banking competition. The results confirm that though the Indian banking market is characterized by monopolistic competition, it has witnessed significant reduction in concentration compared to the results reported by prior studies. The results suggest that the measures taken by the Modi government since 2014 have contributed to increasing competition in the banking sector.

These findings are similar to those by Dutta (2013) who found that banking reforms have helped increase competition in Indian banking.

A policy suggestion emanating from this research would be that the Indian government needs to further liberalize foreign direct investment policy in the banking sector to reap the advantages of competition. As already indicated, the banking sector continues to be dominated by the public sector banks. This is unlikely to change given the geographical spread of these banks across the country.

Future studies could explore the banking competition in India vis-a-vis that of other Asian countries or the BRICS countries so that a comparative picture can emerge. The lessons from Indian banking liberalization over the years could be helpful for other countries in the region if analysis similar to that presented in Table A4 could be attempted for each of the bank ownership groups.

Author Contributions: Conceptualization, M.S.; methodology, S.L. and Z.L.; software, S.L. and Z.L.; validation, S.L., Z.L. and F.M.; formal analysis, Z.L. and F.M.; original draft preparation, M.S.; writing, M.S.; visualization, Z.L. and F.M.; supervision, M.S. and S.L.; project administration, S.L. and M.S.

Funding: This research received no external funding.

Acknowledgments: The authors are very grateful to the anonymous referees whose insights considerably helped improve the quality of the paper.

Conflicts of Interest: The authors declare no conflict of interest.

Appendix A

Table A1. Descriptive statistics for dependent variable.

Variables	P	ROA	Z	GIR	TR
Observations	784	784	784	784	784
Mean	−2.8	−3.85	−2.39	9.76	9.98
Max	−1	−2	−1	15	15
Min	−4	−6	−3	2	4
SD	0.41	0.58	0.49	2.58	2.44
Variance	0.17	0.33	0.24	6.66	5.99
Skewness	1.35	0.39	−0.42	−0.87	−0.74
Kurtosis	3.68	4.67	1.26	2.97	2.62

Table A2. Statistics for control variables.

Variables	FUND	WAGE	CAP	LEV	RISK	SIZE
Observations	784	784	784	784	784	784
Mean	−3	−4.8	−3.94	−4.46	−0.75	12.46
Max	0	−3	−2	0	0	17
Min	−7	−6	−5	−12	−6	6
SD	0.52	0.55	0.43	2.05	0.7	2.5
Variance	0.27	0.31	0.19	4.22	0.49	6.23
Skewness	−2.1	0.66	0.95	−0.09	−2.15	−0.77
Kurtosis	20	3.76	7.83	3.09	15.15	2.74

Table A3. Panel unit root test results. **(A)** ALL BANKS; **(B)** PUBLIC BANKS; **(C)** PRIVATE BANKS; **(D)** FOREIGN BANKS.

(A)		
	Levin-Lin-Chu (lag = 1)	Harris–Tzavalis
Dependent Variable		
P	−3.1146	0.3823
	(0.0009)	(0.0000)
ROA	−1.1360	0.3120
	(0.1280)	(0.0000)
Z	−5.1795	0.3077
	(0.0000)	(0.0000)
GIR	−8.4448	0.7775
	(0.0000)	(0.2053)
TR	−8.0946	0.7952
	(0.0000)	(0.4308)
Control Variable		
FUND	3.2552	0.4119
	(0.9994)	(0.0000)
WAGE	−2.0179	0.4337
	(0.0218)	(0.0000)
CAP	8.7533	0.3354
	(1.0000)	(0.0000)
LEV	−5.0416	0.6355
	(0.0000)	(0.0000)
RISK	−20.9664	0.5021
	(0.0000)	(0.0000)
SIZE	−7.1205	0.8119
	(0.0000)	(0.6682)

Notes: The null and alternative hypotheses are H0: Panels contain unit roots, Ha: Panels are stationary. The p-values are indicated in the brackets. Most of them are smaller than a significant level of 0.05, indicating that we can reject the corresponding H0 and conclude most panels to be stationary.

(B)		
	Levin-Lin-Chu (lag = 1)	Harris–Tzavalis
Dependent Variable		
P	−3.3197	0.4091
	(0.0005)	(0.0000)
ROA	1.4342	0.431
	(0.9242)	(0.0000)
Z	−4.8722	0.3175
	(0.0000)	(0.0000)
GIR	−6.1517	0.7716
	(0.0000)	(0.2623)
TR	−6.0160	0.779
	(0.0000)	(0.3192)
Control Variable		
FUND	29.9577	0.4667
	(1.0000)	(0.0000)
WAGE	−3.3910	0.4342
	(0.0003)	(0.0000)
CAP	10.6714	0.4677
	(1.0000)	(0.0000)
LEV	−4.8137	0.6311
	(0.0000)	(0.0001)
RISK	−3.3426	0.4772
	(0.0004)	(0.0000)
SIZE	−5.4441	0.8107
	(0.0000)	(0.5946)

Table A3. Cont.

(C)

	Levin-Lin-Chu (lag = 1)	Harris–Tzavalis
Dependent Variable		
P	−1.0061 (0.1572)	0.4009 (0.0000)
ROA	0.7258 (0.7660)	0.2187 (0.0000)
Z	−1.1228 (0.1308)	0.3079 (0.0000)
GIR	−3.7480 (0.0001)	0.8342 (0.7409)
TR	−4.0813 (0.0000)	0.8795 (0.9335)
Control Variable		
FUND	2.1392 (0.9838)	0.2952 (0.0000)
WAGE	1.2317 (0.8910)	0.4508 (0.0000)
CAP	11.7123 (1.0000)	0.5500 (0.0000)
LEV	−2.6523 (0.0040)	0.6976 (0.0264)
RISK	0.2849 (0.6121)	0.4711 (0.0000)
SIZE	−3.0872 (0.0010)	0.8456 (0.8054)

(D)

	Levin-Lin-Chu (lag = 1)	Harris–Tzavalis
Dependent Variable		
P	−0.7975 (0.2126)	0.3112 (0.0000)
ROA	−3.8816 (0.0001)	0.2964 (0.0000)
Z	−2.4022 (0.0081)	0.2943 (0.0000)
GIR	−4.7150(0.0000) (0.0000)	0.7288(0.0600) (0.0600)
TR	−3.8617 (0.0001)	0.7213 (0.0428)
Control Variable		
FUND	−4.3949 (0.0000)	0.4286 (0.0000)
WAGE	−0.5895 (0.2778)	0.4245 (0.0000)
CAP	0.3500 (0.6368)	0.2827 (0.0000)
LEV	−0.8784 (0.1899)	0.6036 (0.0000)
RISK	−21.1734 (0.0000)	0.5282 (0.0000)
SIZE	−3.7125 (0.0001)	0.779 (0.3231)

Table A4. Regression of control variables. (**A**) ALL BANKS; (**B**) PUBLIC BANKS; (**C**) PRIVATE BANKS; (**D**) FOREIGN BANKS.

(A)

	Profit		ROA		Z		GIR		TR	
	Coef.	Std. Err.	Coef.	Std. Err.	Coef.	Std. Err.	Coef.	Std. Err.	Coef.	Std. Err.
	OLS Regression									
Constant	−1.902	0.097	−4.08	0.255	−1.11	0.089	−1.902	0.097	−1.11	0.089
FUND	0.235	0.013	−0.303	0.036	0.063	0.012	0.235	0.013	0.063	0.012
WAGE	0.019	0.02	−0.368	0.052	−0.072	0.018	0.019	0.02	−0.072	0.018
CAP	−0.0072	0.024	0.5681	0.065	0.3609	0.022	−0.0072	0.024	0.3609	0.022
LEV	−0.0284	0.004	0.0243	0.01	−0.0368	0.003	−0.0284	0.004	−0.0368	0.003
RISK	0.0851	0.012	−0.041	0.031	0.0069	0.011	0.0851	0.012	0.0069	0.011
SIZE	−0.0066	0.003	−0.0034	0.009	−0.0175	0.003	0.9934	0.003	0.9825	0.003
R-squared	0.4746		0.3422		0.4258		0.9959		0.9961	
SSE	21.0152		145.445		17.763		21.015		17.763	
MSE	0.02705		0.19		0.02		0.03		0.02	
N	784		784		784		784		784	
	GLS Random–effects									
Constant	−1.3558	0.111	−3.3095	0.309	−0.9096	0.109	−1.3558	0.111	−0.9096	0.109
FUND	0.2998	0.013	−0.1812	0.036	0.1599	0.012	0.2998	0.013	0.1599	0.012
WAGE	0.0848	0.026	0.0807	0.072	−0.0201	0.025	0.0848	0.026	−0.0201	0.025
CAP	0.0565	0.03	0.1197	0.084	0.3514	0.029	0.0565	0.03	0.3514	0.029
LEV	−0.011	0.006	0.0588	0.017	−0.0198	0.006	−0.011	0.006	−0.0198	0.006
RISK	0.0897	0.011	−0.0997	0.033	−0.0443	0.011	0.0897	0.011	−0.0443	0.011
SIZE	0.0158	0.006	−0.0015	0.016	0.0088	0.005	1.0158	0.006	1.0088	0.005
R-squared	0.4695		0.1159		0.3526		0.9854		0.9856	
SSE	10.2518		83.922		10.334		10.251		10.334	
MSE	0.0132		0.108		0.0133		0.0132		0.0133	
Root MSE	0.1149		0.3286		0.1153		0.1149		0.1153	
Hausman	32.97		35.65		240.07		32.97		240.07	
(p-value)	(0.0001)		(0.0001)		(0.0001)		(0.0001)		(0.0001)	
N	784		784		784		784		784	
	Fixed effects									
Constant	−1.3378	0.127	−3.6582	0.362	−1.0624	0.125	−1.3378	0.127	−1.0624	0.125
FUND	0.3065	0.013	−0.1496	0.038	0.1761	0.013	0.3065	0.013	0.1761	0.013
WAGE	0.1121	0.029	0.2617	0.084	0.0192	0.029	0.1121	0.029	0.0192	0.029
CAP	0.0561	0.033	−0.0655	0.095	0.3239	0.033	0.0561	0.033	0.3239	0.033
LEV	−0.0091	0.007	0.0575	0.021	−0.0157	0.007	−0.0091	0.007	−0.0157	0.007
RISK	0.088	0.012	−0.1017	0.035	−0.0552	0.012	0.088	0.012	−0.0552	0.012
SIZE	0.0283	0.007	0.0078	0.021	0.0317	0.007	1.0283	0.007	1.0317	0.007
R-squared	0.7677		0.6573		0.7055		0.9982		0.998	
SSE	9.3633		76.3448		9.1797		9.3633		9.1797	
MSE	0.013		0.1057		0.0127		0.013		0.0127	
Root MSE	0.1139		0.3252		0.1128		0.1139		0.1128	
F Test	16.34		11.88		12.27		16.34		12.27	
(p-value)	(0.0001)		(0.0001)		(0.0001)		(0.0001)		(0.0001)	
N	784		784		784		784		784	

Notes: (1) The null and alternative hypotheses for the Hausman test are H0: Random Effects, Ha: Fixed Effects. The p values in the brackets are smaller than a significant level of 0.05, indicating that we reject H0 and conclude to use Fixed Effects models (better than Random Effects models). (2) The null and alternative hypotheses for the F test are H0: No Fixed Effects, Ha: Fixed Effects. The p values in the brackets are smaller than a significant level of 0.05, indicating that we reject H0 and conclude to use Fixed Effects models (better than OLS models).

Table A4. Cont.

(B)

	PROFIT		ROA		Z		GIR		TR	
	Coef.	Std. Err.	Coef.	Std. Err.	Coef.	Std. Err.	Coef.	Std. Err.	Coef.	Std. Err.
					OLS Regression					
Constant	−0.2619	0.2216	−3.9606	0.6436	−0.17	0.195	−0.261	0.221	−0.17	0.195
FUND	0.3744	0.0322	−0.6146	0.0936	0.3426	0.028	0.374	0.032	0.342	0.028
WAGE	0.2797	0.0488	−0.2963	0.1418	0.1348	0.043	0.279	0.048	0.134	0.043
CAP	−0.1015	0.0708	0.5672	0.2057	0.1078	0.062	−0.101	0.07	0.107	0.062
LEV	−0.0181	0.0082	−0.1074	0.0239	−0.023	0.007	−0.018	0.008	−0.023	0.007
RISK	0.2955	0.0619	0.5283	0.1798	0.1502	0.054	0.295	0.061	0.1502	0.054
SIZE	−0.0251	0.0089	−0.0872	0.0257	−0.022	0.007	0.9749	0.008	0.9773	0.007
R-squared	0.4402		0.3229		0.4075		0.9921		0.9938	
SSE	1.9541		16.4902		1.514		1.9541		1.514	
MSE	0.00681		0.0575		0.0053		0.0068		0.0053	
N	294		294		294		294		294	
					GLS Random-effects					
Constant	−1.015	0.2413	−4.4912	0.6996	−0.714	0.215	−1.015	0.241	−0.714	0.215
FUND	0.3276	0.0329	−0.6903	0.0954	0.3089	0.029	0.3276	0.032	0.3089	0.029
WAGE	0.358	0.0606	0.1351	0.174	0.2151	0.053	0.358	0.06	0.2151	0.053
CAP	−0.1703	0.0795	−0.0352	0.2295	0.029	0.07	−0.17	0.079	0.029	0.07
LEV	−0.0155	0.0112	−0.0696	0.032	−0.016	0.009	−0.015	0.011	−0.016	0.009
RISK	0.2176	0.0609	0.4738	0.1774	0.1	0.054	0.2176	0.06	0.1	0.054
SIZE	0.0219	0.0108	−0.0876	0.0311	0.0126	0.009	1.0219	0.01	1.0126	0.009
R-squared	0.4686		0.2915		0.4188		0.9894		0.9913	
SSE	1.4573		12.445		1.1853		1.4573		1.1853	
MSE	0.0051		0.0434		0.0041		0.0051		0.0041	
Root MSE	0.0713		0.2082		0.0643		0.0713		0.0643	
Hausman (p value)	41.34 (0.0001)		14.73 (0.0001)		29.01 (0.0001)		41.34 (0.000)		29.01 (0.0001)	
N	294		294		294		294		294	
					Fixed effects					
Constant	−1.2473	0.2459	−4.7661	0.7327	−0.9452	0.223	−1.247	0.245	−0.9452	0.223
FUND	0.2855	0.0338	−0.6796	0.1008	0.2745	0.03	0.2855	0.033	0.2745	0.03
WAGE	0.4305	0.0674	0.4147	0.2008	0.3001	0.061	0.4305	0.067	0.3001	0.061
CAP	−0.2178	0.0848	−0.3963	0.2528	−0.0391	0.077	−0.217	0.084	−0.0391	0.077
LEV	−0.0306	0.0133	−0.0167	0.0398	−0.0241	0.012	−0.03	0.013	−0.0241	0.012
RISK	0.192	0.0606	0.473	0.1806	0.0789	0.055	0.192	0.06	0.0789	0.055
SIZE	0.0393	0.0115	−0.0709	0.0342	0.0302	0.01	1.0393	0.011	1.0302	0.01
R-squared	0.6416		0.544		0.5959		0.9949		0.9958	
SSE	1.2772		11.3384		1.054		1.2772		1.054	
MSE	0.0048		0.0425		0.0039		0.0048		0.0039	
Root MSE	0.0692		0.2061		0.0628		0.0692		0.0628	
F Test (p value)	7.07 (0.0001)		6.07 (0.0001)		5.83 (0.0001)		7.07 (0.0001)		5.83 (0.0001)	
N	294		294		294		294		294	

Table A4. Cont.

(C)

	PROFIT		ROA		Z		GIR		TR	
	Coef.	Std. Err.	Coef.	Std. Err.	Coef.	Std. Err.	Coef.	Std. Err.	Coef.	Std. Err.
	\multicolumn{10}{c}{OLS Regression}									
Constant	−0.6364	0.1471	−5.0951	0.5282	−0.608	0.1264	−0.636	0.1471	−0.608	0.1264
FUND	0.3949	0.0289	−0.2476	0.1037	0.3727	0.0248	0.3949	0.0289	0.3727	0.0248
WAGE	0.1291	0.0266	−0.1179	0.0955	0.0008	0.0229	0.1291	0.0266	0.0008	0.0229
CAP	−0.0145	0.0335	0.3042	0.1201	0.1587	0.0288	−0.014	0.0335	0.1587	0.0288
LEV	−0.0219	0.004	−0.0751	0.0142	−0.021	0.0034	−0.021	0.004	−0.021	0.0034
RISK	0.2095	0.0554	−0.0892	0.1988	0.1791	0.0476	0.2095	0.0554	0.1791	0.0476
SIZE	−0.0211	0.0051	0.0539	0.0182	−0.011	0.0044	0.9789	0.0051	0.9886	0.0044
R-squared	0.6458		0.2575		0.6864		0.9974		0.9982	
SSE	1.2431		16.0199		0.918		1.2431		0.918	
MSE	0.00612		0.08		0		0.01		0	
N	210		210		210		210		210	
	\multicolumn{10}{c}{GLS Random-effects}									
Constant	−0.3591	0.182	−5.7289	0.7529	−0.492	0.1708	−0.359	0.182	−0.492	0.1708
FUND	0.5072	0.0254	−0.2745	0.1123	0.4263	0.0243	0.5072	0.0254	0.4263	0.0243
WAGE	0.1084	0.0302	0.1109	0.1269	0.035	0.0285	0.1084	0.0302	0.035	0.0285
CAP	0.0179	0.0425	−0.1218	0.1748	0.132	0.0398	0.0179	0.0425	0.132	0.0398
LEV	−0.0101	0.0057	−0.05	0.0229	−0.012	0.0053	−0.01	0.0057	−0.012	0.0053
RISK	0.1338	0.0593	0.0919	0.2515	0.1098	0.056	0.1338	0.0593	0.1098	0.056
SIZE	−0.0139	0.0066	0.0689	0.0267	−0.003	0.0062	0.9861	0.0066	0.9966	0.0062
R-squared	0.763		0.1062		0.7385		0.9968		0.9971	
SSE	0.5505		12.0176		0.5245		0.5505		0.5245	
MSE	0.0027		0.0592		0.0026		0.0027		0.0026	
Root MSE	0.0521		0.2433		0.0508		0.0521		0.0508	
Hausman (p value)	9.71 (0.1372)		7.57 (0.271)		4.94 (0.5521)		9.71 (0.1372)		4.94 (0.5521)	
N	210		210		210		210		210	
	\multicolumn{10}{c}{Fixed effects}									
Constant	−0.2914	0.1943	−5.6543	0.9044	−0.425	0.1903	−0.291	0.1943	−0.425	0.1903
FUND	0.5138	0.0262	−0.2584	0.1221	0.432	0.0257	0.5138	0.0262	0.432	0.0257
WAGE	0.0977	0.0322	0.296	0.1501	0.038	0.0316	0.0977	0.0322	0.038	0.0316
CAP	0.0369	0.0459	−0.4362	0.2135	0.1344	0.0449	0.0369	0.0459	0.1344	0.0449
LEV	−0.0064	0.0063	−0.0398	0.0292	−0.007	0.0061	−0.006	0.0063	−0.007	0.0061
RISK	0.12	0.063	0.2972	0.293	0.0965	0.0616	0.12	0.063	0.0965	0.0616
SIZE	−0.0112	0.0073	0.0539	0.0341	0	0.0072	0.9888	0.0073	0.9992	0.0072
R-squared	0.8584		0.5008		0.8372		0.999		0.9991	
SSE	0.5118		11.0903		0.4908		0.5118		0.4908	
MSE	0.0027		0.0587		0.0026		0.0027		0.0026	
Root MSE	0.052		0.2422		0.051		0.052		0.051	
F Test (p value)	19.29 (0.0001)		6.00 (0.0001)		11.75 (0.0001)		19.29 (0.0001)		11.75 (0.0001)	
N	210		210		210		210		210	

Table A4. Cont.

	(D)									
	PROFIT		ROA		Z		GIR		TR	
	Coef.	Std. Err.	Coef.	Std. Err.	Coef.	Std. Err.	Coef.	Std. Err.	Coef.	Std. Err.
	OLS Regression									
Constant	−2.2339	0.156	−4.3354	0.402	−1.0492	0.149	−2.2339	0.156	−1.0492	0.149
FUND	0.2198	0.021	−0.3492	0.053	0.0393	0.02	0.2198	0.021	0.0393	0.02
WAGE	−0.118	0.039	−0.1008	0.1	−0.0962	0.037	−0.118	0.039	−0.0962	0.037
CAP	0.1057	0.047	0.2666	0.122	0.4141	0.045	0.1057	0.047	0.4141	0.045
LEV	0.0146	0.011	0.0855	0.028	−0.0215	0.01	0.0146	0.011	−0.0215	0.01
RISK	0.0538	0.016	−0.0471	0.043	−0.0072	0.016	0.0538	0.016	−0.0072	0.016
SIZE	0.0022	0.006	0.0419	0.017	−0.0213	0.006	1.0022	0.006	0.9787	0.006
R-squared	0.3767		0.2416		0.495		0.992		0.9916	
SSE	13.225		87.1541		12.0194		13.225		12.0194	
MSE	0.04844		0.32		0.04		0.05		0.04	
N	280		280		280		280		280	
	GLS Random-effects									
Constant	−1.615	0.198	−2.9805	0.506	−0.6561	0.188	−1.615	0.198	−0.6561	0.188
FUND	0.2816	0.02	−0.1593	0.052	0.1248	0.019	0.2816	0.02	0.1248	0.019
WAGE	−0.0083	0.05	0.0661	0.128	−0.0182	0.047	−0.0083	0.05	−0.0182	0.047
CAP	0.1145	0.055	0.1337	0.141	0.3961	0.052	0.1145	0.055	0.3961	0.052
LEV	0.0137	0.014	0.1569	0.037	0.0039	0.013	0.0137	0.014	0.0039	0.013
RISK	0.08	0.018	−0.1246	0.046	−0.0572	0.017	0.08	0.018	−0.0572	0.017
SIZE	0.0169	0.013	0.0031	0.033	−0.0037	0.012	1.0169	0.013	0.9963	0.012
R-squared	0.4306		0.1469		0.3981		0.9698		0.9673	
SSE	7.8402		51.22		7.1054		7.8402		7.1054	
MSE	0.0287		0.1876		0.026		0.0287		0.026	
Root MSE	0.1695		0.4332		0.1613		0.1695		0.1613	
Hausman (p value)	21.83 (0.0013)		13.17 (0.0405)		24.27 (0.0005)		21.83 (0.0013)		8.67 (0.0005)	
N	280		280		280		280		280	
	Fixed effects									
Constant	−1.6299	0.255	−1.9271	0.656	−0.7451	0.243	−1.6299	0.255	−0.7451	0.243
FUND	0.2964	0.021	−0.135	0.054	0.143	0.02	0.2964	0.021	0.143	0.02
WAGE	0.0532	0.056	0.0813	0.146	0.0041	0.054	0.0532	0.056	0.0041	0.054
CAP	0.1107	0.06	0.061	0.154	0.3963	0.057	0.1107	0.06	0.3963	0.057
LEV	0.0035	0.016	0.1711	0.042	0.0073	0.015	0.0035	0.016	0.0073	0.015
RISK	0.0795	0.019	−0.12	0.049	−0.0687	0.018	0.0795	0.019	−0.0687	0.018
SIZE	0.0397	0.018	−0.0388	0.046	0.0179	0.017	1.0397	0.018	1.0179	0.017
R-squared	0.6708		0.5977		0.733		0.9958		0.9956	
SSE	7.1387		47.248		6.4944		7.1387		6.4944	
MSE	0.0281		0.186		0.0256		0.0281		0.0256	
Root MSE	0.1676		0.4313		0.1599		0.1676		0.1599	
F Test (p value)	11.40 (0.0001)		11.29 (0.0001)		11.37 (0.0001)		11.40 (0.0001)		24.27 (0.0001)	
N	280		280		280		280		280	

Table A5. H statistics and F tests of H = 0 and H = 1. (**A**) ALL BANKS; (**B**) PUBLIC BANKS; (**C**) PRIVATE BANKS; (**D**) FOREIGN BANKS.

(**A**)

	PROFIT	ROA	Z	GIR	TR
H statistic	0.4747	0.0466	0.5191	0.4747	0.5191
Test H = 0					
F	322.0077	0.3813	394.2126	322.0077	394.2126
p	0.0000	0.5371	0.0000	0.0000	0.0000
Test H = 1					
F	394.2846	159.7540	338.1969	394.2846	338.1969
p	0.0000	0.0000	0.0000	0.0000	0.0000

Notes: (1) Test H = 0: The null and alternative hypotheses are Ho: H = 0, Ha: H ≠ 0. All p values are smaller than a significant level of 0.05, so we reject Ho: H = 0, except that the ROA equation has a p value of 0.3813 not smaller than 0.05 where we cannot reject Ho: H = 0. (2) Test H = 1: The null and alternative hypotheses are Ho: H = 1, Ha: H ≠ 1. All p values are smaller than a significant level of 0.05, so we reject Ho: H = 1.

(**B**)

	PROFIT	ROA	Z	GIR	TR
H statistic	0.49825	−0.66117	0.5355	0.498251	0.535525
Test H = 0					
F	NA	NA	NA	NA	2238.4359
p	NA	NA	NA	NA	0.0000
Test H = 1					
F	31.3958	51.3694	25.1026	31.3958	25.1026
p	0.0000	0.0000	0.0000	0.0000	0.0000

Notes: (1) Test H = 0: We use NA as the F values are close to F = 0, and therefore their corresponding p values are close to p = 1; H0: H = 0 may NOT be significantly rejected because of NA (or F = 0 and p = 1). (2) Test H = 1: H0: H = 1 is significantly rejected.

(**C**)

	PROFIT	ROA	Z	GIR	TR
H statistic	0.648402	−0.39855	0.6045	0.648402	0.6045
Test H = 0					
F	121.8889	15.29983	89.34615	121.8889	89.34615
p	0.0000	0.000128	0.0000	0.0000	0.0000
Test H = 1					
F	93.74074	68.00511	119.4615	93.74074	119.4615
p	0.0000	2.71×10^{-14}	0.0000	0.0000	0.0000

Notes: (1) Test H = 0: H < 0 is significant as H0: H = 0 is rejected. See the main text for how to explain this. (2) Test H = 1: H0: H = 1 is significantly rejected.

(**D**)

	PROFIT	ROA	Z	GIR	TR
H statistic	0.460325	0.007275	0.543523	0.460325	0.543523
Test H = 0					
F	83.96797	0.003226	128.4961	83.96797	128.4961
p	0.0000	0.954752	0.0000	0.0000	0.0000
Test H = 1					
F	115.4128	58.99892	90.63281	115.4128	90.63281
p	0.0000	3.42×10^{-13}	0.0000	0.0000	0.0000

References

Adjei-Frimpong, Kofi, Christopher Gan, and Baiding Hu. 2016. Competition in the banking industry: Empirical evidence from ghana. *Journal of Banking Regulation* 17: 159–75. [CrossRef]

Andrieș, Alin Marius, and Bogdan Căpraru. 2014. The nexus between competition and efficiency: The European banking industries experience. *International Business Review* 23: 566–79. [CrossRef]

Anginer, Deniz, Asli Demirguc-Kunt, and Min Zhu. 2012. How does competition affect bank systemic risk? *Journal of Financial Intermediation* 23: 1–26. [CrossRef]

Ansari, Jugnu. 2012. *A New Measure of Competition in Indian Loan Market*. Mumbai: CAFRAL.

Apergis, Nicholas. 2015. Competition in the banking sector: New evidence from a panel of emerging market economies and the financial crisis. *Emerging Markets Review* 25: 154–62. [CrossRef]

Apergis, Nicholas, Irene Fafaliou, and Michael L. Polemis. 2016. New evidence on assessing the level of competition in the European Union banking sector: A panel data approach. *International Business Review* 25: 395–407. [CrossRef]

Arrawatia, Rakesh, Arun Misra, Varun Dawar, and Debasish Maitra. 2019. Bank Competition in India: Some New Evidence Using Risk-Adjusted Lerner Index Approach. *Risks* 7: 44. [CrossRef]

Barros, Carlos Pestana, and Zorro Mendes. 2016. Assessing the competition in Angola's banking industry. *Applied Economics* 48: 2785–91. [CrossRef]

Baumol, William J. 1982. Contestable markets: An uprising in the theory of industry structure. *American Economic Review* 72: 1–15.

Beck, Thorsten, Asli Demirgüç-Kunt, and Ross Levine. 2006. Bank concentration, competition, and crises: First results. *Journal of Banking & Finance* 30: 1581–603.

Berg, Sigbjørn Atle, and Moshe Kim. 1998. Banks as multioutput oligopolies: An empirical evaluation of the retail and corporate banking markets. *Journal of Money, Credit and Banking* 1: 135–53. [CrossRef]

Bikker, Jacob A., and Johannes M. Groeneveld. 2000. *Competition and Concentration in the EU Banking Industry*. Amsterdam: De Nederlandsche Bank NV, vol. 33, pp. 62–98.

Bikker, Jacob A., and Katharina Haaf. 2002. Competition, concentration and their relationship: An empirical analysis of the banking industry. *Journal of Banking & Finance* 26: 2191–214.

Bikker, Jacob A., Sherrill Shaffer, and Laura Spierdijk. 2012. Assessing competition with the Panzar-Rosse model: the role of scale, costs, and equilibrium. *Review of Economics and Statistics* 94: 1025–44. [CrossRef]

Bikker, Jacob A., and Laura Spierdijk. 2008. *How Banking Competition Changed over Time*. DNB Working paper, No. 167. Utrecht, The Netherlands: Tjalling C. Koopmans Research Institute.

Bresnahan, Timothy F. 1982. The oligopoly solution concept is identified. *Economics Letters* 10: 87–92. [CrossRef]

Casu, Barbara, and Claudia Girardone. 2006. Bank competition, concentration and efficiency in the Single European Market. *The Manchester School* 744: 441–68. [CrossRef]

Claessens, Stijn, and Luc Laeven. 2004. What drives bank competition? Some international evidence. *Journal of Money, Credit and Banking* 36: 563–83. [CrossRef]

Debnath, Roma Mitra, and Ravi Shankar. 2008. Measuring performance of Indian banks: An application data envelopment analysis. *International Journal of Business Performance Management* 10: 57–85. [CrossRef]

Dinçer, Hasan, and Serhat Yüksel. 2018. Comparative evaluation of BSC-based new service development competencies in Turkish banking sector with the integrated fuzzy hybrid MCDM using content analysis. *International Journal of Fuzzy Systems* 20: 2497–516. [CrossRef]

Dinçer, Hasan, Serhat Yüksel, and İpek Tamara Çetiner. 2019. Strategy Selection for Organizational Performance of Turkish Banking Sector with the Integrated Multi-Dimensional Decision-Making Approach. In *Handbook of Research on Contemporary Approaches in Management and Organizational Strategy*. Philadelphia: IGI Global, pp. 273–91.

Dutta, Nitish. 2013. Competition in Indian Commercial Banking Sector in the liberalized regime: An empirical evaluation. *International Journal of Banking, Risk and Insurance* 17: 24.

Fosu, Samuel. 2013. *Banking Competition in Africa: Sub-Regional Comparative Studies*, rev. ed. Discussion Papers in Economics 13/12. Leicester: Division of Economics, School of Business, University of Leicester.

Gutiérrez de Rozas, Luis. 2007. *Testing for Competition in the Spanish Banking Industry: The Panzar-Rosse Approach Revisited*. Working paper, No. 726. Madrid, Spain: National Central Bank of Spain.

Hair, Joseph F., William C. Black, Barry J. Babin, and Rolph E. Anderson. 2006. *Multivariate Data Analysis*. Upper Saddle River: Pearson University Press, vol. 6.

India Brand Equity Foundation (IBEF). 2019a. *Trends: India Now 6th Largest Economy in the World with High Growth*. New Delhi: India Brand Equity Foundation.

India Brand Equity Foundation (IBEF). 2019b. *Indian Banking Industry Analysis*. New Delhi: India Brand Equity Foundation.

Lau, Lawrence J. 1982. On identifying the degree of competitiveness from industry price and output data. *Economics Letters* 10: 93–99. [CrossRef]

Mishra, Arun. 2011. Competition in Banking: The Indian Experience. Paper presented at the International Conference on Economics and Finance Research, Singapore, February 26–28; IPEDR vol. 4.

Mishra, Pulak, and Deepti Sahoo. 2012. Structure, Conduct and Performance in Indian Banking sector. *Review of Economic Perspectives* 12: 235–64. [CrossRef]

Mohapatra, Amiya, and Srirang Jha. 2018. Bank Recapitalization in India: A Critique of Public Policy Concerns. *FIIB Business Review* 7: 10–15.

Molyneux, Phil, D. Michael Lloyd-Williams, and John Thornton. 1994. Competitive conditions in European banking. *Journal of Banking & Finance* 18: 445–59.

Panzar, John C., and James N. Rosse. 1987. Testing for "monopoly" equilibrium. *The Journal of Industrial Economics* 1: 443–56. [CrossRef]

Pedroni, Peter. 2000. Fully-modified OLS for heterogeneous cointegrated panels. In *Advances in Econometrics Nonstationary Panels Panel Cointegration and Dynamic Panels*. Edited by Badi H. Baltagi and Chihwa Kao. Amsterdam: Elsevier Science, pp. 93–130.

Prasad, Ananthakrishnan, and Saibal Ghosh. 2005. *Competition in Indian Banking*. Washington, DC: International Monetary Fund.

Prasad, Ananthakrishnan, and Saibal Ghosh. 2007. Competition in Indian banking: An empirical evaluation. *South Asia Economic Journal* 8: 265–84. [CrossRef]

Rakshit, Bijoy, and Samaresh Bardhan. 2019. Does bank competition promote economic growth? Empirical evidence from selected South Asian countries. *South Asian Journal of Business Studies* 8: 201–23. [CrossRef]

Reserve Bank of India (RBI). 2017. *Financial Stability Report*. Mumbai: Reserve Bank of India.

Shaffer, Sherrill. 1993. A test of competition in Canadian banking. *Journal of Money, Credit and Banking* 25: 49–61. [CrossRef]

Shaffer, Sherrill. 2002. Conduct in a banking monopoly. *Review of Industrial Organization* 20: 221–38. [CrossRef]

Sinha, Pankaj, and Sakshi Sharma. 2016. Determinants of bank profits and its persistence in Indian Banks: A study in a dynamic panel data framework. *International Journal of System Assurance Engineering and Management* 7: 35–46. [CrossRef]

Yüksel, Serhat, Shahriyar Mukhtarov, and Elvin Mammadov. 2016. Comparing the efficiency of Turkish and Azerbaijani banks: An application with data envelopment analysis. *International Journal of Economics and Financial Issues* 6: 1059–67.

Yüksel, Serhat, Shahriyar Mukhtarov, Elvin Mammadov, and Mustafa Özsarı. 2018. Determinants of Profitability in the Banking Sector: An Analysis of Post-Soviet Countries. *Economies* 6: 41–49. [CrossRef]

Zhao, Tianshu, Barbara Casu, and Alessandra Ferrari. 2010. The impact of regulatory reforms on cost structure, ownership and competition in Indian banking. *Journal of Banking & Finance* 34: 246–54.

© 2019 by the authors. Licensee MDPI, Basel, Switzerland. This article is an open access article distributed under the terms and conditions of the Creative Commons Attribution (CC BY) license (http://creativecommons.org/licenses/by/4.0/).

Article

Role of Bank Regulation on Bank Performance: Evidence from Asia-Pacific Commercial Banks

Zhenni Yang *, Christopher Gan and Zhaohua Li

Department of Financial and Business Systems, Faculty of Agribusiness and Commerce, Lincoln University, Christchurch 7647, New Zealand
* Correspondence: zhenni.yang@lincoln.ac.nz; Tel.: +64-21-183-4896

Received: 30 June 2019; Accepted: 3 August 2019; Published: 7 August 2019

Abstract: The banking industry is an essential financial intermediary, thus the efficient operation of banks is vital for economic development and social welfare. However, the 2008 global financial crisis triggered a reconsideration of the banking systems, as well as the role of government intervention. The literature has paid little attention to the banking industry in the Asia-Pacific region in the context of bank efficiency. This study employs double bootstrap data envelopment analysis to measure bank efficiency and examine the relationship between regulation, supervision, and state ownership in commercial banks in the Asia-Pacific region for the period 2005 to 2014. Our results indicate that excluding off-balance sheet activities in efficiency estimations lead to underestimating of the pure technical efficiency, while overestimating the scale efficiency of banks in the Asia-Pacific region. Cross-country comparisons reveal that Australian banks exhibit the highest levels of technical efficiency, while Indonesian banks exhibit the lowest average. Our bootstrap regression results suggest that bank regulation and supervision are positively related to bank technical efficiency, while state ownership is not significantly related to bank efficiency. Furthermore, our findings show that tighter regulation and supervision are significantly related to higher efficiency for small and large-sized banks.

Keywords: banks; efficiency; data envelopment analysis; Asia-Pacific; regulations

---

1. Introduction

Banking industries, as primary financial intermediaries, provides liquidity and payment services, transforms deposits into loans, and manages and monitors investment projects (Freixas and Rochet 2008). The efficient operation of banks not only enhances economic development, but also influences the income distribution of the economy (Barth et al. 2004). However, the 2008 Global Financial Crisis (GFC) provides evidence that banking industries are not always stable. Before the 2008 GFC, banking industries, especially those in the United States (US), were heavily involved in the real estate bubble and credit boom, through off-balance sheet (OBS) activities. The collapse of the banking industries in 2008 quickly spread to the global financial system (Kim et al. 2013).

In addition to the prevalent OBS activities (DeYoung and Torna 2013; Engle et al. 2014), inefficient regulation and supervision (Brunnermeier 2009) in the banking industries are among other possible reasons for the recently fragile financial system and massive economic turmoil. That GFC also triggered the reconsideration of the official interventions in the financial system (Cihak and Demirgüç-Kunt 2013). In practice, regulation and supervision define capital standards, set requirements for entry into the banking market, frame acceptable ownership structures, and provide business guidelines for the banking industries (Barth et al. 2013).

Compared to countries in other regions, most countries in the Asia-Pacific region have a bank-dominated financial system. Financial systems in the Asia-Pacific region have undergone profound deregulation and privatisation since the 1970s. Following the deregulation, banking industries in the Asia-Pacific region have experienced rapid growth in loans and investments. After the 1997 Asian Financial Crisis (AFC), governments in the region implemented a series of structural changes (and reforms), both in the banking systems, and regulatory and supervisory mechanisms. Following the 2008 GFC, most countries in the Asia-Pacific region had fully implemented the Basel II Accord, and were in a better position to introduce Basel III Accord regulations (International Monetary Fund 2013).

There are two main rationales for the existence of bank regulation and supervision. Firstly, regulation and supervision can mitigate potential conflicts of interest and externalities in the banking system, and thereby benefit the banking industry and social welfare (Kilinc and Neyapti 2012). Secondly, regulation and supervision can maintain the stability of fragile banking systems and function as a safety net for the financial system (Kroszner 1998). However, regulation and supervision are associated with extra costs for the banking systems. It is also difficult to reach equilibrium between different regulatory rules (Freixas and Rochet 2008).

As another major tool of government intervention in the banking industry, state ownership has been widely observed in the banking industry globally. The degree of state ownership in banks depends on factors such as economic and financial development, property rights, and financial openness (La Porta et al. 2002). Theoretically, there are two views supporting government ownership in the financial markets: Development and political views. The development view contends that some financial markets are not sufficiently developed for banks to be functional. Therefore, governments need to participate in the financial institutions to enhance the country's financial and economic development (Gerschenkron 1962). In the political view, state ownership in the banking industry is a way for politicians to affect banks' decisions and achieve their political objectives. When the government owns the bank, it will allocate capital resource to its supporters and gain votes (Shleifer and Vishny 1994; Shleifer 1998).

This paper investigates the impacts of the inclusion of OBS activities in bank efficiency measurement. Furthermore, we examine the relationship between bank regulation, supervision and state ownership with bank efficiency in the Asia-Pacific region. The remainder of the study is organised as the follows: Section 2 provides an overview of the Asia-Pacific banking industries; Section 3 reviews the related literature; Section 4 describes the data and methodology; Section 5 discusses the empirical results; and Section 6 concludes the paper.

2. Overview of Banking Industries in the Asia-Pacific Region

The banking system has dominated the financial system and has played a vital role in the economic development of the Asia-Pacific region over the previous two decades. Before the 1997 AFC, the Asia-Pacific region experienced financial deregulation and reforms, followed by rapid economic growth relative to the US and European countries. Throughout 1990 to 1996, the region experienced significant foreign capital inflow, high levels of domestic consumption, booming investments, and excessive credit expansion.

However, impotent regulation and supervision during the period of financial deregulation and reform exposed the system's weaknesses (Fu et al. 2014) in the region. Except for Australia, most economies in the region were severely affected by the 1997 AFC. More specifically, South Korea, Indonesia, Malaysia, the Philippines, and Thailand were directly affected, while Hong Kong, Singapore, and Japan were indirectly affected and experienced negative economic growth during this period. Following the 1997 AFC, governments in the region began a series of structural reforms and prudential regulatory policies to revive the economy and financial industry. Specifically, the supervisory authorities in the Asian region have contributed to the banks' better asset quality after the 1997 AFC (Rosenkranz and Lee 2019). In compliance with the more conservative regulatory policies, banks in the Asia-Pacific region have mostly increased their capital ratios (Capannelli and Filippini 2010). More surprisingly, the Asia-Pacific banking industry maintained a high return on assets (ROA) ratio during the 2008 GFC. Furthermore, the average ROA in the Asia-Pacific region was almost twice that of the rest of the world, as of the end of 2014; this was largely contributed by the rapid growth of the Chinese and Indonesian banking sectors (McKinsey Company 2016).

3. Literature Review

3.1. Efficiency Measurement

Efficiency is a commonly used concept to describe a firm's performance. The basic idea of efficiency measurement is to compare the observed production to the optimal production which operates on the production frontier. Parametric and nonparametric approaches are often used to conduct the approximation of the frontier and efficiency estimation. Both approaches are benchmarking methods, which exploit the distance function between observed production and the production frontier. Among the various techniques stemming from these two approaches, the two most popular approaches employed in the banking literature are the stochastic frontier analysis (SFA) (a parametric approach) and data envelopment analysis (DEA) (a nonparametric approach) (Fethi and Pasiouras 2010).

3.2. Inclusion of Off-Balance Sheet Activities in Efficiency Estimation

Considering the expansion in banks' business scopes during development of the industry, researchers currently recognise the importance of incorporating the off-balance sheet (OBS) activities in bank efficiency estimations. While most studies directly include OBS activities into efficiency estimations (see for example, Drake 2001; Drake and Hall 2003; Radić et al. 2012; Sufian et al. 2012), only limited numbers of studies provide any justification for the inclusion of OBS activities in efficiency estimations (Rogers 1998; Mester 1996; Clark and Siems 2002; Lieu et al. 2005; Pasiouras 2008a; Lozano-Vivas and Pasiouras 2010, 2014). These studies provide ambiguous evidence on the impacts of OBS activities inclusion in bank efficiency measurement.

Rogers (1998) measured the efficiency of more than 10,000 commercial banks (including branches) in the US over the period 1991 to 1995. The author's results indicate that cost and profit efficiencies of commercial banks would both be underestimated when OBS activities are omitted. Similarly, Clark and Siems (2002) examined the impact of including OBS activities on US bank efficiency over the period 1992 to 1997. They concluded that OBS activities are useful for explaining variations in banks' costs and profits. The cost efficiency is higher with the inclusion of OBS activities, but their results demonstrate little changes in the profit efficiency measurement for the banks. Using the SFA approach, Lieu et al. (2005) measurde the cost efficiency of the Taiwanese banking industry from 1998 to 2001. They found that omitting OBS activities would lead to underestimating a bank's cost efficiency by 55%. In a study of the Greek banking industry from 2000 to 2004, Pasiouras (2008b) found that bank cost efficiencies are not significantly affected by omitting OBS activities as an output.

Using large samples from multiple banking industries around the world, Lozano-Vivas and Pasiouras (2010, 2014) examined the impact of including OBS activities on cost efficiency, profit efficiencies, and Malmquist productivities measurements. They found mixed results. Lozano-Vivas and Pasiouras (2010) explored the cost and profit efficiency for 87 countries banks from 1999 to 2006 and found that cost efficiency would have been higher when considering OBS activities, while the results for profit efficiency were mixed. Using data from 84 countries over the period 1999 to 2006, Lozano-Vivas and Pasiouras (2014) estimated the Malmquist cost and profit productivity for banks. They found that bank profit productivity was higher with OBS activities, while cost productivity was not significantly affected. Moreover, their results suggested that the exclusion of OBS activities should jeopardise the regression results when examining the relationship between environmental factors and bank performance.

3.3. Bank Regulation and Supervision, and Bank Efficiency

Previous studies provide inconclusive evidence with regards to the relationship between regulation, supervision and bank performance using data from various countries or regions. As one of the first studies at the international level, Barth et al. (2004) find that activity restrictions are negatively related to bank efficiency. While market discipline can significantly boost bank efficiency, capital regulation and supervision power are not significantly related to bank performance. In addition, that state ownership is negatively related to bank efficiency. In a study by Barth et al. (2004), bank efficiency was measured with net interest margin and overhead costs (that is, lower net interest margins and overhead costs indicating higher bank efficiency).

Using 715 banks from 95 countries in 2003, Pasiouras (2008a) found empirical evidence to support the implementation of three pillars in the Basel II Accord. The authors' result indicates a positive correlation between capital adequacy regulation, official supervisory power, and market discipline with bank technical efficiency. Furthermore, deposit insurance has no significant relationship with bank efficiency. They also found that government and foreign ownership were associated with lower bank efficiency. In Chortareas et al.'s (2012) study, however, market discipline was found to be negatively related to the European banks' technical efficiency.

After measuring both cost and profit efficiency for banks from 74 countries from 2000 to 2004, Pasiouras et al. (2009) concluded that both official supervision and market discipline were positively related to both efficiency measurement. Additionally, they found that capital regulation would increase cost efficiency while reducing profit efficiency during the period. In contrast, activity restrictions improved profit efficiency but reduced cost efficiency. However, Lozano-Vivas and Pasiouras's (2010) study revealed that supervisory power was negatively related to cost efficiency and positively related to profit efficiency based on a larger dataset from 1999 to 2006.

More recently, Luo et al. (2016) examined the profit efficiency of banks from 140 countries over the period 1999 to 2011, and found that capital regulation, market discipline, and activity restrictions had positive relationships with bank efficiency. However, official supervision power was negatively related to bank efficiency. Focusing on banks from African countries, Triki et al. (2017) suggested that the impacts of regulation and supervision on bank performance depend on the bank size and risks. While other regulatory policies show no significant impact, capital stringency is found to be positively related to large banks with low risks.

Rather than using individual regulatory policies, Gardener et al. (2011) created a comprehensive regulatory index to capture information of the three pillars in the Basel Accord in their study of East Asian banking industries. Their results suggest that bank regulation is negatively related to technical efficiency while positively related to allocative efficiency. Moreover, that those relationships are not significant for state-owned banks, suggesting that regulation and supervision do not impact the performance of state-owned banks.

3.4. State Ownership in the Banking Industry

Most previous studies provide empirical evidence which supports the "political view" of state ownership and argue that state ownership is related to less development in the banking industry (Barth et al. 2001; La Porta et al. 2002); less profitability (Micco et al. 2007; Cornett et al. 2010; Lin and Zhang 2009); and lower profits and cost efficiency (Berger et al. 2005; Bonin et al. 2005; Perera et al. 2007; Margono et al. 2010). However, a few studies find that state-owned banks are more efficient (Gardener et al. 2011; Wang et al. 2014; Dong et al. 2014; Berger et al. 2009) than other types of banks and are related to higher stockholder value (Hossain et al. 2013). Other studies (Barry et al. 2008), however, find no significant difference between state-owned banks and privately-owned banks. Micco et al. (2007) argues that state-owned banks in developing countries have higher costs and lower profits, while those in developed countries have no significant difference in costs and profits. Some studies in the Indonesian banking industry suggest that state-owned banks are found to be less efficient (Perera et al. 2007; Margono et al. 2010; Shaban and James 2018).

In contrast with the previous argument that state ownership impedes bank performance, Gardener et al. (2011) suggest that state-owned banks in developing Asian countries are more efficient than other types of banks. Hossain et al. (2013) also notes that state ownership is a desirable government intervention mechanism used to reduce the negative impact on shareholder value in the Asia-Pacific banking industry. Empirical evidence revealed the better performance of China's four largest state-owned banks (Wang et al. 2014; Dong et al. 2014; Tan and Anchor 2017) over other banks in China. After estimating bank efficiency in Hong Kong, Indonesia, Korea, Malaysia, the Philippines, and Thailand, Barry et al. (2008) found that state-owned banks were not significantly different from privately-owned banks.

4. Data and Methodology

4.1. Data Sources

The bank-level financial data used in this study are comprised of data from unconsolidated statements of individual banks taken from the BvD Bankscope database. When unconsolidated statements are not available, consolidated statements are used instead. Only active commercial banks in Australia, China, Hong Kong, Indonesia, Japan, New Zealand, Singapore, and Thailand were used as sample banks in this study. To capture the overall banking industry characteristics, observations with less than three consecutive years of available data were omitted. Therefore, the sample data decreased from 5610 to 3749 observations for 544 banks. Due to the data validation requirements for DEA approaches, observations with missing, zero, or negative values in the inputs or outputs variables were dropped. As a result, a total sample of 2186 bank-year observations was obtained.

Data on bank regulation and supervision was obtained from the World Bank (2007, 2011). Considering that there were changes in bank regulatory and supervisory policies in most countries following the 2008 GFC, regulation and supervision data from the 2007 survey were used for the period 2005 to 2008. Those regulatory and supervisory data obtained from the 2011 survey were used for the period 2009 to 2014. Bank ownership data were constructed using ownership data provided in the BvD Bankscope database. Other country-level data was obtained using the Global Financial Development Database and World Governance Indicators Database. Appendix A Table A1 provides details of the definition and source of each variable used in this study.

4.2. Efficiency Estimation: Bootstrap DEA Approach

Similar to the conventional benefit/cost theory, the fundamental idea of efficiency measurement is to estimate a ratio of weighted outputs to weighted inputs for each decision-making unit (DMU) (Cook and Seiford 2009). In the efficiency estimation, banks operating on the production frontier are the best-practice banks with efficiency scores of one. Those operating away from the frontier are considered to be inefficient, with efficiency scores less than one. Depending on the distance from the sample banks to the frontier, the DEA approach is employed to estimate relative efficiencies ranging from 0 to 1 (Cook and Seiford 2009) for all individual banks.

Assume there are I banks in the sample data; each bank uses N inputs to produce M outputs. The input X_i for the i-th bank is an $N \times 1$ vector and the output Y_i is an $M \times 1$ vector for the i-th bank. Thus, the production set for bank i can be denoted as (X_i, Y_i). To measure the input-orientated technical efficiencies for bank i, the constant return to ccale (CRS) model solves the following linear programming problem as in Equation (1):

$$\begin{aligned} & \min_{\theta,\lambda} \theta, \\ & \text{s.t. } \theta X_i - X\lambda \geq 0, \\ & \quad -Y_i + Y\lambda \geq 0, \\ & \quad \lambda \geq 0 \end{aligned} \quad (1)$$

where θ is a scalar, and λ is a vector of constant. The efficiency estimated using Equation (1) is the overall technical efficiency.

After taking various external restrictions and influences into consideration, and assuming that there exists scale inefficiency as well as technical inefficiency in the banks during the production process, the variable return to scale (VRS) model can be used to separate the technical inefficiency into pure technical inefficiency and scale inefficiency. To estimate pure technical efficiency for bank i, Equation (2) solves the linear programming problems:

$$\min_{\theta,\lambda} \theta,$$
$$\text{s.t. } \theta X_i - X\lambda \geq 0,$$
$$-Y_i + Y\lambda \leq 0, \quad (2)$$
$$e\lambda = 1$$
$$\lambda \geq 0$$

where θ is a scalar, λ is a vector of constant, and e is an $I \times 1$ vector of ones.

The VRS model measures bank efficiency using a benchmark of similar-sized bank groups (Coelli et al. 2005). After excluding the impact of scale inefficiency, the technical efficiencies estimated using the VRS model are greater or equal to those estimated through the CRS model (Pasiouras 2008a) scale efficiency (SE) can be calculated as:

$$SE = \frac{TE_{CRS}}{PTE_{VRS}} \quad (3)$$

To deal with the issue of asymptotic distribution of estimated efficiency, Simar and Wilson (2000, 2007) proposed a smoothed bootstrapping DEA model to provide a more reliable interpretation of efficiency scores.

To consider the distinctive production opportunities for banks operating in different countries, O'Donnell et al. (2008) introduced the idea of meta-frontier for firms operating in different groups and facing various circumstances. The meta-frontier production possibility set T contains all the feasible input-output combinations for banks from all different groups, which can be expressed in a simple function, as:

$$T = [(X, Y) | X \geq 0, Y \geq 0, X \text{ can produce } Y] \quad (4)$$

The input-orientated efficiency score, which gives the maximum amount of input reduction for bank i is defined as meta-frontier technical efficiency (MTE). Assuming there are K ($K > 1$) countries in the sample, the technical efficiency for bank i in country k can be defined as group technical efficiency (GTE). Specifically, the technology gap ratio (TGR) for bank i in country k is defined as:

$$TGR_k^i(X_i, Y_i) = \frac{MTE(X_i, Y_i)}{GTE_k(X_i, Y_i)} = \frac{\theta}{\theta^k} \quad (5)$$

when TGR_k^i equals 1, the group-frontier is tangent to the meta-frontier. In other words, the larger the TGR_k, the more advanced the technology adopted by banks in country k.

Based on recent literature, our study employed the intermediation approach for input and output selection. Additionally, to analyse the impact of the inclusion of OBS activities, we estimated bank efficiency using four models with different input and output selections and examined whether the incorporation of OBS activities significantly affect bank efficiency measurements in the Asia-Pacific region (see Table 1). To capture the impact of OBS activities on efficiency estimations, "off-balance sheet items" were considered as an additional output to describe the aggregation of guarantees, acceptances and documentary credits, committed credit facilities, managed securitised assets, other exposure to securitisations, and other bank contingent liabilities. Additionally, "loan loss provisions" were also considered to be one of the inputs which indicate problem loans in the banking industry, following Charnes et al. (1990); Altunbas et al. (2000); Drake and Hall (2003); Pasiouras (2008b); and Hall et al. (2012)'s studies.

After obtaining four sets of efficiencies using 4 different models, we employed the Kruskal-Wallis test to examine if the differences between Models 1 and 2, and Models 3 and 4 were significantly different from zero. Furthermore, we used the Skillings-Mack test to test the rankings of the efficiencies from 4 Models. All of the efficiency estimates are bias-corrected using the Bootstrap DEA approach following Simar and Wilson (2007).[1]

Table 1. Input and output specifications for Models 1 to 4.

Model 1	Model 2	Model 3	Model 4
Inputs	Inputs	Inputs	Inputs
Fixed Assets Total Deposits Noninterest Expenses	Fixed Assets Total Deposits Noninterest Expenses	Fixed Assets Total Deposits Noninterest Expenses Loan Loss Provision	Fixed Assets Total Deposits Noninterest Expenses Loan Loss Provision
Outputs	Outputs	Outputs	Outputs
Loans Other Earning Assets	Loans Other Earning Assets Off-balance Sheet Items	Loans Other Earning Assets	Loans Other Earning Assets Off-balance Sheet Items

Source: Adapted from Pasiouras (2008b).

4.3. Bootstrap Truncated Regression Model

To measure the impact of regulation, supervision, and state ownership on bank efficiency, the bootstrap truncated regression model was employed using bias-corrected bank efficiency $\hat{\theta}$ as the dependent variable. Three bias-corrected efficiency measurements were used in the regression model. Specifically, pure technical efficiency (PTE) was used to measure bank efficiency by using minimum inputs to produce a given level of outputs; scale efficiency (SE) was used to measure the efficiency of exploiting the optimal operating scale, and the technology gap ratio (TGR) was used to measure the gap between technology in one country to the best production technology in the Asia-Pacific region. The regression models are specified as follows:

$$PTE_{k,i} = \beta_0 + \beta_1 * REG_k + \beta_2 * Ownership_{k,i} + \beta_3 * Bank_{i,k} + \beta_4 * Country_k + \beta_5 \\ *YEAR\ Dummy + \beta_5 * country\ Dummy + \varepsilon_{k,i} \quad (6)$$

$$SE_{k,i} = \beta_0 + \beta_1 * REG_k + \beta_2 * Ownership_{k,i} + \beta_3 * Bank_{i,k} + \beta_4 * Country_k + \beta_5 \\ *YEAR\ Dummy + \beta_5 * country\ Dummy + \varepsilon_{k,i} \quad (7)$$

$$TGR_{k,i} = \beta_0 + \beta_1 * REG_k + \beta_2 * Ownership_{k,i} + \beta_3 * Bank_{i,k} + \beta_4 * Country_k + \beta_5 \\ *YEAR\ Dummy + \beta_5 * Country\ Dummy + \varepsilon_{k,i} \quad (8)$$

where $PTE_{k,i}$ denotes the bias-corrected pure technical efficiency for bank i in country k, $SE_{k,i}$ denotes the bias-corrected scale efficiency for bank i in country k; $TGR_{k,i}$ denotes the bias-corrected technology gap ratio for bank i in country k. The independent variables are REG_k is a vector of bank regulation and supervision indicators in country k; $Ownership_{k,i}$ is a dummy variable, which equals 1 when the bank is classified as state-owned; $Bank_{i,k}$ is a vector of bank-specific characteristics for bank i in country k, and $Country_k$ is a vector of country-specific characteristics for country k; YEAR Dummy is the year dummy variable from 2005 to 2014; Country Dummy is the country dummy variable for the sample countries; $\varepsilon_{k,i}$ is the error term.

4.3.1. Bank Regulation and Supervision Variables

Together with activity restrictions, the three pillars of the Basel Accord II were used as regulation and supervision variables in the regression models. As discussed in the introduction, the three pillars are capital requirements, official supervision power and market discipline. Activity restrictions in the banking industry were also included to capture restrictions imposed on non-bank activities in

---

[1] More methodology descriptions can be found in the study of Simar and Wilson (2007).

the Asia-Pacific banking sectors. The four indicators of bank regulation and supervision are denoted as capital regulation CAP_k, official supervisory power $SPPOWER_k$, market discipline $MKDSPL_k$, and activity restrictions $ACRS_k$. Bank regulation and supervision data are obtained primarily from the Bank Regulation and Supervision Survey (Barth et al. 2007, 2012).

Based on Barth et al.'s (2001, 2007, 2008, 2012) descriptions, regulation and supervision variables are constructed through assigning "1" or "0" to several survey questions, where regulation and supervision authorities from various countries give answers of "yes" or "no".[2]

CAP_k was the index of capital regulation to measure the initial and overall capital requirements for banks in country k. This index was constructed using answers from five survey questions. The range of the capital requirement was from 0 to 7. A higher value indicates more stringency in the country's capital regulation.

$SPPOWER_k$ assessed the extent of official supervisory power to oversee, monitor, and discipline managers, directors, and auditors of banks in country k. Fourteen questions were surveyed to obtain the value of supervisory power. Variables ranged from 0 to 14 for each country. Similar to capital requirements, higher values show stronger supervisory power from regulatory authorities.

$MKDSPL_k$ measures information disclosure to shareholders, auditors, and the public, and whether any credit ratings are required by regulatory authorities for banks in country k. There were seven questions for this variable. Therefore, the value of market discipline ranged from 0 to 7. A higher value indicates a more informative and transparent banking industry.

$ACRS_k$ was the proxy of non-bank activity restrictions in real estate investment, insurance underwriting and selling, brokering and dealing securities, and all businesses of mutual fund industries in country k. For each category of activities, there were four answers: 1 (unrestricted), 2 (permitted); 3 (restricted); and 4 (prohibited). Thus, the value of $ACRS_k$ ranged from 0 to 12. A higher value of activity restriction indicates more restrictions on nonbank activities in the banking industry.

4.3.2. State Ownership

The variable $Ownership_{k,i}$ was used to examines the relationship between bank ownership and efficiency. Historical ownership data for each sample bank was obtained from the BvD Bankscope database. The global ultimate ownership (GUO) of banks and historical information of direct owners were considered when constructing the variable. Since 20% of the ownership is typically sufficient to have control rights in the banks' operation decisions (La Porta et al. 1999), the benchmark of 20% was used in this study to identify whether the government had control rights. For each bank, shareholders with shares of more than 3% in the bank were considered each year. If the shareholder was a central government, local government, or sole state-owned enterprise in country k, the shareholder was regarded as the government. The dummy variable $Ownership_{k,i}$ equaled one when the aggregate ownership of government in bank i of country k was greater than 20%. Similarly, we also identified foreign-owned banks for comparison. A bank was identified as foreign-owned when a single foreign shareholder owned more than 20% of the bank share. If the bank was neither state-owned nor foreign-owned, it was classified as a privately-owned bank.

4.3.3. Control Variables

To control the impact of other bank-specific characteristics on bank efficiency, this study included a set of bank-specific variables $Bank_{i,k}$ in the regression models. The bank-specific variables were $Banksize_{i,k}$; $EQTA_{i,k}$; $OBSTA_{i,k}$; $LLPTL_{i,k}$; $LIQTA_{i,k}$.

$Banksize_{i,k}$ is calculated as the logarithm of total assets to capture bank scale characteristics. $EQTA_{i,k}$ is proxied as the ratio of total equity divided by total assets, to control the level of capitalisation in banks. The other three variables are used to capture three types of risks in banks. The first variable

---

[2] The World Bank Regulatory and Supervisory survey questions are available upon request.

is $OBSTA_{i,k}$ is calculated as off-balance sheet items divided by total assets. A higher $OBSTA_{i,k}$ value suggests higher risks accompanied by a higher ratio of off-balance sheet activities. The second variable, risk proxy $LLPTL_{i,k}$ is used to capture credit risk, calculated as loan loss provisions over total loans. A higher $LLPTL_{i,k}$ value indicates a higher bank credit risk. The last risk measurement is $LIQTA_{i,k}$, which controls bank liquidity risk levels. $LIQTA_{i,k}$ is calculated as liquid assets over total assets. A higher $LIQTA_{i,k}$ value indicates lower liquidity risk in bank i in country k.

Except for bank-specific variables, country-specific variables were also included in our regression models to account for variations in bank operating environments. We considered five country-level variables: Real GDP growth (GDP_growth_k), inflation rate (INF_k), concentration (HHI_k), banking industry development ($PrCrGDP_k$), and institutional governance environment INS_ENV_k. GDP_growth_k is measured as the annual growth rate of GDP to control for macroeconomic conditions of the country. Additionally, inflation INF_k is measured by the annual rate of the implicit GDP deflator.

Finally, three remaining variables were used to capture the characteristics of the countries' banking industries. The first variable is concentration (Herfindahl Hirschman Index-HHI). HHI_k is calculated as the sum of the square of deposit shares for each bank in all banks of that country. The $PrCrGDP_k$ describes the level of bank claims to the private sector to GDP, which is used to capture the intermediation activities of the banking industry in one country (Pasiouras 2008a). The last variable, institutional governance indicator INS_ENV_k is used to control the institutional environment for countries. Initially, there are six dimensions of governance environment: Voice and accountability (*Voice*), political stability and absence of violence/terrorism (*Stability*), government effectiveness (*Gov_Eff*), regulatory quality (*Reg_Qua*), the rule of law (*Rule_Law*), and control of corruption (*Corruption*). Each of these variables ranges between −2.5 and 2.5. Since these six variables are highly correlated, we employed principal component analysis to create a new variable INS_ENV_k to measure the overall governance environment of each country.

5. Empirical Results

5.1. Descriptive Statistics

Table 2 shows the mean and standard deviation values of each input and output variable for efficiency estimations, from 2005 to 2014. All of the bank data were obtained from the BvD Bankscope database, and data have been adjusted using the GDP deflator in 2005. Table 3 provides the descriptive statistics of the regression models' variables for the full sample data over the period 2005 to 2014. The pairwise correlation coefficients between the independent variables are shown in Appendix A Table A2. Based on the correlation matrix, the absolute values of most of the correlation coefficients are smaller than 0.3 and the maximum absolute value of the correlation coefficients is less than 0.7. Thus, multicollinearity was not a major concern in our regression models.

Table 2. Descriptive statistics of the inputs and outputs of banks in the Asia-Pacific region (2005–2014).

Variables	Mean	SD	Max	Min
Inputs				
Total Deposits	86,068.17	279,580.74 *	3,368,189.83	23.11
Fixed Assets	709.95	2,472.14	32,567.41	0.07
Noninterest Expenses	896.90	2,698.78	31,232.88	0.90
Loan Loss Provisions	209.44	782.56	10,632.95	0.00
Outputs				
Loans	45,788.47	141,244.02	1,759,887.29	6.09
Other Earning Assets	30,315.82	107,021.11	2,247,399.26	9.06
Off-balance Sheet Items	13,047.35	43,863.62	537,704.05	0.00

Notes: All of the bank data are real value in million US dollars adjusted based on the GDP deflator in 2005 for each country from 2005 to 2010. Source: Calculated by the author using data from the BvD Bankscope database. * The large standard deviation value compared to mean value can be observed in the studies of Chortareas et al. (2013); Viverita and Ariff (2011), etc.

Table 3. Descriptive statistics of regression model variables (2005–2014).

Variables	Mean	SD	Max	Min
Regulation and Supervision				
CAP	3.7683	1.7702	5	1
SPPOWER	11.7669	1.1598	14	7
ACRS	8.1163	2.0572	12	3
MKDSPL	5.3054	0.5554	6	4
DEP_INS	0.7239	0.4472	1	0
Ownership				
STATE	0.1003	0.3004	1	0
Bank-specific				
BANKSIZE	16.6697	1.8822	21.9376	10.048
EQTA	0.0876	0.0747	0.81	0.0035
OBSTA	0.1591	0.3874	13.2399	0
LLPTL	0.0061	0.0082	0.0797	0
LIQTA	0.1594	0.1295	0.8454	0.0014
Country-specific				
GDP_growth (%)	3.9979	3.9893	15.2404	−5.4171
INF (%)	2.631	4.378	18.1498	−1.8957
HHI	0.1375	0.0784	1	0.064
PrCrGDP (%)	98.7247	37.2066	219.12	22.31
INST_ENV	−0.6172	2.1847	2.5613	−3.7848

Notes: Bank-specific variables and HHI were calculated using data from the BvD Bankscope database. Data for GDP_growth, INF, and PrCrGDP were obtained from the Global Financial Development Database. Data of INST_ENV is the result of the principal component analysis from 6 indicators of World Governance Indicators. Source: Regulation and supervision data are obtained from the World Bank (2007, 2011).

5.2. Bank Efficiency and Non-Traditional Activities

To examine the impact of including OBS activities on bank efficiency estimations, Table 4 presents the average TE (technical efficiency), PTE (pure technical efficiency), and SE (scale efficiency) scores of 4 different models relative to the meta-frontier. After bias-correction, the TE, PTE and SE estimates had smaller means and standard deviations, which supports Fallah-Fini et al.'s (2012) statement that banks appear to be efficient under traditional DEA approach, but might not be efficient using the bootstrap DEA approach. According to Simar and Wilson (2007) and Fallah-Fini et al. (2012), one possible reason for the existence of such a large bias is that there are not enough observations to construct the correct frontier.

Without considering the asset quality of the banking industry, the comparison between bank efficiency of Models 1 and 2 show that the average TE and PTE scores are higher after with the inclusion of OBS activities. However, the average SE score is lower after incorporating non-traditional activities. Similarly, compared to Model 3, the average TE and PTE estimates are higher, and the average SE estimates are lower in Model 4. To test whether differences in bank efficiencies were significantly different from zero, we followed Lozano-Vivas and Pasiouras (2010), and conducted the Kruskal-Wallis tests to compare between Models 1 and 2, as well as Models 3 and 4. The results are presented in Table 5.

---

[3] Model 1 excludes both off-balance sheet (OBS) and LLP in the efficiency estimation; Model 2 includes OBS and excludes LLP in the efficiency estimation; Model 3 consists of the LLP but excludes the OBS in the estimation; Model 4 includes both OBS and LLP in the estimation.

Table 4. Average technical efficiency, pure technical efficiency, and scale efficiency of 4 efficiency estimation models.[3]

Efficiencies	Without Considering Risk		With Considering Risk	
	Model 1 Without OBS	Model 2 With OBS	Model 3 Without OBS	Model 4 With OBS
Panel A: Bootstrap DEA Approach				
TE	0.5735 (0.1233)	0.5824 (0.1206)	0.6067 (0.1371)	0.617 (0.1354)
PTE	0.8025 (0.1257)	0.8290 (0.1233)	0.8161 (0.1213)	0.8459 (0.1173)
SE	0.7196 (0.1290)	0.7074 (0.1250)	0.7689 (0.2478)	0.7322 (0.1334)
Panel B: Traditional DEA Approach				
TE	0.6337 (0.1376)	0.6481 (0.1392)	0.6725 (0.1609)	0.6891 (0.1609)
PTE	0.8453 (0.1346)	0.8748 (0.133)	0.863 (0.1323)	0.8936 (0.1282)
SE	0.7546 (0.1306)	0.7468 (0.1364)	0.8062 (0.265)	0.7738 (0.1461)

Notes: TE = overall technical efficiency; PTE = pure technical efficiency; SE = scale efficiency. Standard deviations are shown in the parenthesis. Models 1 to 4 use different inputs and outputs specifications (see Table 1). Source: Author's calculations.

Table 5. Kruskal-Wallis test results for efficiencies with and without off-balance sheet (OBS) activities.

Efficiencies	Without Considering Risk		With Considering Risk	
	Model 1 Without OBS	Model 2 With OBS	Model 3 without OBS	Model 4 With OBS
Panel A: Bootstrap DEA Approach				
TE	chi-squared = 6.426 probability = 0.0112		chi-squared = 6.847 probability = 0.0089	
PTE	chi-squared = 112.760 probability = 0.0001		chi-squared = 165.241 probability = 0.0001	
SE	chi-squared = 10.380 probability = 0.0013		chi-squared = 4.106 probability = 0.0427	
Panel B: The Traditional DEA Approach				
TE	chi-squared = 11.130 probability = 0.0008		chi-squared = 11.881 probability = 0.0006	
PTE	chi-squared = 95.529 probability = 0.0001		chi-squared = 109.965 probability = 0.0001	
SE	chi-squared = 6.231 probability = 0.0126		chi-squared = 0.053 probability = 0.8175	

Notes: TE = overall technical efficiency; PTE = pure technical efficiency; SE = scale efficiency. Null hypotheses of the Kruskal-Wallis tests state that two efficiencies are the same and a small p-value suggests a rejection of the null hypothesis. Source: Author's calculation.

Table 6 indicates that efficiency estimates from the four models were significantly different, based on the small p-values for PTE (Panel A), TE (Panel B), and SE (Panel C). Furthermore, based on the information from the ranking statistics (WSumCRank and WSum/SE), we can confirm our observations in Table 4. Model 2 had higher average PTEs and TEs than those in Model 1, and Model 4 had higher PTEs and TEs than those in Model 3. In addition, after the inclusion of OBS activities, the SEs in Model 2 (Model 4) were lower than those in Model 1 (Model 3).

Table 6. Results of Skillings-Mack test for efficiency estimates for the four efficiency estimation models.

Models	Number of Observations	WSumCRank	Standard Error	WSum/SE
Panel A: Overall Technical Efficiency				
Model 1	2505	−3094.51	86.69	−35.7
Model 2	2505	−1266.47	86.69	−14.61
Model 3	2505	1326.88	86.69	15.31
Model 4	2505	3034.1	86.69	35
Skillings Mack = 2210.210				
p-value (No ties) = 0.0000				
Panel B: Pure Technical Efficiency				
Model 1	2505	−3004.66	86.69	−34.66
Model 2	2505	502.71	86.69	5.8
Model 3	2505	−510.46	86.69	−5.89
Model 4	2505	3012.41	86.69	34.75
Skillings Mack = 1857.871				
p-value (No ties) = 0.0000				
Panel C: Scale Efficiency				
Model 1	2505	256.39	86.69	2.96
Model 2	2505	−1742.07	86.69	−20.1
Model 3	2505	948.88	86.69	10.95
Model 4	2505	536.8	86.69	6.19
Skillings Mack = 428.050				
p-value (No ties) = 0.0000				

Notes: WSumCRank is the weighted sum of centred ranks. Standard Error: Standard error of the test. WSum/SE is the weighted sum of cantered ranks divided by the standard error. Smaller WSumCRank or WSum/SE indicates a lower rank among the models. Source: Author's calculations.

Table 7 shows the average meta-frontier PTE score of 0.9039 for Australian banks was the highest, relative to the average level of other countries, followed by Hong Kong (0.8958) and Japan (0.8847). In contrast, Indonesian banks had the lowest average meta-frontier PTE estimate of 0.7312, which suggests that an average bank in Indonesia can reduce inputs by 26.88% compared to the most efficient banks in the Asia-Pacific region, to produce the same level of outputs.

Combining the information of group-frontier PTE and meta-frontier PTE, the range of the TGR scores for the sample countries ranged from 0.8610 (Indonesia) to 0.9227 (Japan). Compared to the meta-frontier PTE, the relatively small range of TGRs suggests that the distances between the country-frontiers and meta-frontier were similar among the sample countries. For example, the average TGR for Australian banks of 0.9091 indicates that Australian banks operating on the frontier can improve and move towards the meta-frontier by reducing inputs by 9.09%.

Table 7. Group-frontier PTE, Meta-frontier PTE, and TGRs for Sample Countries (2005 to 2014).

Countries	Group PTE		Meta PTE		TGR	
	Mean	SD	Mean	SD	Mean	SD
Australia (n = 119)	0.9982	0.0154	0.9039	0.0791	0.9091	0.0828
China (n = 627)	0.9232	0.0524	0.8245	0.1175	0.8930	0.1060
Hong Kong (n = 156)	0.9843	0.0203	0.8958	0.0665	0.9099	0.0630
Indonesia (n = 389)	0.8529	0.1418	0.7312	0.1564	0.8610	0.1292
Japan (n = 941)	0.9588	0.0269	0.8847	0.07	0.9227	0.0688
New Zealand (n = 60)	0.9636	0.0272	0.8603	0.1443	0.8897	0.1266
Singapore (n = 54)	1	0	0.877	0.102	0.8770	0.1020
Thailand (n = 159)	0.9785	0.0284	0.8737	0.066	0.8929	0.0627

Notes: group PTE = group-frontier pure technology efficiency; meta PTE = meta-frontier pure technical efficiency; TGR = technology gap ratio. Source: Author's calculations.

5.3. Bootstrap Truncated Regression Results

5.3.1. Impact of Bank Regulation, Supervision, and Ownership on Bank Efficiency

To examine whether bank regulation, supervision, and state ownership in banks have significant influences on bank performance, the second-stage bootstrap regression model (Simar and Wilson 2007) was employed in this study. The pairwise correlated coefficients of the independent variables indicated no major issues of multicollinearity in the regression (see Appendix A Table A2). Additionally, robust standard errors were used in all the regression models to address potential heteroskedasticity problems. Year dummy and country dummy variables were included in the regression model to capture the impact of time and other unspecified country-specific characteristics.

Table 8 shows the regression results of the relationship between regulation, supervision and bank efficiencies (that is, PTE—pure technical efficiency, SE—scale efficiency, and TGR—technology gap ratio) using the full sample data of 2186 bank-year observations. Overall, the regression results show that regulation and supervision policies are positively related to pure technical efficiency and technology gap ratio of banks in the Asia-Pacific region. Following the first pillar of the Basel Accord, the capital requirement had a positive relationship with PTE and TGR at a 1% significance level. Consistent with previous empirical studies (Lozano-Vivas and Pasiouras 2010; Barth et al. 2013; Luo et al. 2016), stricter capital requirements can reduce the incentive to engage in risky behavior, and therefore improve the bank performance. The positive relationship between capital regulation and scale efficiency was insignificant.

Table 8. Bootstrap truncated regressionrResults: Full sample data.

Variables	Model 4			Model 1		
	Pure Technical Efficiency	Scale Efficiency	Technology Gap Ratio	Pure Technical Efficiency	Scale Efficiency	Technology Gap Ratio
Regulation and Supervision						
CAPITAL	0.0413 ***	−0.0008	0.0414 ***	0.0143	−0.0051	0.0024
	(3.3049)	(0.1182)	(2.7251)	(1.4627)	(0.6653)	(0.2161)
SPPOWER	0.0112 **	0.0052	0.0304 ***	0.0162 ***	−0.0027	0.0346 ***
	(2.2398)	(1.2695)	(4.3678)	(3.6520)	(0.7370)	(5.8246)
MKDSPL	0.0934 **	0.0802 **	0.2591 ***	0.0797 **	0.0811 **	0.1682 ***
	(2.0006)	(2.1102)	(3.6960)	(2.0011)	(2.3647)	(2.7786)
ACRS	0.0252 **	−0.0035	0.0536 ***	0.0180 **	−0.0011	0.0281 **
	(2.4088)	(0.4291)	(3.2889)	(2.0262)	(0.1505)	(1.9672)
DEP_INS	−0.0180	0.0119	−0.0015	0.0003	0.0502 ***	−0.0039
	(0.7791)	(0.6636)	(0.0447)	(0.0132)	(3.2407)	(0.1462)

Table 8. Cont.

	Model 4			Model 1		
Variables	Pure Technical Efficiency	Scale Efficiency	Technology Gap Ratio	Pure Technical Efficiency	Scale Efficiency	Technology Gap Ratio
Bank Ownership						
STATE	−0.0146 (1.2922)	0.0101 (1.1599)	−0.0209 (1.3806)	−0.0078 (0.8073)	0.0024 (0.2894)	−0.0130 (1.0847)
Bank-specific						
BANKSIZE	0.0387 *** (13.1486)	−0.0307 *** (18.0733)	0.0496 *** (8.6720)	0.0353 *** (16.1771)	−0.026 *** (16.1730)	0.0397 *** (11.4585)
EQTA	0.5016 *** (7.7435)	0.1470 *** (3.2061)	0.5327 *** (5.9613)	0.4708 *** (8.8300)	0.1332 *** (2.7354)	0.4169 *** (6.4345)
LIQTA	−0.1147 *** (2.8748)	0.0359 (1.3852)	−0.1367 ** (2.3743)	−0.0752 ** (2.1534)	0.0044 (0.1807)	−0.0435 (1.0027)
OBSTA				−0.0261 (1.2194)	0.0113 * (1.7808)	−0.0161 (1.1607)
LLPTL				−0.1660 (0.4644)	−1.568 *** (4.4302)	−0.4978 (1.2061)
Country-specific						
GDP_growth	0.0028 (1.2052)	−0.0007 (0.4408)	0.0034 (0.9910)	0.0053 *** (3.0187)	0.0009 (0.6334)	0.0110 *** (4.3530)
INF	0.0021 (1.5009)	0.0040 *** (3.1245)	−0.0074 *** (3.2805)	0.0024** (2.0932)	0.0040 *** (3.3899)	−0.0059 *** (3.5733)
HHI	0.1704 (1.3020)	0.1153 (1.3683)	−0.0530 (0.3083)	0.0569 (0.5487)	−0.0385 (0.6604)	−0.1445 (1.1137)
PrCrGDP	−0.0014 *** (2.9624)	−0.0000 (0.1594)	−0.0016 ** (2.4151)	−0.0000 (0.0459)	−0.0006 ** (2.3849)	0.0008 * (1.8283)
INST_ENV	−0.0403 (1.3761)	−0.0369 (1.5343)	−0.0264 (0.6527)	−0.066 *** (2.7279)	−0.0249 (1.1007)	−0.0481 (1.4502)
Constant	(2.4733) −0.3658	(0.7818) 0.8555 ***	(3.7280) −1.7831 ***	(2.5700) −0.4160	(1.5091) 0.8127 ***	(2.3282) −1.2376 **
Sigma	(0.9459) 0.1028 ***	(2.7512) 0.0996 ***	(2.9241) 0.1154 ***	(1.2686) 0.0925 ***	(2.9727) 0.0892 ***	(2.3473) 0.1055 ***
Country Dummy	Yes	Yes	Yes	Yes	Yes	Yes
Year Dummy	Yes	Yes	Yes	Yes	Yes	Yes

Note: This table reports the coefficients of regulation and supervision variables, state ownership, and other control variables in the Simar and Wilson (2007) bootstrap truncated regression models. Z-statistics are shown in the parentheses. See Appendix A Table A1 for definitions and information about the independent variables. *, **, *** indicates 10%, 5% and 1% levels of significance, respectively. Source: Author's calculations.

Similar to the capital requirement, the second pillar of the Basel Accord (that is, the official supervision power), is positively related to both PTE and TGR at 5% significance level. Under the "official supervision approach," greater official supervision power is believed to increase credit flow to firms which are well-connected with banks (Levine 2004) and enhances bank performance. Furthermore, a powerful official supervision regime can improve bank efficiency through increased competition in the banking industry (Barth et al. 2008). Empirically, our result is consistent with Pasiouras (2008a) and Luo et al.'s (2016) findings on global banking industries. Hirtle et al. (2016) found similar results in the US bank-holding companies. Official supervisory power is not significantly related to banks' scale efficiency.

The significantly positive coefficients of market discipline on PTE, SE, and TGR estimates support the "private monitoring approach" hypothesis, in which regulation and supervision policies promoting private monitoring in banks can induce better performance. By requiring banks to disclose adequate information to the public, market discipline can encourage private sectors to monitor banks with lower information and transaction costs (Barth et al. 2008). Table 8 shows that market discipline is the only regulation and supervision variable which is significantly (at a 5% significance level) related to the scale efficiency of banks in the Asia-Pacific region.

Banks with more activity restrictions tend to have higher performance, in both pure technical efficiency and technology gap ratios. These findings are similar to Barth et al.'s (2004) discussion that restricting banks engagement in security underwriting, insurance underwriting, and real estate investments would limit the conflicts of interest between stakeholders. Furthermore, narrowing the range of activities can reduce risky behaviours caused by moral hazards (Boyd et al. 1998) and positively affect bank performance. There is no evidence to suggest a significant relationship between activity restrictions and scale efficiency.

The existence of a deposit insurance scheme in each country has no significant relationship with bank performance according to our results. Additionally, state ownership is not significantly related to bank performance in the Asia-Pacific region. Bank-specific characteristics exhibit significant relationships with bank efficiencies. For example, bank size is positively related to technical efficiency and technical gap ratio, indicating that larger banks have better management and technology in their production processes. However, bank scale efficiency tends to be lower for larger banks, possibly due to the fact that most banks in the Asia-Pacific region expanded too quickly and operated at decreasing returns to scale during the 10-year sample period.

In addition, banks with higher capital ratios performed better in all three efficiency estimates. When banks hold more capital, managers tend to be more risk-averse in terms of operation, and therefore these banks would exhibit better performance. Our results are consistent with most of the previous studies in bank performance (see Demirgüç-Kunt and Huizinga 1999; Goddard et al. 2004; Sufian and Habibullah 2010; Fiordelisi et al. 2011; and Pessarossi and Weill 2015).

The level of liquid assets (LIQTA) in banks has a negative relationship with technical efficiency and technical gap ratio, but no significant correlation with scale efficiency. One possible reason for a higher level of liquid assets could be that banks would raise more liquid assets to reduce risks during times of uncertainty and unfavourable industry conditions (Radić et al. 2012). Thus, banks tend to have a lower performance during those times. Moreover, liquid assets are believed to be less profitable than illiquid assets and reduce investment opportunities for banks managers. The negative relationship between liquid ratio and technical gap ratio implies that holding more liquid assets would widen the distance from the group frontiers to the meta-frontier in banking industry.

The coefficients of GDP growth are not significantly related to bank performance, while a higher inflation rate has a positive relationship with scale efficiency and a negative impact on technology gap ratio. The concentration (HHI) of the banking industry appears unrelated to bank performance in the Asia-Pacific region. Furthermore, the negative coefficients of PrCrGDP indicate a negative relationship between private credit from banks to GDP and bank performance, suggesting that financial markets with more lending to private credit have relatively lower bank performance. The overall institutional environment of banks exhibits no significant relationship with bank performance in the Asia-Pacific region.

5.3.2. Regulation, Supervision, and Bank Size

After categorising banks into three size groups—small, medium and large, based on banks' total assets, we conducted further analysis to examine if the impacts of regulation, supervision, and state ownership on bank efficiency would be different in different sized groups. Table 9 shows the regression results for each bank groups, using meta-frontier efficiency from Model 4 as the dependent variable. Our findings in Table 9 suggest that stricter regulation and supervision policies are mostly positively related to small-sized banks, but not to medium or large-sized banks.

The first three columns in Table 9 compare the impact of regulation, supervision, and state ownership on pure technical efficiency for three sized bank groups. Tighter capital regulation and market discipline are significantly related to higher pure technical efficiency of small banks at a 1%

significant level. At the 10% significance level, activity restriction is positively associated with the pure technical efficiency of small banks. While official supervisory power has no significant relationship with the technical efficiency of small and medium banks, it is positively related to large bank efficiency at a 5% significance level. None of the regulatory and supervisory policies are significantly related to the pure technical efficiency of medium-sized banks.

Columns 4 to 6 in Table 9 summarise the regression results on scale efficiency for different-sized banks. The official supervision power and market discipline are significantly related to the scale efficiency of small banks. Additionally, market discipline is also positively related to large-sized banks' scale efficiency. There is no significant impact of bank regulation and supervision on medium-sized banks. Compared to the pure technical efficiency, scale efficiencies of banks are less affected by regulation and supervision. The deposit insurance scheme is positively related to the small-sized banks' scale efficiency at the 10% significance level.

The relationships of regulation and supervision and bank technology gap ratio are shown in columns 7 to 9 in Table 9. All four regulatory and supervisory indicators are positively related to the technology gap ratio of small banks. For large banks, official supervisory power is positively associated with the technology gap ratio. The medium-sized banks' technology gap ratios are not affected by any of the regulation and supervision indicators.

Table 9. Bootstrap truncated regression results: Different-sized bank groups.

Variables	(Columns 1–3) Pure Technical Efficiency			(Columns 4–6) Scale Efficiency			(Columns 7–9) Technology Gap Ratio		
	Small	Medium	Large	Small	Medium	Large	Small	Medium	Large
Regulation and Supervision									
CAPITAL	0.0757 *** (2.9635)	0.0171 (1.0773)	0.0045 (0.4986)	0.0202 (1.1485)	−0.0067 (0.3498)	−0.0185 (1.1844)	0.0839 ** (2.4592)	0.0172 (0.8045)	−0.0052 (0.3606)
SPPOWER	0.0100 (0.9637)	0.0011 (0.1682)	0.0081 ** (2.1796)	0.0310 *** (2.9870)	−0.0019 (0.2548)	−0.0014 (0.3157)	0.0301 ** (2.0693)	0.0115 (1.4927)	0.0186 *** (3.9669)
MKDSPL	0.2654 *** (2.6430)	−0.0521 (0.7393)	−0.0582 (1.3764)	0.1474 * (1.8145)	0.0507 (0.6432)	0.1194 ** (2.0539)	0.5115 *** (3.0413)	−0.0102 (0.1138)	0.0492 (1.0305)
ACRS	0.0398 * (1.8009)	−0.0010 (0.0700)	0.0053 (0.6782)	0.0229 (1.3651)	−0.0230 (1.3770)	0.0039 (0.3400)	0.0711 * (1.9474)	0.0124 (0.6400)	0.0150 (1.4497)
DEP_INS	−0.0671 (1.2391)	−0.0296 (0.8829)	−0.0042 (0.2506)	0.0676* (1.6483)	−0.0079 (0.2217)	−0.0093 (0.4429)	−0.0989 (1.2326)	−0.0052 (0.1297)	0.0157 (0.7598)
Ownership									
STATE	0.0194 (0.6326)	−0.0185 (1.1080)	0.0106 (1.3256)	0.0259 (0.9567)	0.0139 (0.6755)	−0.0105 (1.3329)	0.0077 (0.1578)	0.0011 (0.0628)	0.0073 (0.9588)
Bank-specific									
EQTA	0.3548 *** (4.3773)	0.0093 (0.0592)	0.1332 (0.6794)	0.2146 *** (3.7184)	0.1388 (1.2648)	−0.5144 ** (2.3111)	0.3188 *** (2.9380)	−0.0429 (0.2479)	−0.2266 (1.1389)
LIQTA	−0.0703 (0.9504)	−0.1182 ** (2.0130)	−0.1880 *** (3.6610)	0.0058 (0.1367)	0.0468 (0.8438)	−0.0002 (0.0052)	−0.1221 (1.1268)	−0.2056 *** (2.8275)	−0.1114 ** (2.4968)
Country-specific									
GDP_growth	0.0117 ** (2.2114)	−0.0041 (1.4506)	−0.0006 (0.3212)	−0.0060 * (1.6692)	0.0004 (0.1465)	0.0021 (1.1888)	0.0234 *** (2.8115)	−0.0068 ** (2.1655)	−0.0031 (1.4766)
INF	0.0019 (0.6360)	0.0032 * (1.6664)	−0.0005 (0.3732)	0.0059 ** (2.2244)	0.0070 *** (3.0186)	0.0038 ** (2.3868)	−0.0071 (1.4969)	−0.0100 *** (4.1489)	−0.0030 ** (2.2244)
HHI	0.0844 (0.2927)	0.2166 (1.4563)	0.0134 (0.1662)	0.3355 (1.3775)	0.2716 (1.4077)	−0.1003 (1.2404)	0.0661 (0.1283)	−0.2207 (1.4719)	−0.2000 *** (2.7198)
PrCrGDP	−0.0005 (0.4741)	−0.0013** (2.4554)	−0.0007* (1.7261)	0.0002 (0.2486)	−0.0005 (0.9370)	−0.0009** (2.4464)	−0.0004 (0.2328)	−0.0015** (2.3008)	−0.0004 (1.0400)
INST_ENV	−0.1690 *** (2.7521)	−0.0534 (1.1384)	0.0559 * (1.9522)	0.0351 (0.6148)	−0.0643 (1.3926)	−0.0944 *** (3.4470)	−0.2765 *** (3.2453)	0.0462 (0.8689)	0.0597 ** (2.3521)
Constant	−0.7725 (0.9831)	1.5390 *** (2.9823)	1.2107 *** (4.0531)	−0.7807 (1.1678)	0.7517 (1.2258)	0.4405 (1.0432)	−2.3958* (1.7966)	1.1413 (1.6180)	0.4574 (1.2343)
sigma	0.1270 *** (19.2102)	0.0885 *** (16.7169)	0.0558 *** (11.2685)	0.1095 *** (25.7747)	0.0995 *** (30.6333)	0.0699 *** (25.7247)	0.1480 *** (12.9352)	0.0868 *** (11.7518)	0.0501 *** (17.0131)
Country Dummy	Yes	Yes	Yes	Yes	Yes	Yes	Yes	Yes	Yes
Year Dummy	Yes	Yes	Yes	Yes	Yes	Yes	Yes	Yes	Yes

Notes: This table reports the bootstrap truncated regression results in different-sized bank groups. Z-statistics are shown in parentheses. The pure technical efficiency, scale efficiency, and technology gap ratio scores are estimated in Model 4. See Table A1 for definitions and information on the independent variables. *, **, *** indicate 10%, 5% and 1% levels of significance, respectively. Source: Author's calculations.

5.4. Robustness Check: Tobit Regression and Fractional Logit Regression

This study employs the Simar and Wilson (2007) bootstrap truncated regression model to examine the relationship between bank regulation, supervision, ownership and bank efficiency. In previous studies, different types of regression models were used in the second stage after obtaining the DEA efficiency estimates. For example, most of the previous studies (Pasiouras 2008a; Sufian 2009; Gardener et al. 2011; Ab-Rahim et al. 2012; Huang and Fu 2013) used the Tobit regression to identify determinants of bank efficiency. Alternatively, Ramalho et al. (2010) suggested that fractional logit regression is the most natural way for second-stage regression.

To check the robustness of our regression results, we applied both fractional logit regression and Tobit regression in the second stage, to examine the relationship between regulation, supervision, ownership and bank performance (see Table 10). In both regressions, we used technical efficiency, scale efficiency, and technology gap ratio in Model 4 as the dependent variables, with the same independent variables as in the previous analysis.

Columns 1 to 3 in Table 10 show the results of fractional logit regression, which are similar to the results in Table 8. Regulation and supervision are positively related to bank pure technical efficiency and technology gap ratios. Additionally, market discipline is positively associated with bank scale efficiency in the Asia-Pacific region. However, we observe that the coefficient estimates in the fractional logit regression are larger than those in the truncated regression, and there are some variations in the Z-value compared to bootstrap truncated regression results.

Columns 4 to 6 in Table 10 display the Tobit regression results of bank efficiency. Even though the coefficients of variables have the same signs, we observe that supervision power and market discipline are not significantly related to pure technical efficiency. All four regulation and supervision indices exhibited positive relationships with the technology gap ratio of banks. Similar to the discussion in Section 5.3, deposit insurance schemes and state ownership were not significantly related to bank performance in both fractional logit and Tobit regression models.

Table 10. Robustness test results: Fractional logit regression and tobit regression.

Variables	Fractional Logit Regression			Tobit Regression		
	Pure Technical Efficiency	Scale Efficiency	Technology Gap Ratio	Pure Technical Efficiency	Scale Efficiency	Technology Gap Ratio
	Regulation and Supervision					
CAPITAL	0.2069 *** (3.6605)	−0.0081 (0.2649)	0.1789 *** (2.8087)	0.0201 *** (2.8396)	0.0010 (0.1533)	0.0164 ** (2.5060)
SPPOWER	0.0506 * (1.7768)	0.0269 * (1.7727)	0.1205 *** (3.8051)	0.0026 (1.0131)	0.0043 (1.1047)	0.0079 *** (3.2451)
MKDSPL	0.4634 * (1.9161)	0.4098 ** (2.3118)	1.0504 *** (3.6772)	0.0313 (1.2163)	0.0680 * (1.8896)	0.0926 *** (3.3342)
ACRS	0.1274 ** (2.3162)	−0.0152 (0.4514)	0.2119 *** (3.1935)	0.0132 ** (2.3242)	−0.0032 (0.4276)	0.0153 *** (2.5911)
DEP_INS	−0.0607 (0.6188)	0.0562 (0.7962)	−0.0130 (0.1182)	0.0049 (0.4296)	0.0116 (0.7011)	−0.0011 (0.0902)
Ownership						
STATE	−0.0719 (0.8184)	0.0565 (0.7775)	−0.0997 (1.1219)	−0.0103 (1.3123)	0.0073 (0.9210)	−0.0098 (1.2725)
	Bank-specific					
BANKSIZE	0.1973 *** (10.6387)	−0.146 *** (9.7058)	0.2134 *** (8.7663)	0.0221 *** (15.0755)	−0.028 *** (18.8324)	0.0179 *** (11.9368)
EQTA	2.5618 *** (5.8482)	0.8073 ** (2.4078)	2.2581 *** (4.6255)	0.2827 *** (7.5429)	0.0929 ** (2.4482)	0.1958 *** (5.5274)
LIQTA	−0.6041 ** (2.2406)	0.1807 (0.9800)	−0.6323 ** (2.0175)	−0.082 *** (2.8372)	0.0269 (1.1919)	−0.077 *** (2.8936)

Table 10. Cont.

Variables	Fractional Logit Regression			Tobit Regression		
	Pure Technical Efficiency	Scale Efficiency	Technology Gap Ratio	Pure Technical Efficiency	Scale Efficiency	Technology Gap Ratio
			Country-specific			
GDP_growth	0.0168 (1.3993)	−0.0036 (0.5275)	0.0172 (1.2214)	0.0033 *** (2.5957)	−0.0002 (0.1132)	0.0051 *** (3.9388)
INF	0.0102 (1.4189)	0.0200 *** (3.7307)	−0.031 *** (3.5093)	0.0019 * (1.8685)	0.0032 *** (2.8496)	−0.004 *** (4.3943)
HHI	0.7608 (1.2715)	0.5872 * (1.6500)	−0.0714 (0.1111)	0.0670 (1.4434)	0.0585 (1.0167)	0.0087 (0.2193)
PrCrGDP	−0.0075 ** (2.4916)	0.0000 (0.0279)	−0.0071 ** (2.0615)	−0.001 *** (3.2615)	−0.0001 (0.4575)	−0.0006 ** (2.5366)
institutional_env	−0.1883 (1.3395)	−0.2061 ** (2.0546)	−0.1553 (0.8973)	−0.0441 ** (2.1493)	−0.0287 (1.2977)	−0.0086 (0.4657)
Constant	−4.4315 ** (2.1735)	1.4683 (1.0551)	−9.105 *** (3.6945)	0.3335 * (1.6557)	0.8862 *** (3.0197)	−0.0705 (0.3283)
Sigma				0.0810 *** (39.7257)	0.0958 *** (56.2804)	0.0755 *** (34.1237)
Country Dummy	Yes	Yes	Yes	Yes	Yes	Yes
Year Dummy	Yes	Yes	Yes	Yes	Yes	Yes

Note: This table reports the relationship between bank regulation and supervision on efficiencies of banks using fractional logit regression (columns 1–3) and ordinary least square regression (columns 4–6). Z-values are shown in the parenthesis. PTE, SE, and TGR estimates from Model 4 are used as the dependent variables. Statistically significance at 10% level. *, **, *** indicates 10%, 5% and 1% levels of significance, respectively. Source: Author's calculations.

6. Conclusions

This study examined the impacts of off-balance sheet activities on bank efficiency measurement, and investigated the relationship between regulation, supervision, state ownership and bank efficiency. Our results showed that omitting off-balance sheet activities while estimating bank efficiency using bootstrap DEA approach would significantly underestimate the pure technical efficiency and overall technical efficiency, while overestimating the scale efficiency of banks. Furthermore, we identified the positive relationship between regulation, supervision, and bank efficiency, especially in small-sized banks. However, no significant relationship between state ownership with bank performance was found in this study.

Our findings have imperative policy implications. Firstly, our results have highlighted the impact of including non-traditional bank activities when measuring bank efficiency. Precise information relating to bank performance is essential for policy-making decisions, such as capital requirements and information disclosure. Correctly estimated efficiency could reveal the banks' intrinsic value and potential investment return in the future. Such information could further assist investors' and bank managers' decision making. Secondly, regulatory and supervisory authorities could impose customized regulatory and supervisory policies on different sized banks. While smaller banks benefit more from stricter policies, regulatory authorities could relax the requirements for medium and large-sized banks to exploit operational efficiency. Finally, since state ownership is found to be insignificantly related to bank performance, it could be an appropriate tool for governments to intervene in the banking industry during financial turmoil to maintain the intermediary function of banks.

There exist several limitations of the current study. First, we used the nonparametric DEA approach to estimate bank efficiency. Compared to the parametric approaches, the DEA method assumes the random error to be zero, which could affect the precision of efficiency estimation. Second, due to the data availability of bank regulation and supervision, we used the 2007 and 2011 World Bank Regulatory and Supervisory Survey to cover the 10-year sample period. Therefore, the timeliness and frequency of data could have potentially limited the validity of our results. Last, our sample covered eight countries in the Asia-Pacific region based on data availability. There were five developed countries and three developing countries. Even though these countries can capture the diversity and common characteristics of the Asia-Pacific banking industries, questions remain whether our results can be applied to all banking industries in the region.

In future studies, we recommend different approaches, such as the stochastic frontier analysis approach, to estimate bank efficiency to avoid potential biases arising from the zero-error assumption of the DEA approach. Future researchers can collect more detailed bank-specific and country-specific data from more sample countries. Using these detailed data, future researchers can explore the timely changes in regulatory policies and their impacts on bank performance, and provide evidence which can be used to benefit the stakeholders in all the banks in the Asia-Pacific region.

Author Contributions: Z.Y. contributed to the research design and data analysis, writing, and formal analysis of the research. C.G. and Z.L. supervised the research. Z.Y. and C.G. helped with the modifying of the manuscript and final editorial clarifications and corrections. All authors contributed to the writing, reviewing, and correction of this manuscript.

Funding: This research received no external funding.

Acknowledgments: Baiding Hu has provided valuable insights into the methodology and statistical analysis of the the study.

Conflicts of Interest: The authors declare no conflict of interest.

Appendix A

Table A1. Definition and data source of variables used in the regression models.

Variables	Definition	Data Source
Regulation and supervision		
CAP_k	Initial and overall capital requirements for banks in country k	World Bank (2007, 2011)
$SPPOER_k$	Extent of official supervision power to oversee, monitor, and discipline managers, directors, and auditors of banks in country k	World Bank (2007, 2011)
$MKDSPL_k$	Information disclosure to regulators, shareholders, auditors, and public and whether any credit ratings are required for banks in country k	World Bank (2007, 2011)
$ACRS_k$	Bank activity restrictions in real estate investment, insurance underwriting and selling, brokering and dealing securities, and all aspects of mutual fund industries in country k	World Bank (2007, 2011)
Ownership Variable		
$Ownership_{k,i}$	State ownership of the bank, equals1 when bank is state-owned, otherwise 0.	Caculated based on information from BvD Bankscope
Bank-specific Variables		
$Banksize_{i,k}$	Bank size, calculated as logarithm of the total assets of the bank.	BvD Bankscope
$EQTA_{i,k}$	Bank capitalisation, calculated as total equity divided by total assets.	BvD Bankscope
$LIQTA_{i,k}$	Bank liquidity risk, calculated by liquid assets divided by total assets.	BvD Bankscope
$OBS_{i,k}$	Bank operating risk, calculated as off-balance sheet items divided by total assets.	BvD Bankscope
$LLPTL_{i,k}$	Bank credit risk, calculated as loan loss provisions over the total loans.	BvD Bankscope

Table A1. *Cont.*

Variables	Definition	Data Source
Country-specific Variables		
GDP_growth_k	Real GDP growth in the country.	Global Financial Development Database
INF_k	Annual rate of the implicit GDP deflator.	Global Financial Development Database
HHI_k	Herfindall Hirschman Index, calculated as sum of square for deposit shares for each bank in all banks in the country.	Calculated by author using data from BvD Bankscope
$PrCrGDP_k$	Bank claims to the private sector to GDP.	Global Financial Development Database
INS_ENV_k	Institutional governance index, consists of voice and accountability, political stability and absence of violence or terrorism, government effectiveness, regulatory quality, the rule of law, control of corruption.	Calculated using data from World Governance Indicators database

Table A2. Pairwise correlation between independent variables in the regression.

	CAPITAL	SPPOWER	MKDSPL	ACRS	DEP_INS	STATE	BANKSIZE	OBS	EQTA	LLPTL	LIQTA	GDP_growth	INF	HHI	PrCrGDP	INST_ENV
CAPITAL	1															
SPPOWER	0.045 *	1														
MKDSPL	0.159 *	−0.605 *	1													
ACRS	−0.115 *	0.276 *	−0.195 *	1												
DEP_INS	−0.028	0.443 *	−0.6268 *	−0.4598 *	1											
STATE	0.0327	0.063 *	0.0530 *	0.1850 *	−0.1857 *	1										
BANKSIZE	0.0798 *	−0.181 *	0.2173 *	−0.0841 *	−0.0456 *	0.1107 *	1									
OBS	0.0323	−0.008	0.0997 *	−0.0077	−0.1063 *	0.0313	−0.0343	1								
EQTA	0.0531 *	0.005	−0.005	−0.0643 *	−0.0728 *	−0.0166	−0.5176 *	0.1393 *	1							
LLPTL	−0.0767 *	0.128 *	−0.0735 *	0.2122 *	−0.0966 *	0.1313 *	−0.2009 *	0.1486 *	0.1034 *	1						
LIQTA	0.0918 *	−0.1684 *	0.2815 *	0.0308	−0.3004 *	0.1378 *	−0.2498 *	0.1665 *	0.2936 *	0.2042 *	1					
GDP_growth	0.0105	−0.123 *	0.4185 *	0.3590 *	−0.6253 *	0.2624 *	−0.1484 *	0.1336 *	0.1739 *	0.1930 *	0.4659 *	1				
INF	−0.048 *	0.150 *	−0.138 *	0.3437 *	−0.178 *	0.2353 *	−0.3816 *	0.1099 *	0.2590 *	0.3138 *	0.3962 *	0.4841 *	1			
HHI	−0.146 *	−0.361 *	0.3589 *	−0.492 *	−0.0829 *	−0.0412	−0.0023	0.1325 *	0.1559 *	−0.085 *	0.2369 *	0.1600 *	0.0737 *	1		
PrCrGDP	0.1333 *	−0.696 *	0.6954 *	−0.367 *	−0.275 *	−0.143 *	0.4023 *	0.0626 *	−0.126 *	−0.255 *	0.0214	−0.0542 *	−0.513 *	0.3332 *	1	
INST_ENV	−0.120 *	−0.180 *	−0.08 *	−0.641 *	0.5179 *	−0.3513 *	0.2866 *	−0.1868 *	−0.2115 *	−0.379 *	−0.398 *	−0.6621 *	−0.62 *	0.302 *	0.3866 *	1

Notes: See Table A1 for definitions for variables. * indicates 5% level of significance. Source: Author's calculation.

References

Ab-Rahim, Rossazana, Nor Ghani Md-Nor, Shamsubarida Ramlee, and Nur Zaimah Ubaidillah. 2012. Determinants of cost efficiency in malaysian banking. *International Journal of Business and Society* 13: 355–74.

Altunbas, Yener, Ming-Hau Liu, Philip Molyneux, and Rama Seth. 2000. Efficiency and risk in Japanese banking. *Journal of Banking & Finance* 24: 1605–28. [CrossRef]

Barry, Thierno, Santos Jose Dacanay III, Laetitia Lepetit, and Amine Tarazi. 2008. Ownership Structure and Bank Efficiency in the Asia Pacific Region. *SSRN*. [CrossRef]

Barth, James R., Gerard Caprio Jr., and Ross Levine. 2001. Banking systems around the globe: Do regulation and ownership affect performance and stability? In *Prudential Supervision: What Works and What Doesn't*. Chicago: University of Chicago Press, pp. 31–96.

Barth, James R., Gerard Caprio Jr., and Ross Levine. 2004. Bank regulation and supervision: What works best? *Journal of Financial Intermediation* 13: 205–48. [CrossRef]

Barth, James R., Gerard Caprio Jr., and Ross Levine. 2007. *The Microeconomic Effects of Different Approaches to Bank Supervision. The Politics of Financial Development*. Palo Alto: Stanford University Press.

Barth, James R., Gerard Caprio Jr., and Ross Levine. 2008. *Rethinking Bank Regulation: Till Angels Govern*. Cambridge: Cambridge University Press.

Barth, James R., Gerard Caprio Jr., and Ross Levine. 2012. *The Evolution and Impact of Bank Regulations*. Washington: The World Bank.

Barth, James R., Chen Lin, Yue Ma, Jesús Seade, and Frank M. Song. 2013. Do bank regulation, supervision and monitoring enhance or impede bank efficiency? *Journal of Banking & Finance* 37: 2879–92. [CrossRef]

Berger, Allen N., George R. G. Clarke, Robert Cull, Leora Klapper, and Gregory F. Udell. 2005. Corporate governance and bank performance: A joint analysis of the static, selection, and dynamic effects of domestic, foreign, and state ownership. *Journal of Banking & Finance* 29: 2179–221. [CrossRef]

Berger, Allen N., Iftekhar Hasan, and Mingming Zhou. 2009. Bank ownership and efficiency in China: What will happen in the world's largest nation? *Journal of Banking & Finance* 33: 113–30.

Bonin, John P., Iftekhar Hasan, and Paul Wachtel. 2005. Bank performance, efficiency and ownership in transition countries. *Journal of Banking & Finance* 29: 31–53. [CrossRef]

Boyd, John H., Chun Chang, and Bruce D. Smith. 1998. Moral Hazard under Commercial and Universal Banking. *Journal of Money, Credit and Banking* 30: 426–68. [CrossRef]

Brunnermeier, Markus K. 2009. Financial crisis: Mechanism, prevention and management. *Macroeconomic Stability and Financial Regulation: Key Issue for the G* 20: 91–104.

Capannelli, Giovanni, and Carlo Filippini. 2010. Economic Integration in East Asia and Europe: Lessons from a Comparative Analysis. *The Singapore Economic Review* 55: 163–84. [CrossRef]

Charnes, Abraham, William W. Cooper, Zhimin Huang, and Dee Bruce Sun. 1990. Polyhedral Cone-Ratio DEA Models with an illustrative application to large commercial banks. *Journal of Econometrics* 46: 73–91. [CrossRef]

Chortareas, Georgios E., Claudia Girardone, and Alexia Ventouri. 2012. Bank supervision, regulation, and efficiency: Evidence from the European Union. *Journal of Financial Stability* 8: 292–302. [CrossRef]

Chortareas, Georgios E., Claudia Girardone, and Alexia Ventouri. 2013. Financial freedom and bank efficiency: Evidence from the European Union. *Journal of Banking & Finance* 37: 1223–31.

Cihak, Martin, and Asli Demirgüç-Kunt. 2013. *Rethinking the State's Role in Finance*. Washington: The World Bank.

Clark, Jeffery Arthur, and Tom Siems. 2002. X-efficiency in banking: Looking beyond the balance sheet. *Journal of Money, Credit, and Banking* 34: 987–1013. [CrossRef]

Coelli, Timothy J., Dodla Sai Prasada Rao, Christopher J. O'Donnell, and George Edward Battese. 2005. *An introduction to Efficiency and Productivity Analysis*. Berlin: Springer Science & Business Media.

Cook, Wade D., and Larry M. Seiford. 2009. Data envelopment analysis (DEA)—Thirty years on. *European Journal of Operational Research* 192: 1–17. [CrossRef]

Cornett, Marcia Millon, Lin Guo, Shahriar Khaksari, and Hassan Tehranian. 2010. The impact of state ownership on performance differences in privately-owned versus state-owned banks: An international comparison. *Journal of Financial Intermediation* 19: 74–94. [CrossRef]

Demirgüç-Kunt, Ash, and Harry Huizinga. 1999. Determinants of commercial bank interest margins and profitability: some international evidence. *The World Bank Economic Review* 13: 379–408. [CrossRef]

DeYoung, Robert, and Gökhan Torna. 2013. Nontraditional banking activities and bank failures during the financial crisis. *Journal of Financial Intermediation* 22: 397–421. [CrossRef]

Dong, Yizhe, Robert Hamilton, and Mark Tippett. 2014. Cost efficiency of the Chinese banking sector: A comparison of stochastic frontier analysis and data envelopment analysis. *Economic Modelling* 36: 298–308. [CrossRef]

Drake, Leigh. 2001. Efficiency and productivity change in UK banking. *Applied Financial Economics* 11: 557–71. [CrossRef]

Drake, Leigh, and Maximilian J. B. Hall. 2003. Efficiency in Japanese banking: An empirical analysis. *Journal of Banking & Finance* 27: 891–917. [CrossRef]

Engle, Robert, Fariborz Moshirian, Sidharth Sahgal, and Bohui Zhang. 2014. Banks non-interest Income and Global Financial Stability. CIFR Paper No. 015/2014. Rochester: SSRN. [CrossRef]

Fallah-Fini, Saeideh, Konstantinos Triantis, Jesus M. de la Garza, and William L. Seaver. 2012. Measuring the efficiency of highway maintenance contracting strategies: A bootstrapped non-parametric meta-frontier approach. *European Journal of Operational Research* 219: 134–45. [CrossRef]

Fethi, Meryem Duygun, and Fotios Pasiouras. 2010. Assessing bank efficiency and performance with operational research and artificial intelligence techniques: A survey. *European Journal of Operational Research* 204: 189–98. [CrossRef]

Fiordelisi, Franco, David Marques-Ibanez, and Phil Molyneux. 2011. Efficiency and risk in European banking. *Journal of Banking & Finance* 35: 1315–26.

Freixas, Xavier, and Jean-Charles Rochet. 2008. *Microeconomics of Banking*. Cambridge: MIT Press.

Fu, Xiaoqing Maggie, Yongjia Rebecca Lin, and Philip Molyneux. 2014. Bank efficiency and shareholder value in Asia Pacific. *Journal of International Financial Markets, Institutions and Money* 33: 200–22. [CrossRef]

Gardener, Edward, Philip Molyneux, and Hoai Nguyen-Linh. 2011. Determinants of efficiency in South East Asian banking. *The Service Industries Journal* 31: 2693–719. [CrossRef]

Gerschenkron, Alexander. 1962. *Economic Backwardness in Historical Perspective: A book of Essays*. Cambridge: Belknap Press of Harvard University Press.

Goddard, John, Philip Molyneux, and John OS Wilson. 2004. The profitability of European banks: A cross-sectional and dynamic panel analysis. *The Manchester School* 72: 363–81. [CrossRef]

Hall, Maximilian J. B., Karligash A. Kenjegalieva, and Richard Simper. 2012. Environmental factors affecting Hong Kong banking: A post-Asian financial crisis efficiency analysis. *Global Finance Journal* 23: 184–201. [CrossRef]

Hirtle, Beverly, Anna Kovner, and Matthew Plosser. 2016. *The Impact of Supervision on Bank Performance*. FRB of NY Staff Report No. 768. Rochester: SSRN.

Hossain, Mahmud, Pankaj K. Jain, and Santanu Mitra. 2013. State ownership and bank equity in the Asia-Pacific region. *Pacific-Basin Finance Journal* 21: 914–31. [CrossRef]

Huang, Mei-Ying, and Tsu-Tan Fu. 2013. An examination of the cost efficiency of banks in Taiwan and China using the metafrontier cost function. *Journal of Productivity Analysis* 40: 387–406. [CrossRef]

International Monetary Fund. 2013. *Asia and Pacific: Shifting Risks, New Foundations for Growth*. Washington: Internaional Monetary Fund, Available online: https://www.imf.org/en/Publications/REO/APAC/Issues/2017/03/09/Shifting-Risks-New-Foundations-for-Growth (accessed on 3 September 2018).

Kilinc, Mustafa, and Bilin Neyapti. 2012. Bank regulation and supervision and its welfare implications. *Economic Modelling* 29: 132–41. [CrossRef]

Kim, Teakdong, Bonwoo Koo, and Minsoo Park. 2013. Role of financial regulation and innovation in the financial crisis. *Journal of Financial Stability* 9: 662–72. [CrossRef]

Kroszner, Randall S. 1998. Rethinking bank regulation: A review of the historical evidence. *Journal of Applied Corporate Finance* 11: 48–58. [CrossRef]

La Porta, Rafael, Florencio Lopez-de-Silanes, and Andrei Shleifer. 1999. Corporate ownership around the world. *The Journal of Finance* 54: 471–517. [CrossRef]

La Porta, Rafael, Florencio Lopez-de-Silanes, and Andrei Shleifer. 2002. Government ownership of banks. *The Journal of Finance* 57: 265–301. [CrossRef]

Levine, Ross. 2004. *The Microeconomic Effects of Different Approaches to Bank Supervision*. Working Paper No. 237. Stanford: Stanford Center for International Development.

Lieu, Pang-Tien, Tsai-Lien Yeh, and Yung-Ho Chiu. 2005. Off-balance sheet activities and cost inefficiency in Taiwan's Banks. *The Service Industries Journal* 25: 925–44. [CrossRef]

Lin, Xiaochi, and Yi Zhang. 2009. Bank ownership reform and bank performance in China. *Journal of Banking & Finance* 33: 20–29. [CrossRef]

Lozano-Vivas, Ana, and Fotios Pasiouras. 2010. The impact of non-traditional activities on the estimation of bank efficiency: International evidence. *Journal of Banking & Finance* 34: 1436–49. [CrossRef]

Lozano-Vivas, Ana, and Fotios Pasiouras. 2014. Bank Productivity Change and Off-Balance-Sheet Activities across Different Levels of Economic Development. *Journal of Financial Services Research* 46: 271–94. [CrossRef]

Luo, Yun, Sailesh Tanna, and Glauco De Vita. 2016. Financial openness, risk and bank efficiency: Cross-country evidence. *Journal of Financial Stability* 24: 132–48. [CrossRef]

Margono, Heru, Subhash C. Sharma, and Paul D. Melvin Ii. 2010. Cost efficiency, economies of scale, technological progress and productivity in Indonesian banks. *Journal of Asian Economics* 21: 53–65. [CrossRef]

McKinsey Company. 2016. Weathering the Storm: Asia-Pacific Banking Review 2016. Available online: https://www.mckinsey.com/industries/financial-services/our-insights/weathering-the-storm-asia-pacific-banking-review-2016 (accessed on 20 August 2017).

Mester, Loretta J. 1996. A study of bank efficiency taking into account risk-preferences. *Journal of Banking & Finance* 20: 1025–45.

Micco, Alejandro, Ugo Panizza, and Monica Yanez. 2007. Bank ownership and performance. Does politics matter? *Journal of Banking & Finance* 31: 219–41.

O'Donnell, Christopher J., D. S. Prasada Rao, and George E. Battese. 2008. Metafrontier frameworks for the study of firm-level efficiencies and technology ratios. *Empirical Economics* 34: 231–55. [CrossRef]

Pasiouras, Fotios. 2008a. International evidence on the impact of regulations and supervision on banks' technical efficiency: An application of two-stage data envelopment analysis. *Review of Quantitative Finance and Accounting* 30: 187–223. [CrossRef]

Pasiouras, Fotios. 2008b. Estimating the technical and scale efficiency of Greek commercial banks: The impact of credit risk, off-balance sheet activities, and international operations. *Research in International Business and Finance* 22: 301–18. [CrossRef]

Pasiouras, Fotios, Sailesh Tanna, and Constantin Zopounidis. 2009. The impact of banking regulations on banks' cost and profit efficiency: Cross-country evidence. *International Review of Financial Analysis* 18: 294–302. [CrossRef]

Perera, Shrimal, Michael Skully, and Jayasinghe Wickramanayake. 2007. Cost Efficiency in South Asian Banking: The Impact of Bank Size, State Ownership and Stock Exchange Listings. *International Review of Finance* 7: 35–60. [CrossRef]

Pessarossi, Pierre, and Laurent Weill. 2015. Do capital requirements affect cost efficiency? Evidence from China. *Journal of Financial Stability* 19: 119–27. [CrossRef]

Radić, Nemanja, Franco Fiordelisi, and Claudia Girardone. 2012. Efficiency and risk-taking in pre-crisis investment banks. *Journal of Financial Services Research* 41: 81–101. [CrossRef]

Ramalho, Esmeralda A., Joaquim J. S. Ramalho, and Pedro D. Henriques. 2010. Fractional regression models for second stage DEA efficiency analyses. *Journal of Productivity Analysis* 34: 239–55. [CrossRef]

Rogers, Kevin E. 1998. Nontraditional activities and the efficiency of US commercial banks. *Journal of Banking & Finance* 22: 467–82. [CrossRef]

Rosenkranz, Peter, and Junkyu Lee. 2019. *Nonperforming Loans in Asia: Determinants and Macrofinancial Linkages*. Asian Development Bank Economics Working Paper Series, No. 574. Rochester: SSRN.

Shaban, Mohamed, and Gregory A. James. 2018. The effects of ownership change on bank performance and risk exposure: Evidence from Indonesia. *Journal of Banking & Finance* 88: 483–97. [CrossRef]

Shleifer, Andrei. 1998. State versus private ownership. *Journal of Economic Perspectives* 12: 133–50. [CrossRef]

Shleifer, Andrei, and Robert W. Vishny. 1994. Politicians and firms. *The Quarterly Journal of Economics* 109: 995–1025. [CrossRef]

Simar, Léopol, and Paul Wilson. 2000. Statistical Inference in Nonparametric Frontier Models: The State of the Art. *Journal of Productivity Analysis* 13: 49–78. [CrossRef]

Simar, Léopold, and Paul W. Wilson. 2007. Estimation and inference in two-stage, semi-parametric models of production processes. *Journal of Econometrics* 136: 31–64. [CrossRef]

Sufian, Fadzlan. 2009. Determinants of bank efficiency during unstable macroeconomic environment: Empirical evidence from Malaysia. *Research in International Business and Finance* 23: 54–77. [CrossRef]

Sufian, Fadzlan, and Muzafar Shah Habibullah. 2010. Bank-specific, Industry-specific and Macroeconomic Determinants of Bank Efficiency: Empirical Evidence from the Thai Banking Sector. *Margin: The Journal of Applied Economic Research* 4: 427–61. [CrossRef]

Sufian, Fadzlan, Junaina Muhamad, A. N. Bany-Ariffin, Mohamed Hisham Yahya, and Fakarudin Kamarudin. 2012. Assessing the effect of mergers and acquisitions on revenue efficiency: Evidence from Malaysian banking sector. *Vision: The Journal of Business Perspective* 16: 1–11. [CrossRef]

Tan, Yong, and John Anchor. 2017. The impacts of risk-taking behaviour and competition on technical efficiency: Evidence from the Chinese banking industry. *Research in International Business and Finance* 41: 90–104. [CrossRef]

Triki, Thouraya, Imen Kouki, Mouna Ben Dhaou, and Pietro Calice. 2017. Bank regulation and efficiency: What works for Africa? *Research in International Business and Finance* 39: 183–205. [CrossRef]

Viverita, and Mohamed Ariff. 2011. Efficiency measurement and determinants of Indonesian bank efficiency. *Academy of Financial Services*, May 30.

Wang, Ke, Wei Huang, Jie Wu, and Ying-Nan Liu. 2014. Efficiency measures of the Chinese commercial banking system using an additive two-stage DEA. *Omega* 44: 5–20. [CrossRef]

World Bank. 2007. *Bank Regulation and Supervision*. Washington: World Bank.

World Bank. 2011. *Bank Regulation and Supervision*. Washington: World Bank.

© 2019 by the authors. Licensee MDPI, Basel, Switzerland. This article is an open access article distributed under the terms and conditions of the Creative Commons Attribution (CC BY) license (http://creativecommons.org/licenses/by/4.0/).

Article

Revenue Diversification, Risk and Bank Performance of Vietnamese Commercial Banks

Khanh Ngoc Nguyen

Faculty of Banking, Banking Academy, Hanoi 100000, Vietnam; khanhnguyensaxion@gmail.com

Received: 28 June 2019; Accepted: 26 August 2019; Published: 28 August 2019

Abstract: In the future, when the process of economic integration in the banking sector is more powerful, and competitive, diversifying revenue is an inevitable and objective trend to help the banks increase profits, minimize risks and improve their competitive position in the system. The research is on the relationship between revenue diversification, risk and bank performance using data from audited financial statements and annual reports of 26 commercial banks listed and unlisted in Vietnam during the period 2010–2018. The research method uses Generalized Method of Moment (GMM) modeling techniques to solve endogenous problems, variance and autocorrelation in the research model. Research results show that diversification negatively impacts profitability and the higher the diversification, the higher the risk of commercial banks. However, the more diversified listed banks, the more increased the bank's stability. The banks show the weakness and lack of experience of the banking system in developing a reasonable profit transformation model. The revenue diversification of banks is currently passive and moves slowly. Interest income is still the motivation of bank development, boosting profit growth. Growth, as well as the contribution from service activities, is not commensurate with potentials; although there are many positive points, they are not enough to cover risks from net interest income activities.

Keywords: revenue diversification; bank risks; bank performance; net interest income; non-interest income

---

1. Introduction

In recent times, the Vietnamese banking system has changed significantly. Some banks have merged and foreign banks have been allowed to participate in the banking sector. Great and healthy banks are strongly encouraged to seek the consolidation and development of universal banking services to become essential in the banking sector. The merger or consolidation of banks has created a new wave of competitive pressure and contributed to restructuring the banking sector. From specialized credit operations, banks have begun to change by switching to non-traditional activities to diversify revenues, minimize risks as well as seek new opportunities for themselves. Business strategies of banks are reflecting a continuously great change in income structure. Interest income is still the dominant revenue source in the income structure of the industry; however, it has been on a downward trend in recent years. Non-interest income has increased from 18% in 2015 to 23% at the end of 2017. However, this is still a relatively low number compared to other countries in the region such as the Philippines, Myanmar and Singapore, whose non-interest income rate is up to 35–40% (Source: World Bank (2018)). This shows that non-traditional activity is still a potential activity for commercial banks in Vietnam. In the future, when the process of economic integration in the banking sector is more powerful, the banking system will become more competitive; thus, diversifying revenue is an inevitable and objective trend that will help the banks increase profits, minimize risks and improve their competitive position in the system.

The bank performance in research documents is often used as an economic performance, which refers to a bank's ability to minimize costs (cost savings) or maximize profits (profit efficiency). Some recent research highlights the importance of bank diversification. The traditional view in the banking sector is that revenue from non-interest activities is more stable than interest income; thus, the bank's risk will be reduced when diversification (Berger 1995; Elsas et al. 2010), Laeven and Levine (2007) and (Stiroh and Rumble 2006) argued that non-interest income contributed to profit growth and lowered risks. Boot and Schmeits (2000); Elsas et al. (2010) showed that by diversifying income, products or different markets, banks could reduce the risk of bankruptcy due to different business activities related to different risk levels. Similarly, Sanya and Wolfe (2011) showed that diversification helped banks increase profits and reduce risks. Rossi et al. (2009); and Lee et al. (2014) argued that bank risks were reduced through the revenue diversification and increase of bank performance.

However, there are many researches that does not support the banks' diversification strategy. Some argue that the high cost of diversification increases risks and reduces profits when the banks perform encroaching on their amateur activities, or that the diversification will cause adverse impacts on the bank performance due to managing many operational areas. (Gamra and Plihon 2011; Stiroh and Rumble 2006) also showed that the greater reliance on non-interest income has led to higher volatility in bank income and higher risks but not higher returns. The bank's expansion of non-interest income means increasing fixed costs, leading to increased leverage in banking operations and higher risks (De Jonghe 2010; Fiordelisi et al. 2011). This argument is supported by experimental studies such as Lepetit et al. (2008) and Baele et al. (2007). The above studies show that diversification owns both advantages and disadvantages. However, whether banks have diversified or not, diversification has been going on because of its necessity for the purpose of seeking profits as well as enhancing the competitiveness of the banks in the context of international economic integration. All these reforms aim to modernize the banking activities and to improve the financial service products. In this paper, the author analyzed the main factors that determine the level of non-interest income for Vietnamese banks, then, the author studied the impact of non-interest income on the banking profitability, and finally, the association between non-interest income and the level of risk taking was explored. To the best of the author's knowledge, there has not been any study that has analyzed the impact of diversification on bank performance and risk within the Vietnam context. Therefore, this paper tries to fill the gap in the literature by providing a comprehensive study.

2. Theoretical Background and Literature Review

Studies of diversification between banks in the US and Europe, in general, showed that it was related to non-interest income structure of commercial banks. Revenue diversification has a negative impact on the profit risk of US banks (DeYoung and Roland 2001; Stiroh 2004a). However, the diversification enhanced the level of profit risk of European banks (Baele et al. 2007; Chiorazzo et al. 2008). DeYoung and Rice (2004) analyzed the impact of non-interest income on the profits and risks of US banks and showed that despite income diversification boosted profitability, a banking diversification strategy increased the fluctuation of income. Acharya et al. (2006) carried out research on 105 banks in Italy during the period 1993–1999, and concluded that diversification did not guarantee superior performance and or reduce risks for banks. In particular, for high-risk banks, diversification reduced profits and created more risky loans; for low-risk banks, diversification created an ineffective balance between profits and risks. Laeven and Levine (2007) conducted banking research of 13 Western European countries and concluded that revenue diversification had two negative impacts on risks. Baele et al. (2007) studied the effects of revenue diversification on bank performance and risks. Research data were tabular data from banks from 17 European countries in the period 1989–2004. Research results showed that banks with a higher non-interest income ratio of total revenue had a better bank performance. In addition, diversifying revenues from different activities will increase the risks of the banking system. Rossi et al. (2009) showed that diversification increased profitability and reduced bank risks. Elsas et al. (2010) studied the impact of diversification on bank business performance, using developed countries' data, namely, Australia, Canada, France, Germany, Italy, United Kingdom, United States, Spain and Switzerland, during the period 1996–2008.

The results demonstrated that revenue diversification improved bank profitability even during the 2007–2008 financial crisis. Sanya and Wolfe (2011) studied the impact of risk diversification and bank performance in 11 emerging economies, concluding that revenue diversification reduced bankruptcy risk and increased profits for banks.

DeYoung and Torna (2013) analyzed the impact of revenue diversification on the failure of banks during the financial crisis. The research showed that switching to non-traditional banking activities had a significant impact on the bank's ability to fail in the crisis, depending on the bank's financial condition. While banks are more involved in non-traditional activities, it will reduce the risk of failure of credit institutions; the banks with financial degradation when participating in these activities will increase their probability of failure. Delpachitra and Lester (2013) used panel data of 09 listed by Australian banks in the period 2000–2009 to study the impact of the diversification of banking activities. Experimental results showed that revenue and diversification of non-interest income reduced profitability and did not improve the bank's default risk. Research results show that non-interest income activities will not benefit the bank. Meanwhile, Williams and Prather (2010) focused on the impact of non-interest income on the bank's profitability risk. As a result, non-interest income was riskier than profit income but brought diversified benefits to bank shareholders. (Li and Zhang 2013) studied the increasing dependence on the non-interest income of Chinese banks in the period 1986–2008. Research results showed that diversification of non-interest income brought benefits for banks, but also increased risks to the system.

Meslier et al. (2014) used panel data of 39 global and commercial banks in the Philippines during the period 1999–2005 to study the role and value of bank diversification. Research results indicated that non-interest income increased bank profits and regulated bank risks. In the same view, Lee et al. (2014) studied the impact of non-interest income on bank profits and risks, using bank data of 22 countries in Asia with 967 private banks in the period 1995–2009. By implementing the GMM regression method, the results showed that non-credit activities of Asian banks' minimized risks, but did not increase profitability. Brighi et al. (2014) used panel data of 52 Corporate Organization Banks (BHCs) in Italy in the period of 2006–2011 to test the impact of revenue diversification on bank performance. Unlike studies on diversification that focused on its impact on equity and debt value and portfolio strategy of profitability, risk and scientists conducted other ways to test the impact of non-interest business activities on the bank's performance. Diversification increased bank profits on the basis of risk adjustment.

3. Data and Methodology

3.1. Data Collection

The data used in the study were collected from the audited financial statements and annual reports of 26 commercial banks, including 12 listed banks and 14 unlisted banks in Vietnam in the period of 2010–2018. After that, the researcher selected banks owning full financial statements, including balance sheet, income statement, cash flow statement and notes to financial statements. In addition, data were also collected from the website http://finance.vietstock.vn, from the State Bank of Vietnam, websites of commercial banks under study, General Statistics Office of Vietnam, Ministry of Finance. After collection, the data were imported into an Excel file and edited and encoded in this file. The next step is to conduct data cleaning to detect errors; empty cells that lack information, wrong information and complete the data matrix. Then, the researcher used Stata 13 software to calculate and process data according to the model.

3.2. Data Analysis

This study applied a dynamic panel data approach proposed by Arellano and Bover (1995); Blundell and Bond (2000) used GMM modeling techniques to solve endogenous problems, variance and autocorrelation. With the foundation of theoretical studies and empirical studies, like Stiroh (2004a);

Mercieca et al. (2007); Lepetit et al. (2008); Chiorazzo et al. (2008); Lee et al. (2014); Geambasu et al. (2013) the study to determine the following basic models:

$$\text{Performance (ROA, ROE)}_{i,t} = \alpha_{i,t} + \beta_1 \text{INT}_{i,t} + \beta_2 \text{HHI}_{i,t} + \sum_{s=3}^{8} \beta_s \lambda_{i,t} + \varepsilon_{i,t} \quad (1)$$

$$\text{Bank Risk (Z-score)}_{i,t} = \alpha_{i,t} + \beta_1 \text{INT}_{i,t} + \beta_2 \text{HHI}_{i,t} + \sum_{s=3}^{8} \beta_s \lambda_{i,t} + \varepsilon_{i,t} \quad (2)$$

In which i represents the number of banks in the research sample, $i = 1 \ldots 28$; t represents the time ($t = 2010–2018$), β represents the regression coefficient λ which is the control variable matrix, ε which is the error. Measuring efficiency by ROA, ROE; INT represents the ratio of net interest income, HHI represents the revenue diversification variable. Control variables include: natural logarithm of total assets; loan outstanding balance/asset ratio; equity/asset ratio; non-performing loan/loan outstanding balance ratio; asset growth; liquidity ratio (see Table 1).

- Bank performance (ROA, ROE)

Bank performance from the point of view of shareholders of a bank is obtaining profit by maximizing the revenue and minimizing the costs. Economic theories show that, in the situation of perfect competition, profit maximization is equal to minimizing costs. In practice, however, it can interfere factors such as changes in the regulatory framework that would disturb obtain desired performance. The factors that could explain the deviation from profit maximization can be grouped into two categories: incorrect incentives and inefficiency (Bikker and Bos 2008). Bank's economic efficiency was measured by comparing its performance to that of the best-practice bank. Economic efficiency, as defined by Aigner et al. (1977), refers to a bank's ability to minimize its cost or maximize its profit. Similarly, profit efficiency is determined by comparing its profit to what the best-practice bank would produce given the same bundle of inputs Berger and Mester (1997). All performance measures, regardless of their specific objectives, use accounting and market data to assess the financial condition of an institution at a point in time, as well as to determine how well it has been managed over a period of time (Jianu et al. 2017). Profitability can be used as a summary index of performance (De Andres and Vallelado 2008; Liang et al. 2013). There are two methods commonly used to measure the performance of businesses in general and banks in particular, including returns on assets (ROA), defined as the return on the average total assets. ROE is defined as the ratio of returns on equity. Measure of bank performance differs from that of Laeven and Levine (2007), who used Tobin's Q (i.e., the sum of the market value of common equity plus the book value of preferred shares divided by the book value of total assets). Given the limited data on the market value of banks, this study uses ROA to measure bank performance and to derive excess value. Bank performance measures should be limited to ROA or ROE and should not cover other measures such as cost efficiency and asset quality cost to income ratio (CTI, an inverse proxy for bank (cost) efficiency), and loan loss reserves divided by gross loans (LLR, an inverse proxy for asset quality or bank stability) (Beck et al. 2013; Vennet 2002). In banking activities, increasing profits means banks face more and more risks. Therefore, in addition to the goal of increasing profits, banks need to diversify to spread risks (Chiorazzo et al. 2008; Stiroh 2004a, 2004b).

- Revenue diversification (HHI)

The degree of banking diversification is measured by the ratio of net interest income and non-interest income (Lepetit et al. 2008; Stiroh 2004a, 2004b). Mercieca et al. (2007) conducted the measurement of diversification by building Herfindahl-Hirschman Index (HHI) for each bank. This method measures the ratio between diversification and the main business activities of the bank. HHI (Rev) will be calculated by the following formula:

$$HHI_{Rev} = \left(\frac{NON}{NETOP}\right)^2 + \left(\frac{NET}{NETOP}\right)^2$$

In which, NETOP = NON + NET; NON represents non-interest income, NET represents net interest income. This formula indicates that if the bank focuses on increasing profits, its diversification will be decreased. Stiroh and Rumble (2006) clearly saw that revenue diversification was offset by the increase in non-interest activity; however, it also increased banks' risk. Demirgüç-Kunt and Huizinga (2010) also claimed that higher degrees of increased non-interest income led to higher risks for banks.

- Bank risk (Z-score)

As previously stated, we proxy bank risk using two complementary metrics that are intuitive and easily measured: the NPL (Non-Performing Loan) and the Z-score (Demirgüç-Kunt and Huizinga 2010; Köhler 2015; Laeven and Levine 2009). Z-score is an inverse proxy for a firm's probability of failure (insolvency risk), combining profitability, leverage, and return volatility into a single measure. A higher Z-score indicates higher bank stability and less overall bank risk (Hsieh et al. 2013; Kick and von Westernhagen 2009). The Z-score is considered a better measure of bank risk than the NPL, because non-performing loans are traditionally backward looking and highly procyclical (Bikker and Metzemakers 2005; Laeven and Majnoni 2003). This is a criticism that does not concern the Z-score as much because changes in bank riskiness are captured through the variance component of this index (Delis et al. 2011). In addition, the Z-score represents a more universal measure of bank risk that captures more than credit risk alone (Agoraki et al. 2011). Risk measurement method is formed based on the theoretical background of bankruptcy risk measurement of Roy (1952); Boyd and Runkle (1993) and Lepetit and Strobel (2015) and the theory of bank diversification of Mercieca et al. (2007); Chiorazzo et al. (2008) and Lee et al. (2014). Until now, Roy's Z-score (1952) is considered an index of bank's bankruptcy prediction which is widely used in previous studies. Higher Z-Score index indicates lower possibility of bankruptcy (Lepetit and Strobel 2015). It will be calculated by the following formula:

$$Z-score = \frac{ROA + ETA}{SDROA}$$

- Bank size (SIZE)

According to Demsetz and Strahan (1997), diversification has a positive relationship with the size of bank assets, the larger the size of bank deposits, the higher the loan balance for customers. Bank size is measured by logarithms by total assets. Curi et al. (2015) and Berger et al. (2010) argued that there was a nonlinear relationship between size and business performance. The effect of bank size on performance is still controversial. McAllister and McManus (1993) argued that large banks often had the advantage of size and had more opportunities to diversify risks than small banks. Therefore, large banks will have lower costs and higher profits (Goddard et al. 2004). On the other hand, Vallascas and Keasey (2012) argued that large banks were more motivated to make more risky investments. Therefore, large banks may be less effective than small banks.

- Gross interest revenue (INT)

INT is often used to express the impact of interest rate risk on the possibility of bankruptcy of commercial banks because interest income is the main source of income. The ratio increases due to an increase in interest income or a decrease in total assets. This shows that the bank is at high risk when net interest income is reduced or investment and lending on risky accounts. According to Halling and Hayden (2006), INT has a contravariant relationship with Z-score.

- Capitalization ratio, measured as the ratio of equity to total assets (ETA)

This variable shows the level of financial leverage of a bank. High leverage ratio means high risk. This variable is also used in most recent studies such as Sanya and Wolfe (2011); Chiorazzo et al. (2008) and (Stiroh 2004b). High-capitalized banks are less risky and so generate lower profits (Hughes and Mester 1998). The contrary relationship between capital and profits emphasizes that higher insurance costs can prevent bankruptcy risks with low capital asset ratio, indicating a positive relationship between capital asset ratio and performance (Berger 1995). Experimental evidence by Demirgüç-Kunt and Huizinga (1999); Goddard et al. (2004) showed that the best banking activities are to maintain a high level of equity equivalent to bank assets at a ratio higher capital tending to face costs lower than funds due to lower possibility of bankruptcy. Porter and Chiou (2013) investigated the relationships between investment capital risks and bank risks and proposed that banks could supplement capital by increasing the risk of the income asset portfolio and off-balance sheet activity, that is, by implementing a more aggressive diversification strategy.

- Ratio of loans to total assets (LTA)

The ratio of total outstanding loans to total assets represents the effects of loan strategy to performance and bank risk adjustment as studied by Sanya and Wolfe (2011); Chiorazzo et al. (2008) and Stiroh (2004a). This ratio increases, meaning that the expansion of credit activities negatively affects the profitability and credit risk will increase accordingly; thus, there will be a positive correlation between total loans to mobilized capital for bank risk.

- Ratio of Non-performing loan (NPL)

Credit quality is often measured by the non-performing loan to total outstanding loan ratio of commercial banks. The bank with a large loss must increase its capital to meet management requirements and minimize the bankruptcy risk. Aggarwal and Jacques (2001) argued that the decline in asset quality is synonymous with a higher degree of risk. Therefore, there is a positive relationship between credit risk and bankruptcy risk and adjusting expected bank profits. Ineffective loans meaning the high non-performing loan ratio reduce asset quality and quickly increase bank risk (González-Hermosillo 1999).

- Liquidity Ratio (LIQ)

To measure bank liquidity, the research uses the loan to deposit ratio (LTD). If this ratio is too high, banks may not have sufficient liquidity to meet the client's capital needs; if this ratio is too low, banks may not achieve the expected revenue. Some empirical studies showed that the higher the liquidity, the higher the bank's asset risk (Demirgüç-Kunt and Huizinga 2010; Norden and Weber 2010).

- Asset growth (GTA)

Asset growth shows that the attitude of managers when facing with bank risk, GTA is calculated by the growth rate of total bank assets. Bank managers often expect more rapid growth and more stable profits (Chiorazzo et al. 2008; Stiroh 2004a). This variable positively affects risks because rapid asset growth can increase the bank's investment portfolio risk.

Table 1. Research variables.

Classification	Variable	Definition	Source
Dependent variables	ROA	Returns on assets	(Chiorazzo et al. 2008; Stiroh 2004a, 2004b)
	ROE	Returns on equity	
	Z-score	Z-score = $\frac{ROA+ETA}{SDROA}$ ETA = Equity to Assets SDROA = ROA standard deviation	Mercieca et al. (2007); Chiorazzo et al. (2008); Lee et al. (2014)
	INT	Net interest margin/total income	Halling and Hayden (2006)
Independent variables	HHI	Revenue diversification $HHI_{Rev} = \left(\frac{NON}{NETOP}\right)^2 + \left(\frac{NET}{NETOP}\right)^2$ NETOP = NON + NET; NON represents non-interest income, NET represents net interest income	(Stiroh 2004a, 2004b); Lepetit et al. (2008); Mercieca et al. (2007)
	SIZE	Natural logarithm of total assets	Curi et al. (2015); and Berger et al. (2010)
	LTA	Loan to total Asset ratio	Sanya and Wolfe (2011); Chiorazzo et al. (2008) Vallascas and Keasey (2012)
Control variable	ETA	Equity to total Assets ratio	Demirgüç-Kunt and Huizinga (1999); Goddard et al. (2004); Porter and Chiou (2013)
	NPL	Non-performing loan/loan outstanding balance	Aggarwal and Jacques (2001); Gonzalez-Hermosillo (1999)
	GTA	Asset growth	(Chiorazzo et al. 2008); Stiroh (2004b)
	LIQ	Liquidity ratio = loan outstanding balance/customer deposits	(Demirgüç-Kunt and Huizinga 2010); (Norden and Weber 2010)

Source: Summary of the author.

4. Results and Discussion

4.1. Descriptive Statistics

This study aims to assess the impact of revenue diversification on risks and performance of 26 Vietnamese commercial banks in the period of 2010–2018. Table 2, descriptive statistics of research variables, including dependent variables and independent variables used in the GMM (Generalized Method of Moments) system model. In which performance is measured by ROA, ROE; bank risk (Z-score); revenue diversification (HHI), net interest income ratio (INT) and control variables (SIZE, LTA, ETA, NPL, GTA, LIQ). Statistical results show that banks' asset use efficiency is approximately 0.7% on average. Meanwhile, the profitability on average equity is 8.7%. The risk coefficient Z-score reaches 40.552 on average, showing that banks in the Vietnamese banking system operate safely under the policy regulation of the State Bank of Vietnam. Average revenue diversification is 0.803, net interest income accounts for 81.5% of total revenue (Table 2). This is a challenge for banks in the context of digital economy development. Loan outstanding balance accounts on average of 54.8% of total loan outstanding balance, the liquidity ratio reaches 0.873. Non-performing loan ratio of commercial banks is 2.5% on average; equity/asset ratio reaches 9.2%, ensuring compliance with the regulations of the State Bank of Vietnam and satisfying Basel II standards.

Table 2. Descriptive statistics of research variables.

Variable	Mean	Standard Deviation	Min	Max
Bank performance				
ROA	0.007	0.007	−0.055	0.040
ROE	0.087	0.079	−0.458	0.565
Risk of bank				
Z-score	40.522	78.975	2.455	557.332
Independent variables				
HHI	0.736	0.134	0.500	0.984
INT	0.815	0.137	0.136	0.992
Control variable				
SIZE	8.038	0.503	6.915	9.129
LTA	0.548	0.138	0.145	0.827
LIQ	0.873	0.255	0.363	2.388
ETA	0.092	0.040	0.023	0.255
NPL	0.025	0.017	0.000	0.114
GTA	0.521	4.279	−0.392	65.375

Source: Financial reporting of 26 Vietnamese commercial banks in the period of 2010–2018. Note: ROA (return on assets); ROE (return on equity); INT (net interest income/total income); HHI (revenue diversification); SIZE (natural logarithm of total assets); LTA (loan to total asset ratio); ETA (equity to total asset ratio); NPL (non-performing loan/loan outstanding balance); GTA (asset growth); LIQ (liquidity ratio = loan outstanding balance/customer deposits).

In this research, dependent variable is performance which was measured using ROA, ROE and bank risk (Z-score); independent variables are revenue diversification and net interest income. In order to solve the research problems, the paper conducts regression of panel data with Pooled model, fixed effects model (FEM) and random effects model (REM). However, the study first conducted a correlation analysis to detect autocorrelation and partially identify multidimensional defects of independent variables affecting regression models. The results of Table 3 show that there is no autocorrelation, facilitating the implementation of subsequent verification steps.

Table 3. Correlation analysis.

	ROA	ROE	Z-Score	HHI	SIZE	LTA	LIQ	ETA	NPL	INT	GTA
ROA	1										
ROE	0.798	1									
Z-score	−0.166	−0.195	1								
HHI	0.072	−0.002	−0.140	1							
SIZE	0.087	0.330	0.071	−0.246	1						
LTA	0.185	0.215	−0.018	0.091	0.430	1					
LIQ	0.209	0.233	−0.002	0.027	−0.036	0.372	1				
ETA	0.266	−0.189	−0.084	0.114	−0.647	−0.170	0.028	1			
NPL	−0.024	−0.107	0.019	−0.038	−0.122	0.009	−0.098	0.140	1		
INT	0.255	0.201	−0.142	0.860	−0.107	0.199	0.101	−0.003	−0.045	1	
GTA	0.067	0.046	−0.013	0.032	−0.002	−0.044	0.049	0.030	−0.037	0.035	1

Source: Author's calculations. Note: ROA (return on assets); ROE (return on equity) used to measure the performance of commercial banks. Independent variables including: net interest income/total income ratio (INT); revenue diversification (HHI) measured by: HI = $(NON/NETOP)^2 + (NET/NETOP)^2$. NETOP = NON + NET; NON represents non-interest income, NET represents net interest income. Natural logarithm of total assets (SIZE); loan to total asset ratio (LTA); liquidity ratio = loan outstanding balance/customer deposits (LIQ); equity to total assets (ETA); non-performing loan (NPL); asset growth (GTA); Research data is extracted from audited financial statements in the period 2010–2018, published publicly on the electronic portal of banks and publicly announced at the State Securities Commission of Vietnam.

4.2. The Impact of Revenue Diversification on the Performance of Commercial Banks

Research conducts regression of the GMM and GMM models to assess the impact of revenue diversification on the performance of the banking system (26 banks), listed banks (12 banks), and unlisted banks (14 banks). Research results are shown in Tables 4 and 5. The research results show that revenue diversification negatively affects the performance of the Vietnamese banking system measured by ROA and ROE (Lepetit et al. 2008; Mercieca et al. 2007; Stiroh 2004a). The assessment of the role of diversification for listed and unlisted banks performance also gives similar results. Berger et al. (2010) also argued that if banks focused too much on profits, they would reduce diversification. However, this result is contrary to Rossi et al. (2009), arguing that revenue diversification significantly improves overall profitability; Banks with higher revenue diversification, will have higher profitability in both short and long term. Similarly, Meslier et al. (2014) found that revenue diversification, increased the profitability of Philippine banks. Net interest income is the main income source of banks; it is the key motivation of the bank's development in the medium and long term. In addition to credit activities, trading in foreign exchange, gold and securities are affected by fluctuations; thus, it is difficult to avoid the risk of losses, and negatively impacting the bank performance. The bank's revenue from services currently is still mainly from card fees, credit card fees, intermediary services of real estate transaction payment, international payment and ATM and Internet Banking and Mobile Banking fees. Banks continue to raise fees to increase revenue from services. Non-interest activities also have positive results, increasing the proportion of income structure. However, not all banks have a large revenue from services, including large-scale banks and banks developing retail services.

Pressure to implement Basel II forces banks to divert in operations. Credit activities seem to be growing slowly, banks switch to develop services to increase revenue, but it is difficult to expect strong growth in a short time. Some large-scale banks that lead the retail sector, show signs of declining revenue from services. Growth, as well as contributions from service activities, is not commensurate with potential; although there are many positive points, they are not enough to cover risks from net interest income activities. The system of Vietnamese commercial banks needs to improve and promote the non-credit service quality, especially e-banking services in the context of constantly changing consumer habits and increasing technology acceptance level. It is necessary to restructure revenue between credit and non-credit services effectively in accordance with the financial capacity and development objectives and business development orientation of each bank, making the most of supporting policies from the State Bank of Vietnam and the government. Promote implementation of comprehensive and breakthrough solutions to manage credit growth stably, effectively and minimize risks as well as ensure the safety of the banking system.

Table 4. Pooled, Fixed effect model—the impact of revenue diversification on performance.

Variable	Banking System (26) ROA Pooled	Banking System (26) ROA Fixed Effect	Banking System (26) ROE Pooled	Banking System (26) ROE Fixed Effect	Listed Bank (12) ROA Pooled	Listed Bank (12) ROA Fixed Effect	Listed Bank (12) ROE Pooled	Listed Bank (12) ROE Fixed Effect	Unlisted Banks (14) ROA Pooled	Unlisted Banks (14) ROA Fixed Effect	Unlisted Banks (14) ROE Pooled	Unlisted Banks (14) ROE Fixed Effect
HHI	−0.0295 *	−0.0354 *	−0.2702 *	−0.3172 *	−0.0626 *	−0.0768 *	−0.5159 *	−0.6968 *	0.0068	0.0068	0.0074	0.1186
	0.0059	0.0079	0.0689	0.0902	0.0073	0.0090	0.0786	0.0979	0.0067	0.0088	0.0991	0.1292
SIZE	0.0069 *	0.0100 *	0.0633 *	0.0302	0.0110 *	0.0134 **	0.1154 *	0.0831 **	0.0007	−0.0003	−0.0214	−0.0896 **
	0.0012	0.0025	0.0140	0.0291	0.0021	0.0039	0.0224	0.0384	0.0014	0.0031	0.0209	0.0456
LTA	−0.0044	−0.0053	−0.0626	−0.0432	−0.0213 *	−0.0242 *	−0.2496 *	−0.2528 *	−0.0030	−0.0059	−0.0351	0.0078
	0.0036	0.0048	0.0424	0.0545	0.0065	0.0083	0.0692	0.0865	0.0033	0.0051	0.0479	0.0742
LIQ	0.0049 *	0.0079 *	0.0705 *	0.1139 *	0.0044	0.0192 *	0.0642 **	0.2157 *	0.0046 *	0.0044 **	0.0606 *	0.0815 *
	0.0017	0.0022	0.0198	0.0253	0.0032	0.0049	0.0345	0.0476	0.0015	0.0019	0.0214	0.0281
ETA	0.1129 *	0.1001 *	0.2097	−0.1647	0.1824 *	0.1223 *	0.7100 *	−0.0377	0.0488 *	0.0319 ***	−0.4645 **	−0.7668 *
	0.0128	0.0156	0.1496	0.1792	0.0200	0.0253	0.2141	0.2031	0.0137	0.0169	0.2017	0.2478
NPL	−0.0090	0.0297	−0.1766	0.1741	−0.0439	−0.0183	−0.5856	−0.0511	0.0439 **	0.0491 **	0.4892	0.1365
	0.0235	0.0252	0.2758	0.2890	0.0417	0.0770	0.4471	0.7309	0.0207	0.0225	0.3050	0.3299
INT	0.0410 *	0.0458 *	0.3656 *	0.3915 *	0.0855 *	0.0967 *	0.7182 *	0.8706 *	0.0015	−0.0044	0.0501	−0.1018
	0.0057	0.0066	0.0667	0.0754	0.0079	0.0120	0.0851	0.1060	0.0060	0.0069	0.0879	0.1012
GTA	0.0000	0.0001	0.0003	0.0011	0.0000	0.0001	−0.0005	0.0005 **	0.0030 *	0.0033 **	0.0319 ***	0.0449 **
	0.0001	0.0001	0.0010	0.0010	0.0000	0.0000	0.0009	0.0002	0.0013	0.0013	0.0192	0.0196
Intercept factor	−0.0721	−0.0983	−0.5634	−0.3071	−0.1113	−0.1374	−1.0079	−0.8094	−0.0152	0.0004	0.1744	0.7439
	0.0109	0.0207	0.1275	0.2378	0.0176	0.0324	0.1891	0.2912	0.0132	0.0258	0.1945	0.3789
Observation	234	234	234	234	108	108	108	108	126	126	126	126
Group	26	26	26	26	13	13	13	13	14	14	14	14
R2	0.3884	0.3276	0.2776	0.2342	0.6666	0.5165	0.5740	0.4724	0.3302	0.3359	0.1707	0.1031

*, ** and *** represent significance at the 1%, 5% and 10% levels, respectively. Note: ROA (Return on assets); ROE (Return on equity) used to measure the performance of commercial banks. Independent variables including: net interest income/total income ratio (INT); revenue diversification (HHI) measured by: HI = (NON/NETOP)^2 + (NET/NETOP)^2. NETOP = NON + NET; NON represents non-interest income, NET represents net interest income. Natural logarithm of total assets (SIZE); loan to total asset ratio (LTA); liquidity ratio = loan outstanding balance/customer deposits (LIQ); equity to total asset ratio (ETA); non-performing loan ratio (NPL); asset growth (GTA). Research data is extracted from audited financial statements in the period 2010–2018, published publicly on the electronic portal of banks and publicly announced at the State Securities Commission of Vietnam.

Table 5. GMM model—the impact of revenue diversification on performance.

Variable	Banking System (26) ROA GMM	Banking System (26) ROA GMM for System	Banking System (26) ROE GMM	Banking System (26) ROE GMM for System	Listed Bank (12) ROA GMM	Listed Bank (12) ROA GMM for System	Listed Bank (12) ROE GMM	Listed Bank (12) ROE GMM For System	Unlisted Banks (14) ROA GMM	Unlisted Banks (14) ROA GMM for System	Unlisted Banks (14) ROE GMM	Unlisted Banks (14) ROE GMM for System
HHI	0.0258 *	−0.0337 *	0.2598 **	−0.2747 *	0.0220	−0.0620 *	−0.0445 *	−0.5633 *	0.0073	−0.0483 **	0.0910	−0.1853 *
	0.0086	0.0049	0.1290	0.0686	0.0405	0.0096	0.4597	0.1060	0.0087	0.0208	0.0789	0.0736
SIZE	0.0185 *	0.0057 *	0.1403 *	0.0496 *	0.0207 *	0.0128 *	0.1185	0.0983 ***	0.0163 **	−0.0043	0.1965 *	0.0648
	0.0051	0.0012	0.0446	0.0142	0.0037	0.0035	0.0379	0.0533	0.0059	0.0053	0.0616	0.0506
LTA	−0.0140	−0.0036	−0.1693 **	−0.0692 *	−0.0223	−0.0258 *	−0.1748 **	−0.2776 **	−0.0094	−0.0009	−0.1139	−0.0191
	0.0094	0.0023	0.0764	0.0275	0.0143	0.0085	0.1452	0.1137	0.0096	0.0019	0.0845	0.0302
LIQ	0.0159 **	0.0052 *	0.2053 *	0.0742 *	0.0177 ***	0.0106 *	0.2137	0.1193 *	0.0094 *	0.0051 *	0.1273 *	0.0980 *
	0.0059	0.0011	0.0550	0.0111	0.0085	0.0038	0.0915	0.0305	0.0031	0.0014	0.0216	0.0253
ETA	0.1381 *	0.1097 *	0.4423 **	0.0396	0.1768 *	0.1861 *	0.4128	0.7597	0.1104 **	0.0197	0.6750 ***	0.2105
	0.0318	0.0100	0.1932	0.1847	0.0176	0.0353	0.2628	1.0128	0.0494	0.0461	0.3621	0.4195
NPL	0.0270	−0.0030 *	0.1746	−0.2440 *	−0.0451	0.0569	−0.4725	0.1890	0.0633	0.0800 ***	0.4399	0.3005
	0.0309	0.0350	0.3600	0.2464	0.0761	0.1213	0.8594	2.0757	0.0360	0.0476	0.3121	0.3089
INT	−0.0095	0.0443 *	−0.1568	0.3277 *	−0.0047	0.0870 *	0.1249	0.7680 *	−0.0037	0.0387 *	−0.0414	−0.0540
	0.0007	0.0000	0.0000	0.0006	0.0377	0.0001	0.4539	0.0981	0.0050	0.0151	0.0505	0.0378
GTA	−0.0003	−0.0631 **	0.0061	0.0009	0.0003	0.0001	0.0078	0.0010	−0.0008	0.0007	0.0035	0.0322
	0.0007	0.0109	0.0060	0.0006	0.0004	0.0001	0.0061	0.0008	0.0023	0.0022	0.0210	0.0288
Intercept factor		−0.0676		−0.4039		−0.1341		−0.9222		0.0355		−0.6603
		0.0088		0.1324		0.0335		0.4486		0.0515		0.4678
Observation	234	234	234	234	108	108	108	108	126	126	126	126
Group	26	26	26	26	13	13	13	13	14	14	14	14
F-statistic	4.90		7.63		45.42		16.05		42.30			
Wald Test		322.51		205.69		496.45		1822.82		87.99		499.41
AR (2)	0.43		0.11		0.56		0.05		−0.39		0.55	
Sargan test	11.04		6.85		6.80		7.03		12.01		6.91	
Hansen	16.70		16.95		4.80		7.45		1.53		2.49	

*, **, and *** represent significance at the 1%, 5% and 10% levels, respectively. Note: ROA (return on assets); ROE (return on equity) used to measure the performance of commercial banks. Independent variables including: net interest income/total income ratio (INT); revenue diversification (HHI) measured by: HI = (NON/NETOP)^2 + (NET/NETOP)^2. NETOP = NON + NET; NON represents non-interest income, NET represents net interest income. Natural logarithm of total assets (SIZE); loan to total asset ratio (LTA); liquidity ratio = loan outstanding balance/customer deposits (LIQ); equity to total asset ratio (ETA); non-performing loan ratio (NPL); asset growth (GTA). Research data is extracted from audited financial statements in the period 2010–2018, published publicly on the electronic portal of banks and publicly announced at the State Securities Commission of Vietnam.

The larger the bank's asset size (SIZE), the more likely it is to increase revenue and profit, grow strongly in assets and be able to use capital more efficiently than small banks. Berger et al. (2010) and Curi et al. (2015) also found that both bank scale and squared bank regression increased cost efficiency, suggesting that large banks managed cost more efficiently than small banks, meaning their business performance was better. The banks with good liquidity are usually large-scale banks with state capital. The liquidity of these banks is usually better than the rest. In fact, the better the banking liquidity, the higher the profitability of the credit institutions, along with an increasing credit risk. The leaders of the banks all have the same view that high risk provision is made because the non-performing loan ratio has not decreased much over the same period because the new non-performing loan is arisen in the macroeconomic context that has not had much improvement, business operations of the bank still face many difficulties. Moreover, for restructured debt, when the repayment period expired, could not be paid by many customers. It can be seen that the views on debtors–creditors in Vietnam are unusual, leading to difficulties in dealing with non-performing loan. In addition, the legal framework is incomplete, overlapping and contradictory; "criminalization" thinking of cases of losing public property is still heavy. Meanwhile, the handling of secured assets is complicated; the debt trading market has not yet been formed.

In general, banks satisfy the Basel II standard and the state bank regulation on Equity to Total Asset Ratio (ETA), which is a higher, reducing the dependence from funding flows and make profits of banks higher. This shows the bank's ability to absorb losses and handle risks. Banks with capital strength will face lower bankruptcy risk costs, thus, risk provisioning is also lower (Berger 1995; Bourke 1989; Hassan and Bashir 2003). Vietnamese banks have made great progress and made positive contributions to the socioeconomic development. However, along with that development, the shortcomings in the management of banks as well as difficulties also arise in many aspects of operation, including the issue of equity-that is the capital component which is extremely important in operating capital of commercial banks. Therefore, it is necessary to have strong changes in the recognition and management of bank equity from the state management agencies as well as commercial banks.

4.3. The Impact of Revenue Diversification on the Risk of Commercial Banks

Similar to Section 4.2, in this section, the study conducts regression of the GMM model and GMM for system for Panels data to assess the impact of revenue diversification on risk of Vietnamese commercial banking system. Research results for the Pooled OLS, Fixed effects method (FEM) and GMM Model are shown in Tables 6 and 7. Experimental research shows that revenue diversification negatively affects the Z-Score risk measurement index, which means that the higher the revenue diversification, the higher the bank risk. This seems inconsistent with previous studies by (Mercieca et al. 2007); (Chiorazzo et al. 2008) and (Lee et al. 2014). However, it is consistent with the research of Stiroh and Rumble (2006); the benefit of revenue diversification is offset by the increase in non-interest activity. On the other hand, it also adjusts the risk of banks. Demirgüç-Kunt and Huizinga (2010) and Li and Zhang (2013) argued that a higher level of increased non-interest income means increased revenue diversification leads to higher risks for banks. This shows the weakness and lack of experience of the banking system in building a reasonable profit transformation model. The current bank revenue diversification is passive and slow to change; economic efficiency is not high and still depends heavily on credit activities.

The higher the Equity to total asset ratio (ETA) variable, the lower the bankruptcy risk of commercial banks. This higher ratio helps to reduce the dependence from external fund inflows and banks' profits higher, indicating the potential risk to the bank's credit activities; banks should actively fund to absorb losses and handle risks. Banks with capital strength will face lower bankruptcy risk costs, thus, risk provisioning is also lower (Berger 1995; Bourke 1989; Hassan and Bashir 2003). Experimental evidence by Demirgüç-Kunt and Huizinga (1999) and Goddard et al. (2004) shows that banking operations are best to maintain high levels of equity to total asset ratio because banks with the high ratio of capitalized tend to face less risk of bankruptcy. However, Porter and Chiou (2013) had the same view with this research result given that banks supplemented capital by increasing the risk of the income asset portfolio and off-balance sheet activities. The Vietnamese banking system has made great progress, but there are still shortcomings in the management of banks as well as difficulties that arise in many aspects, including the issue of equity. This is a capital component, which is extremely important in operating capital of commercial banks. Therefore, it is necessary to have strong changes in the recognition and management of bank equity from the state management agencies, as well as commercial banks.

Table 6. Pooled fixed effect model—the impact of revenue diversification on bank risk.

Variable	Z-Score					
	Banking System (26)		Listed Bank (12)		Unlisted Banks (14)	
	Pooled	Fixed Effect	Pooled	Fixed Effect	Pooled	Fixed Effect
HHI	−16.9592	−73.4480 **	−4.0018	12.7742 **	−60.2815	−120.0412 ***
	80.3413	35.2882	17.3641	6.3749	165.1179	69.0823
SIZE	2.0199	−44.6604 *	12.8728 *	−8.3746 *	49.0409	−113.4627 *
	16.3511	11.3639	4.9417	1.9541	34.7700	24.3848
LTA	−12.3307	−7.7556 **	−21.3642	10.1551 **	0.6757	−12.2934
	49.4180	21.3316	15.2882	4.2530	79.7648	39.6514 *
LIQ	7.4200	22.6653 **	10.5988	7.5995 *	1.2986	30.7564
	23.1193	9.8921	7.6130	2.5419	35.5776	15.0461
ETA	−158.2371	146.6115	41.7001	161.9017 *	−1.2293	−66.1437
	174.3350	70.0892	47.3005	16.7084	335.9920	132.4654
NPL	131.4755	83.9041	112.3704	79.8889 *	−249.7761	−35.9672
	321.3336	113.0256	98.7605	27.4320	508.0504	176.3655
INT	−64.5546	108.6839 *	32.9859 ***	−5.0104	−107.0849	172.7163 *
	77.6919	29.4989	18.7928	5.6554	146.3749	54.0877
GTA	−0.1333	−0.1017	−0.1624	0.0075	51.7277	−8.2381
	1.2220	0.3890	0.2018	0.0504	31.9143	10.4810
Intercept factor	101.0566	333.9465	−108.9888	60.6610	−200.9881	876.6272
	148.5109	92.9856	41.7590	16.1334	324.0319	202.5602
Observation	234	234	234	234	234	234
Group	26	26	12	12	14	14
R2	0.0285	0.2843	0.1597	0.2363	0.1214	0.0673

*, ** and *** represent significance at the 1%, 5% and 10% levels, respectively. Note: bank risk measured by Z-score = (ROA + ETA)/SDROA; ETA = equity/asset, SDROA = ROA standard deviation. Independent variables including: net interest income/total income ratio (INT); Revenue diversification (HHI) measured by: HHI = $(NON/NETOP)^2 + (NET/NETOP)^2$. NETOP = NON + NET; NON represents non-interest income, NET represents net interest income. Natural logarithm of total assets (SIZE); loan to total asset ratio (LTA); equity to total asset ratio (ETA); non-performing loan (NPL); asset growth (GTA); liquidity ratio = loan outstanding balance/customer deposits (LIQ). Research data is extracted from audited financial statements in the period 2010–2018, published publicly on the electronic portal of banks and publicly announced at the State Securities Commission of Vietnam.

Table 7. GMM model—the impact of revenue diversification on bank risk.

Variable	Z-Score					
	Banking System (26)		Listed Bank (12)		Unlisted Banks (14)	
	GMM	GMM for System	GMM	GMM for System	GMM	GMM for System
HHI	67.4423	−27.0381 *	5.3984	−50.5815 *	−15.0852	−138.2848 **
	62.7267	5.9107	23.7921	18.5574	60.0802	63.8694
SIZE	−53.1374	−0.9251	−14.3257 *	11.2364 **	−211.3938	71.1272 *
	45.8868	4.3233	2.7267	4.6223	150.8904	28.0055
LTA	−28.2702	−11.7999	19.3898	−18.2607	−49.0586	19.0482
	43.4823	9.6310	10.8840	19.4630	65.3754	49.5226
LIQ	23.6764	12.4501 ***	12.5640 **	−6.1353	76.2397	−3.1114
	24.6322	6.8079	5.0670	13.2196	52.9093	12.4002
ETA	−26.0547	−21.7340	123.5465 *	140.7288 *	−534.9738	668.2044 *
	230.9513	55.9014	36.6224	50.2955	621.2281	196.4053
NPL	116.3247	112.3741 ***	107.8816 ***	−602.4066	−254.4825	−560.2787
	151.6507	62.2863	56.9173	436.3195	181.4965	739.3324
INT	−22.5291	−11.5127	2.7492	89.7978 *	65.2403	−118.3618 *
	1.1798	0.1422	22.6803	28.0515	63.4773	38.7996
GTA	67.4423	61.6590	−0.2922	−0.3418	−29.0838	39.6196 ***
	62.7267	43.5201	0.5190	0.4346	29.2333	22.0640
Intercept		−27.0381		−85.9714		−590.5181
factor		5.9107		51.9649		250.3589
Observation	234	234	108	108	126	126
Group	26	26	13	13	14	14
F-statistic	6.61		17.74		137.16	
Wald Test		207.01		198.80		160.11
AR (2)	1.03		0.21		1.08	
Sargan test	35.78		17.09		31.13	
Hansen	10.50		4.76		2.24	

*, ** and *** represent significance at the 1%, 5% and 10% levels, respectively. Note: bank risk measured by Z-score = (ROA + ETA)/SDROA; ETA = Equity/total asset, SDROA = ROA standard deviation. Independent variables including: net interest income/total income ratio (INT); revenue diversification (HHI) measured by: HHI = $(NON/NETOP)^2 + (NET/NETOP)^2$. NETOP = NON + NET; NON represents non-interest income, NET represents net interest income. Natural logarithm of total assets (SIZE); loan to total asset ratio (LTA); equity to total asset ratio (ETA); non-performing loan (NPL); asset growth (GTA); liquidity ratio = loan outstanding balance/customer deposits (LIQ). Research data is extracted from audited financial statements in the period 2010–2018, published publicly on the electronic portal of banks and publicly announced at the State Securities Commission of Vietnam.

The research results of the Loan to Total asset ratio (LTA) are similar to those of Sanya and Wolfe (2011); Chiorazzo et al. (2008) and Stiroh (2004b), suggesting that the increase in this ratio means that the expansion of credit activities will increase credit risk accordingly; hence, there will be a positive correlation between total loan on capital mobilized to bank risk. The use of the relationship between loan and deposit is as a measure of liquidity is based on the premise that credit is the least flexible asset among the bank's profitable assets. Therefore, when the bank's liquidity decreases, bank risk tends to increase. The good management of credit risk (or reducing non-performing loan ratio) currently will help reduce the provision rate in the future.

The Loan to Deposit ratio (LIQ) is one of the commonly used liquidity ratios in many countries in banking management and monitoring activities to improve the quality of liquidity risk management of the banks, ensure the stability and safety of the system. The research results show that although liquidity increases, the banking system remains stable and safe, unlike Demirgüç-Kunt and Huizinga (2010) and (Norden and Weber 2010). This shows that the positive signal from the banking system in ensuring liquidity, safety to help banks prevent risks. Liquidity risk of Vietnamese commercial banks is minimized thanks to the SBV's efforts in continuously reducing the interest rate ceiling and encouraging large banks to support small banks. The signs of assessment of improving liquidity risk are reflected in Interbank Offered Rate rapidly increasing, mainly in a short time, reduced overnight transactions, no public interest rate races and no sign of a decline in deposits even if banks are forced to restructure. Banks have taken the initiative and flexible solutions to enhance capital mobilization as well as restructuring capital to ensure safety ratios such as short-term, medium and long-term loan rate to be 40% and must prepare to raise capital to satisfy Basel II standard. The interest rate level depends on the inflation variable and exchange rate. Therefore, the State Bank of Vietnam should maintain the interest rate level as current. Banks with good capital conditions should reduce interest rates, support customers and not expect a large-scale interest rate reduction. In addition, banks need to diversify products to mobilize deposits, be flexible in deposit terms, improve service quality and develop networks to reach and meet customers' needs better.

In theory, the larger the scale of the bank, the greater the capacity to withstand the risk (Lehar 2005; Poghosyan and Čihak 2011). However, this is not true for the reality in Vietnam, where large-scale banks have declining asset quality while the scale of credits and customers increases rapidly. Meanwhile, risk management capacity, control system, and forecast are still limited. In recent times, banks have had many changes in lending policies as well as appraising, monitoring and controlling disbursed loans to customers to ensure the NPL ratio remains less than 3%. However, the handling of non-performing loans is still a difficult issue. Risks to operations may stem from credit policies, unsatisfactory processes, people and internal systems, inactivity or external actors. The risks may be due to the information technology system, internal fraud, organizational model, regulations and the process of handling the work. Banks need to strengthen credit risk prevention, raise a cautious sense of loans to customers, really care about controlling loans after disbursing such as reviewing and improving cross monitoring procedures in bank for loans, thereby helping banks identify problematic loans and negotiate with customers in order to avoid transferring debt groups, avoid profiteering activities for the bank's loan officers.

5. Check Robust

Because banks can choose whether or not to diversify, the issue of endogeneity between diversification and bank performance is regularly discussed in the literature (Berger et al. 2010; Elsas et al. 2010; Laeven and Levine 2007). Hence, I test the robustness of the results by controlling for possible endogeneity, following Elsas et al. (2010) approach of using lagged instrumental variables. Although lagging variables are not fully exogenous, they are predetermined. To be valid instruments, these variables must be correlated with one endogenous variable (diversification) but not the other (bank efficiency). Tables 8–10 shows the results of estimations using lagged diversifications as the instrumental variables for current diversifications, and employing a two-stage least squares (2SLS) estimated. The tables also present the results of the Hansen test for endogeneity (De-Min 1973; Hausman 1978). According to Schultz et al. (2010), the existence of endogeneity would bias fixed-effects parameter estimates, and other estimators would need to be used. On the other hand, if endogeneity does not exist, estimates that deal with endogeneity such as the 2SLS would be less efficient than the fixed-effects panel regression. Most of the tests for the validity of instrumental variables (Sargan test) and the second-order autocorrelation of residuals (Arellano-Bond test) give the evidence not to reject the null hypothesis at the significance level of 5%. Hence, we could rely on the regression results for decision making.

Table 8. Poole, fixed effect model—Check Robustness of ROA, ROE regression.

| Variable | Banking System (26) | | | | Listed Bank (12) | | | | Unlisted Banks (14) | | | |
| | ROA | | ROE | | ROA | | ROE | | ROA | | ROE | |
	Pooled	Fixed Effect	Pooled	Fixed Effect	Pooled	Fixed Effect	Pooled	Fixed Effect	Pooled	Fixed Effect	Pooled	Fixed Effect
HHI	−0.0295	−0.0354	−0.2702	−0.3172	−0.0626 *	−0.0768 *	−0.5159 *	−0.6968 *	0.0068	0.0068	0.0074	0.1186
	0.0206	0.0265	0.1672	0.2426	0.0073	0.0090	0.0786	0.0979	0.0059	0.0076	0.0961	0.0828
SIZE	0.0069 *	0.0100 **	0.0633 *	0.0302	0.0110 *	0.0134 *	0.1154 *	0.0831 **	0.0007	−0.0003	−0.0214	−0.0896
	0.0014	0.0049	0.0222	0.0658	0.0021	0.0039	0.0224	0.0384	0.0017	0.0054	0.0474	0.1416
LTA	−0.0044	−0.0053	−0.0626	−0.0432	−0.0213 *	−0.0242 **	−0.2496 *	−0.2528 *	−0.0030	−0.0059	−0.0351	0.0078
	0.0038	0.0054	0.0432	0.0754	0.0065	0.0083	0.0692	0.0865	0.0030	0.0068 ***	0.0388	0.0774
LIQ	0.0049 *	0.0079 *	0.0705 *	0.1139 *	0.0044	0.0192 *	0.0642 **	0.2157 *	0.0046 *	0.0044	0.0606 **	0.0815 **
	0.0015	0.0033	0.0178	0.0350	0.0032	0.0049	0.0345	0.0476	0.0016	0.0021	0.0253	0.0369
ETA	0.1129 *	0.1001 *	0.2097	−0.1647	0.1824 *	0.1223 *	0.7100 *	−0.0377	0.0488 *	0.0319	−0.4645	−0.7668
	0.0186	0.0304	0.2593	0.4240	0.0200	0.0253	0.2141	0.2031	0.0191	0.0269	0.5113	0.7437
NPL	−0.0090	0.0297	−0.1766	0.1741	−0.0439	−0.0183	−0.5856	−0.0511	0.0439	0.0491	0.4892 ***	0.1365
	0.0279	0.0475	0.2656	0.3555	0.0417	0.0770	0.4471	0.7309	0.0281	0.0425	0.2889	0.3633
INT	0.0410 *	0.0458	0.3656 **	0.3915	0.0855 *	0.0967 *	0.7182 *	0.8706 **	0.0015	−0.0044	0.0501	−0.1018 ***
	0.0226	0.0300	0.1822	0.2723	0.0079	0.0120	0.0851	0.1060	0.0037	0.0047	0.0546	0.0513
GTA	0.0000	0.0001 *	0.0003	0.0011 *	0.0000	0.0001	−0.0005	0.0005 **	0.0030 ***	0.0033 **	0.0319 *	0.0449 **
	0.0000	0.0000	0.0002	0.0002	0.0001	0.0000	0.0009	0.0002	0.0017	0.0015	0.0189	0.0176
Intercept factor	−0.0721	−0.0983	−0.5634	−0.3071	−0.1113	−0.1374	−1.0079	−0.8094	−0.0152	0.0004	0.1744	0.7439
	0.0135	0.0425	0.2047	0.5489	0.0176	0.0324	0.1891	0.2912	0.0162	0.0440	0.4497	1.1692
Observation	234	234	234	234	108	108	108	108	126	126	126	126
Group	26	26	26	26	13	13	13	13	14	14	14	14
R2	0.3884	0.3276	0.2776	0.2342	0.6666	0.5165	0.5740	0.4724	0.3731	0.3359	0.1707	0.1031

*, **, and *** represent significance at the 1%, 5% and 10% levels, respectively. Note: bank risk measured by Z-score = (ROA + ETA)/SDROA; ETA = Equity/total asset, SDROA = ROA standard deviation. Independent variables including: net interest income/total income ratio (INT); revenue diversification (HHI) measured by: HHI = (NON/NETOP)^2 + (NET/NETOP)^2. NETOP = NON + NET; NON represents non-interest income, NET represents net interest income. Natural logarithm of total assets (SIZE); loan to total asset ratio (LTA); liquidity ratio = loan outstanding balance/customer deposits (LIQ); equity to total asset ratio (ETA;); non-performing loan ratio (NPL); asset growth (GTA). Research data is extracted from audited financial statements in the period 2010–2018, published publicly on the electronic portal of banks and publicly announced at the State Securities Commission of Vietnam.

Table 9. GMM model—the impact of revenue diversification on bank risk.

Variable	Banking System (26)		Listed Bank (12)		Unlisted Banks (14)	
	Pooled	Fixed Effect	Pooled	Fixed Effect	Pooled	Fixed Effect
HHI	−16.9592	−73.4480	−4.0018	12.7742 **	−60.2815	−120.0412 ***
	73.7673	89.7649	12.3356	5.1253	165.1179	69.0823
SIZE	2.0199	−44.6604	12.8728	−8.3746 **	49.0409	−113.4627 *
	13.7446	34.0561	4.8588	3.0237	34.7700	24.3848
LTA	−12.3307	−7.7556	−21.3642	10.1551	0.6757	−12.2934
	42.9020	15.1637	14.7637	5.8711	79.7648	39.6514
LIQ	7.4200	22.6653	10.5988	7.5995 ***	1.2986	30.7564 **
	20.7262	16.6958	8.3724	4.1961	35.5776	15.0461
ETA	−158.2371	146.6115 **	41.7001	161.9017 **	−1.2293	−66.1437
	129.8217	73.8420	53.7398	55.9156	335.9920	132.4654
NPL	131.4755	83.9041	112.3704	79.8889 **	−249.7761	−35.9672
	187.9586	109.4308	80.4284	32.0927	508.0504	176.3655
INT	−64.5546	108.6839	32.9859	−5.0104	−107.0849	172.7163
	80.3877	106.9252	12.6504	3.4738	146.3749	54.0877 *
GTA	−0.1333	−0.1017	−0.1624	0.0075	51.7277	−8.2381
	0.1526	0.1010	0.0588	0.0122	31.9143	10.4810
Intercept factor	101.0566	333.9465	−108.9888	60.6610	−200.9881	876.6272
	145.9379	244.6197	38.3586	21.5519	324.0319	202.5602
Observation	234	234	108	234	126	126
Group	26	26	12	12	14	14
R2	0.0285	0.2843	0.1549	0.2363	0.1214	0.0673

*, ** and *** represent significance at the 1%, 5% and 10% levels, respectively. Note: bank risk measured by Z-score = (ROA + ETA)/SDROA; ETA = Equity/total asset, SDROA = ROA standard deviation. Independent variables including: net interest income/total income ratio (INT); Revenue diversification (HHI) measured by: HHI = $(NON/NETOP)^2 + (NET/NETOP)^2$. NETOP = NON + NET; NON represents non-interest income, NET represents net interest income. Natural logarithm of total assets (SIZE); loan to total asset ratio (LTA); equity to total asset ratio (ETA); non-performing loan/loan outstanding balance ratio (NPL); asset growth (GTA); liquidity ratio = loan outstanding balance/customer deposits (LIQ). Research data is extracted from audited financial statements in the period 2010–2018, published publicly on the electronic portal of banks and publicly announced at the State Securities Commission of Vietnam.

Table 10. GMM system—Check Robustness of regression.

Variable	Banking System (26)			Listed Bank (12)			Unlisted Bank (14)		
	ROA	ROE	Z	ROA	ROE	Z	ROA	ROE	Z
HHI	0.0278 ***	0.0538	12.7007	0.0810 *	0.7393 *	−10.2105 *	0.0253	0.2882 *	−344.3881 *
	0.0140	0.1940	218.0181	0.0125	0.7220	129.8393	0.0460	0.3814	298.8000
SIZE	0.0125 *	0.1111 *	4.2403	0.0177	0.3412 *	2.2228	0.0035	0.0514	135.0938
	0.0039	0.0316	11.6422	0.0206	0.1059	16.5757	0.0118	0.1677	130.8438
LTA	−0.0025	−0.0765 ***	−46.4334	−0.0259	−0.5018 **	−28.9225	0.0053	0.0925	−127.5582
	0.0055	0.0455	37.3457	0.0216	0.1875	38.5953	0.0457	0.1535	95.4969
LIQ	0.0085 *	0.1219 *	−8.7072	−0.0019	−0.0621	−8.2921	0.0100	0.0990	−45.9132
	0.0023	0.0424	13.1264	0.0223	0.1128	28.7639	0.0143	0.0985	55.7641
ETA	0.1338	0.4357 ***	−201.2829	0.2243	0.2943	176.1328	0.0695	0.4077	462.6792
	0.0330	0.2208	288.0752	0.1317	1.5209	157.9478	0.1051	0.8222	523.0208
NPL	0.0320	0.4733	344.0908	−0.0987	2.7899	−126.4210	0.0947	0.5805	890.7104 *
	0.0552	0.6523	385.1840	0.3723	2.4728	309.3013	0.0832	0.9339	564.6832
INT	−0.0194 *	0.0054	−48.1336	−0.1024 **	−0.5525	−0.8150	−0.0150	−0.1670	405.9794
	0.0155	0.1725	280.0172	0.0407	0.7624	162.4012	0.0396	0.2945	359.3684
GTA	0.0005	0.0129	−1.7425	0.0023	−0.0030	7.3651 **	0.0040	0.0771	31.9446
	0.0019	0.0162	4.3208	0.0021	0.0277	2.6692	0.0094	0.0581	39.7768
Intercept factor	−0.1176	−0.9705	72.6049	−0.1157	−2.5399	18.0472	−0.0498	−0.6264	−1064.648
	0.0340	0.2637	169.2970	0.1679	0.7531	136.3234	0.1038	1.3944	1049.401
Observation	234	234	234	108	108	108	126	126	126
Group	26	26	26	12	12	12	14	14	14
F-statistic	5.25	3.54	1.10	1.12	2.94	3.97	1.24	2.26	11.02
AR (2)	0.01	0.14	0.50	−0.28	0.25	−0.48	−1.09	0.16	−0.76
Hansen test	21.18	20.86	11.68	1.50	1.95	3.3	7.44	8.25	1.01

*, ** and *** represent significance at the 1%, 5% and 10% levels, respectively. Note: bank risk measured by Z-score = (ROA + ETA)/SDROA; ETA = Equity/asset, SDROA = ROA standard deviation. Independent variables including: net interest income/total income ratio (INT); Revenue diversification (HHI) measured by: HHI = $(NON/NETOP)^2 + (NET/NETOP)^2$. NETOP = NON + NET; NON represents non-interest income, NET represents net interest income. Natural logarithm of total assets (SIZE); loan to total asset ratio (LTA); equity to total asset ratio (ETA); non-performing loan/loan outstanding balance ratio (NPL); asset growth (GTA); liquidity ratio = loan outstanding balance/customer deposits (LIQ). Research data is extracted from audited financial statements in the period 2010–2018, published publicly on the electronic portal of banks and publicly announced at the State Securities Commission of Vietnam.

6. Conclusions

The bank is the capital circulatory system of the economy; thus, assessing the financial condition of commercial banks is an important step in the risk management process to forecast the economic situation. Credit risk is one of the causes of the weaknesses of the commercial banking system, leading to restructuring in recent years. The process of restructuring the commercial banking system is still going on; the question raised is: which management method should be used to assess and forecast bank revenue and bankruptcy risks? Determining how the revenue diversification affects performance and safety, stabilizing the banking system to help banks time to provide interventions as well as appropriate solutions. In the world, there have been many researches work on this issue and have given meaningful experimental results, approaching in many different research aspects, the impact results may be similar or different depending on bank characteristics, geographical location and national political economy. However, in Vietnam, most of the studies have not yet produced quantitative research models and have rarely been published in journals or on other financial information channels. Therefore, the analysis of the impact of revenue diversification on performance and bank risk is an extremely urgent issue. The research model is based on the grouped factors of revenue diversification (INT, HHI). In particular, revenue diversification is measured by indexes of Mercieca et al. (2007); $HHI = (NON/NETOP)^2 + (NET/NETOP)^2$. Performance measured by financial performance (ROA, ROE), the bank risk using the index Z-score = (ROA + ETA)/SDROA to measure as the study of Roy (1952); Boyd and Runkle (1993); Chiorazzo et al. (2008); Lepetit and Strobel (2015); Lee et al. (2014). Using the quantitative analysis method with tests to evaluate the fixed effects model (FEM) and the random effects model (REM) to extract research result. The results of GMM system research have verified the negative impact of revenue diversification on bank performance. However, the revenue diversification at listed banks is different when the impact reduces risks for the banks. Interest income is still the motivation for the development of banks; the more this income increases, the more profits and systemic risks increase. The benefit of revenue diversification is offset by the increase in non-interest activity; however, it also adjusts the risk of banks (Demirgüç-Kunt and Huizinga 2010; Li and Zhang 2013). This shows the weakness and lack of experience in the banking system in building a reasonable profit transformation model. The pressure to implement Basel II forces banks to shift in business operations, restructure credit activities, and restructure revenue. In fact, banks which cannot promote credit will turn to promote the development of services to increase revenue; however, it is difficult to expect a strong increase in a short time. Some large-scale banks that lead the retail sector show signs of declining revenue from services. Growth, as well as the contribution from service activities, is not commensurate with potentials; although there are many positive points, they are not enough to cover risks from net interest income activities. Therefore, the Vietnamese commercial banking system needs to improve and enhance the non-credit service quality, especially e-banking services, to meet the trend of competition in banking digitization and the trend of consumer consumption. The better the banking liquidity is, the higher the profitability of the credit institutions. However, there have been positive solutions in ensuring liquidity and safety such as adjusting interest rates, diversifying capital mobilization products, flexible in deposit terms and improving service quality have helped the bank to prevent risks and ensure the safety and stability of the system.

Funding: This research received no external funding.

Conflicts of Interest: The author declares no conflict of interest.

References

Acharya, Viral V., Iftekhar Hasan, and Anthony Saunders. 2006. Should banks be diversified? Evidence from individual bank loan portfolios. *The Journal of Business* 79: 1355–412. [CrossRef]

Aggarwal, Raj, and Kevin T. Jacques. 2001. The impact of FDICIA and prompt corrective action on bank capital and risk: Estimates using a simultaneous equations model. *Journal of Banking & Finance* 25: 1139–60.

Agoraki, Maria-Eleni K., Manthos D. Delis, and Fotios Pasiouras. 2011. Regulations, competition and bank risk-taking in transition countries. *Journal of Financial Stability* 7: 38–48. [CrossRef]

Aigner, Dennis, C. A. Knox Lovell, and Peter Schmidt. 1977. Formulation and estimation of stochastic frontier production function models. *Journal of Econometrics* 6: 21–37. [CrossRef]

Arellano, Manuel, and Olympia Bover. 1995. Another look at the instrumental variable estimation of error-components models. *Journal of Econometrics* 68: 29–51. [CrossRef]

Baele, Lieven, Olivier De Jonghe, and Rudi Vander Vennet. 2007. Does the stock market value bank diversification? *Journal of Banking & Finance* 31: 1999–2023. [CrossRef]

Beck, Thorsten, Olivier De Jonghe, and Glenn Schepens. 2013. Bank competition and stability: Cross-country heterogeneity. *Journal of Financial Intermediation* 22: 218–44. [CrossRef]

Berger, Allen N. 1995. The relationship between capital and earnings in banking. *Journal of Money, Credit and Banking* 27: 432–56. [CrossRef]

Berger, Allen N., and Loretta J. Mester. 1997. *Efficiency and Productivity Change in the US Commercial Banking Industry: A Comparison of the 1980s and 1990s*. Philadelphia: Federal Reserve Bank of Philadelphia.

Berger, Allen N., Iftekhar Hasan, and Mingming Zhou. 2010. The effects of focus versus diversification on bank performance: Evidence from Chinese banks. *Journal of Banking & Finance* 34: 1417–35.

Bikker, Jacob, and Jaap W. B. Bos. 2008. *Bank Performance: A Theoretical and Empirical Framework for the Analysis of Profitability, Competition and Efficiency*. London: Routledge.

Bikker, Jacob A., and Paul A. J. Metzemakers. 2005. Bank provisioning behaviour and procyclicality. *Journal of International Financial Markets, Institutions and Money* 15: 141–57. [CrossRef]

Blundell, Richard, and Stephen Bond. 2000. GMM estimation with persistent panel data: an application to production functions. *Econometric Reviews* 19: 321–40. [CrossRef]

Boot, Arnoud W. A., and Anjolein Schmeits. 2000. Market discipline and incentive problems in conglomerate firms with applications to banking. *Journal of Financial Intermediation* 9: 240–73. [CrossRef]

Bourke, Philip. 1989. Concentration and other determinants of bank profitability in Europe, North America and Australia. *Journal of Banking & Finance* 13: 65–79.

Boyd, John H., and David E. Runkle. 1993. Size and performance of banking firms: Testing the predictions of theory. *Journal of Monetary Economics* 31: 47–67. [CrossRef]

Brighi, Paola, Valeria Venturelli, and Centro Studi Banca e Finanza. 2014. The effect of revenue and geographic diversification on bank performance. Paper Presented at the European Financial Management Association 2014 Annual Meetings, Lugano, Switzerland, June 25–28.

Chiorazzo, Vincenzo, Carlo Milani, and Francesca Salvini. 2008. Income diversification and bank performance: Evidence from Italian banks. *Journal of Financial Services Research* 33: 181–203. [CrossRef]

Curi, Claudia, Ana Lozano-Vivas, and Valentin Zelenyuk. 2015. Foreign bank diversification and efficiency prior to and during the financial crisis: Does one business model fit all? *Journal of Banking & Finance* 61: S22–S35.

De Andres, Pablo, and Eleuterio Vallelado. 2008. Corporate governance in banking: The role of the board of directors. *Journal of Banking & Finance* 32: 2570–80.

De Jonghe, Olivier. 2010. Back to the basics in banking? A micro-analysis of banking system stability. *Journal of Financial Intermediation* 19: 387–417. [CrossRef]

Delis, Manthos D., Philip Molyneux, and Fotios Pasiouras. 2011. Regulations and productivity growth in banking: Evidence from transition economies. *Journal of Money, Credit and Banking* 43: 735–64. [CrossRef]

Delpachitra, Sarath, and Laurence Lester. 2013. Non-Interest Income: Are Australian Banks Moving Away from their Traditional Businesses? *Economic Papers: A Journal of Applied Economics and Policy* 32: 190–99. [CrossRef]

De-Min, Wu. 1973. Alternative tests of independence between stochastic regressors and disturbances. *Econometrica (pre-1986)* 41: 733.

Demirgüç-Kunt, Ash, and Harry Huizinga. 1999. Determinants of commercial bank interest margins and profitability: Some international evidence. *The World Bank Economic Review* 13: 379–408. [CrossRef]

Demirgüç-Kunt, Asli, and Harry Huizinga. 2010. Bank activity and funding strategies: The impact on risk and returns. *Journal of Financial Economics* 98: 626–50. [CrossRef]

Demsetz, Rebecca S., and Philip E. Strahan. 1997. Diversification, size, and risk at bank holding companies. *Journal of Money, Credit, and Banking* 29: 300–13. [CrossRef]

DeYoung, Robert, and Tara Rice. 2004. Noninterest income and financial performance at US commercial banks. *Financial Review* 39: 101–27. [CrossRef]

DeYoung, Robert, and Karin P. Roland. 2001. Product mix and earnings volatility at commercial banks: Evidence from a degree of total leverage model. *Journal of Financial Intermediation* 10: 54–84. [CrossRef]

DeYoung, Robert, and Gökhan Torna. 2013. Nontraditional banking activities and bank failures during the financial crisis. *Journal of Financial Intermediation* 22: 397–421. [CrossRef]

Elsas, Ralf, Andreas Hackethal, and Markus Holzhäuser. 2010. The anatomy of bank diversification. *Journal of Banking & Finance* 34: 1274–87.

Fiordelisi, Franco, David Marques-Ibanez, and Phil Molyneux. 2011. Efficiency and risk in European banking. *Journal of Banking & Finance* 35: 1315–26.

Gamra, Saoussen Ben, and Dominique Plihon. 2011. Revenue diversification in emerging market banks: implications for financial performance. *arXiv*, arXiv:1107.0170.

Geambasu, Cristina, Robert Sova, Iulia Jianu, and Liviu Geambasu. 2013. Risk measurement in post-modern portfolio theory: differences from modern portfolio theory. *Economic Computation & Economic Cybernetics Studies & Research* 47: 113–32.

Goddard, John, Phil Molyneux, and John OS Wilson. 2004. Dynamics of growth and profitability in banking. *Journal of Money, Credit and Banking* 36: 1069–90. [CrossRef]

González-Hermosillo, Ms Brenda. 1999. *Determinants of ex-Ante Banking System Distress: A Macro-Micro Empirical Exploration of Some Recent Episodes*. Washington: International Monetary Fund.

Halling, Michael, and Evelyn Hayden. 2006. Bank Failure Prediction: A Two-Step Survival Time Approach. Available online: https://ssrn.com/abstract=904255 (accessed on 25 May 2019).

Hassan, M. Kabir, and Abdel-Hameed M. Bashir. 2003. Determinants of Islamic banking profitability. Paper Presented at the 10th ERF Annual Conference, Morocco, Kuwait City, Kuwait, March 10–12.

Hausman, Jerry A. 1978. Specification tests in econometrics. *Econometrica: Journal of the Econometric Society* 46: 1251–71. [CrossRef]

Hsieh, Meng-Fen, Pei-Fen Chen, Chien-Chiang Lee, and Shih-Jui Yang. 2013. How does diversification impact bank stability? The role of globalization, regulations, and governance environments. *Asia-Pacific Journal of Financial Studies* 42: 813–44. [CrossRef]

Hughes, Joseph P., and Loretta J. Mester. 1998. Bank capitalization and cost: Evidence of scale economies in risk management and signaling. *Review of Economics and Statistics* 80: 314 25. [CrossRef]

Jianu, Ionel, Iulia Jianu, and Carmen Țurlea. 2017. Measuring the company's real performance by physical capital maintenance. *Economic Computation and Economic Cybernetics Studies and Research* 51: 21.

Kick, Thorsten Beck Heiko Hesse Thomas, and Natalja von Westernhagen. 2009. *Bank Ownership and Stability: Evidence from Germany*. Boston: VOX CEPRs Policy Portal.

Köhler, Matthias. 2015. Which banks are more risky? The impact of business models on bank stability. *Journal of Financial Stability* 16: 195–212. [CrossRef]

Laeven, Luc, and Ross Levine. 2007. Is there a diversification discount in financial conglomerates? *Journal of Financial Economics* 85: 331–67. [CrossRef]

Laeven, Luc, and Ross Levine. 2009. Bank governance, regulation and risk taking. *Journal of Financial Economics* 93: 259–75. [CrossRef]

Laeven, Luc, and Giovanni Majnoni. 2003. Loan loss provisioning and economic slowdowns: too much, too late? *Journal of Financial Intermediation* 12: 178–97. [CrossRef]

Lee, Chien-Chiang, Shih-Jui Yang, and Chi-Hung Chang. 2014. Non-interest income, profitability, and risk in banking industry: A cross-country analysis. *The North American Journal of Economics and Finance* 27: 48–67. [CrossRef]

Lehar, Alfred. 2005. Measuring systemic risk: A risk management approach. *Journal of Banking & Finance* 29: 2577–603.

Lepetit, Laetitia, and Frank Strobel. 2015. Bank insolvency risk and Z-score measures: A refinement. *Finance Research Letters* 13: 214–24. [CrossRef]

Lepetit, Laetitia, Emmanuelle Nys, Philippe Rous, and Amine Tarazi. 2008. Bank income structure and risk: An empirical analysis of European banks. *Journal of Banking & Finance* 32: 1452–67.

Li, Li, and Yu Zhang. 2013. Are there diversification benefits of increasing noninterest income in the Chinese banking industry? *Journal of Empirical Finance* 24: 151–65. [CrossRef]

Liang, Qi, Pisun Xu, and Pornsit Jiraporn. 2013. Board characteristics and Chinese bank performance. *Journal of Banking & Finance* 37: 2953–68.

McAllister, Patrick H., and Douglas McManus. 1993. Resolving the scale efficiency puzzle in banking. *Journal of Banking & Finance* 17: 389–405.

Mercieca, Steve, Klaus Schaeck, and Simon Wolfe. 2007. Small European banks: Benefits from diversification? *Journal of Banking & Finance* 31: 1975–98.

Meslier, Céline, Ruth Tacneng, and Amine Tarazi. 2014. Is bank income diversification beneficial? Evidence from an emerging economy. *Journal of International Financial Markets, Institutions and Money* 31: 97–126. [CrossRef]

Norden, Lars, and Martin Weber. 2010. Funding modes of German banks: structural changes and their implications. *Journal of Financial Services Research* 38: 69–93. [CrossRef]

Poghosyan, Tigran, and Martin Čihak. 2011. Determinants of bank distress in Europe: Evidence from a new data set. *Journal of Financial Services Research* 40: 163–84. [CrossRef]

Porter, Robert L., and Wan-Jiun Paul Chiou. 2013. How has capital affected bank risk since implementation of the Basel accords. *Banks and Bank System* 1: 1–52.

Rossi, Stefania P. S., Markus S Schwaiger, and Gerhard Winkler. 2009. How loan portfolio diversification affects risk, efficiency and capitalization: A managerial behavior model for Austrian banks. *Journal of Banking & Finance* 33: 2218–26.

Roy, Andrew Donald. 1952. Safety first and the holding of assets. *Econometrica: Journal of the Econometric Society* 20: 431–49. [CrossRef]

Sanya, Sarah, and Simon Wolfe. 2011. Can banks in emerging economies benefit from revenue diversification? *Journal of Financial Services Research* 40: 79–101. [CrossRef]

Schultz, Emma L., David T. Tan, and Kathleen D. Walsh. 2010. Endogeneity and the corporate governance-performance relation. *Australian Journal of Management* 35: 145–63. [CrossRef]

Stiroh, Kevin J. 2004a. Diversification in banking: Is noninterest income the answer? *Journal of Money, Credit, and Banking* 36: 853–82. [CrossRef]

Stiroh, Kevin J. 2004b. Do community banks benefit from diversification? *Journal of Financial Services Research* 25: 135–60. [CrossRef]

Stiroh, Kevin J., and Adrienne Rumble. 2006. The dark side of diversification: The case of US financial holding companies. *Journal of Banking & Finance* 30: 2131–61.

Vallascas, Francesco, and Kevin Keasey. 2012. Bank resilience to systemic shocks and the stability of banking systems: Small is beautiful. *Journal of International Money and Finance* 31: 1745–76. [CrossRef]

Vennet, Rudi Vander. 2002. Cost and profit efficiency of financial conglomerates and universal banks in Europe. *Journal of Money, Credit and Banking* 34: 254–82. [CrossRef]

Williams, Barry, and Laurie Prather. 2010. Bank risk and return: the impact of bank non-interest income. *International Journal of Managerial Finance* 6: 220–44. [CrossRef]

World Bank. 2018. Management's Discussion & Analysis and Financial Statements (Fiscal 2018). Available online: http://documents.worldbank.org/curated/en/473291538159094998/Annual-Report-2018-Managements-Discussion-and-Analysis-and-Financial-Statements-Fiscal-2018 (accessed on 25 May 2019).

© 2019 by the author. Licensee MDPI, Basel, Switzerland. This article is an open access article distributed under the terms and conditions of the Creative Commons Attribution (CC BY) license (http://creativecommons.org/licenses/by/4.0/).

Article

Can Higher Capital Discipline Bank Risk: Evidence from a Meta-Analysis

Quang T. T. Nguyen [1,*], Son T. B. Nguyen [2] and Quang V. Nguyen [3]

[1] University of Economics—The University of Danang, Danang 55000, Vietnam
[2] University of Foreign Language Studies—The University of Danang, Danang 55000, Vietnam
[3] Ho Chi Minh National Academy of Politics—Region III, Danang 55000, Vietnam
* Correspondence: quangntt@due.udn.vn

Received: 23 July 2019; Accepted: 15 August 2019; Published: 20 August 2019

Abstract: Capital regulation has been among the most important tools for regulators to maintain the credibility and stability of the financial systems. However, the question whether higher capital induce banks to take lower risk remains unanswered. This paper examines the effect of capital on bank risk employing a meta-analysis approach, which considers a wide range of empirical papers from 1990 to 2018. We found that the negative effect of bank capital on bank risk, which implies the discipline role of bank capital, is more likely to be reported. However, the reported results are suffered from the publication bias due to the preference for significant estimates and favored results. Our study also shows that the differences in the previous studies' conclusions are primarily caused by the differences in the study design, particularly the risk and capital measurements; the model specification such as the concern for the dynamic of bank risk behaviors, the endogeneity of the capital and unobserved time fixed effects; along with and the sample characteristics such as the sample size, and whether banks are bank holding companies or located in high-income countries.

Keywords: bank capital; bank risk; meta-analysis; Bayesian model-averaging; capital regulation

1. Introduction

Three decades have passed since the first introduction of the Basel I Accord in 1988. Since then, capital regulation has been among the most important tools for regulators to maintain the credibility and stability of the financial systems. The capital regulation emphasizes the role of capital in disciplining the bank risk such that it requires banks to hold an adequate amount of capital to cover their risk. Over time, the accord has been regularly revised to enhance the quality of banking supervision and further ensure the credibility and stability of the international banking system. The latest version of Basel Accord—Basel III—is a response of the regulators to the massive failure of the banking system during the global financial crisis of 2007–2009. The new framework gives more focus on the role of capital by strengthening the regulatory capital base in both quality and quantity and introducing new minimum requirements for the non-risk-based capital (the leverage ratio), the common equity tier 1 capital, the capital conservation buffers as well as the capital surcharges for global systemically important banks (G-SIB) (BIS 2018). The average total capital to asset ratio of banks across countries has gradually increased from just 8.55% in 2000 to 10.31% in 2015. The average risk-weighted regulatory capital ratio also raises from 13.3% to 16.95% during the same period (World Bank 2018). While it is favorable for banks to have more capital, there remains debates on whether higher capital induce banks to take lower risk.

There have been two opposing views on the effect of capital on bank risk. One stream believes that capital represents the shareholders' benefits. Thus, it will motivate banks to manage risk properly and efficiently. Consequently, banks tend to take less risk given the higher level of capital. This stream is often regarded as the "moral hazard hypothesis" (Admati et al. 2013; Gale 2010). The other stream, which is often referred as the "regulatory hypothesis", argues that capital is costly, the enforcement of regulatory actions such as capital requirements increase the cost of capital (regulatory cost). Hence, they are induced to increase their risks to generate higher return (Altunbas et al. 2007; Shrieves and Dahl 1992).

Given different views on the effect of bank capital, numerous studies have relied on empirical evidence to solve the puzzle. Our survey of the literature yields around 100 empirical studies (until August 2018) studying the effect of bank capital on bank risk. However, the findings are inconclusive. These findings are important to the Basel Committee (who acts as the primary global standard setter for the prudential regulation of banks) and central banks' governors for policy design to maintain the stability of the banking and financial system. Therefore, this study investigates empirical research on the impact of bank capital on bank risk to identify (1) whether bank capital increase or reduce bank risk; and (2) why there are variations in previous studies' conclusions.

For that purpose, we employ a meta-analysis method. Since the term first coined by Glass in 1976 (Glass 1976), the meta-analysis has gained popularity and widely adopted in psychological research and major review articles in many fields, including finance and banking. These studies focus on controversial topics such as bank efficiency (Aiello and Bonanno 2016, 2018), bank competition and stability (Zigraiova and Havranek 2016), financial development and economic growth (Valickova et al. 2015), and the policy impact (Fidrmuc and Lind 2018; Gechert 2015). Meta-analysis is useful for review articles by providing a systematic review of the literature and not suffering from potential selective bias as qualitative literature surveys (Glass 1976; King and He 2005).

Our meta-dataset comprises 910 observations from 89 papers during the period from 1990 to 2018. We found that the negative effect of bank capital on bank risk, which implies the discipline role of bank capital, is more likely to be reported. However, the reported results are suffered from the publication bias due to the preference for significant estimates and favoured results. Our study also shows that the differences in the previous studies' conclusions are primarily caused by the differences in the study design, particularly the risk and capital measurements; the model specification such as the concern for the dynamic of bank risk behaviors, the endogeneity of the capital and unobserved time fixed effects; along with and the sample characteristics such as sample size, and whether banks are bank holding companies or located in high-income countries. Even using the same risk measurements, the effect also varies due to the different model settings and samples.

Our study contributes to the literature in several ways. First, to the best of our knowledge, our study is the first to apply a meta-analysis to investigate the effect of bank capital on bank risk. Second, the study covers a comprehensive empirical literature over the past three decades. Third, rather than estimating the variations in the effect of bank capital on bank risk using the traditional fixed and random effect models, we apply Bayesian model-averaging techniques to address the model uncertainty. Fourth, our study is useful for academics in researching the way to constrain bank risk and for policy makers to design a proper banking regulation to promote the financial stability.

The remainder of the paper is structured as follows. Section 2 describes the data and methods used in the study. Section 3 reports the results. Section 4 conducts some further analysis including regressions for different risk measurements as well as calculating the "benchmark" and "best-practice" estimates for different risk measurements and samples. Finally, Section 5 concludes the paper with implications for future research and policy makers.

2. Data and Methodology

2.1. Data

Our data comes from previous papers that investigate the effect of bank capital on risk. We searched for all articles and working papers from online databases including Web of Science, ABI, Scopus, ScienceDirect Elsevier, JSTOR, Wiley Online Library, Crossref, Taylor & Francis, Springer, HAL, and Palgrave Macmillan. Searching key words are "bank", "risk", and "capital" in the title. Publication date is restricted to range from 1990 to 2018, since studies on the topic increase significantly after the introduction of Basel I standard in 1988. Initially, we obtained 268 results. Then, we manually searched the top journals in finance (These are A* journals in finance (code 1502) in the ABDC journal list 2018, available at http://www.abdc.edu.au/master-journal-list.php), checked the reference lists in the found articles, and searched the Google Scholar database so that we did not omit important articles. We retrieved an additional 49 papers. We finish searching on 17 August 2018 with a total of 317 papers.

Then, we skimmed these papers and applied some criteria to obtain the final dataset. For this purpose, the paper should: (i) conduct empirical analysis; (ii) be written in English; (iii) estimate the coefficient β in equation (1); and (iv) have enough information to apply meta regression analysis (coefficient β and its standard deviations, or p-value). After filtering, our dataset comprised of 89 papers with 910 observations. The full list of surveyed papers is provided in Appendix A.

Specifically, papers considered should empirically examine the following model:

$$Risk_{it} = \alpha + \beta Capital_{it} + \sum_{k=1}^{K} \gamma_k X_{kit} + \varepsilon_{it} \qquad (1)$$

where i is a bank index, t is a time index, and X is a set of control variables. The interest is in the coefficient β, which reflects the effect of bank capital on risk.

2.2. Standardized Effect Sizes

Given the broad scope of the measures for bank risk and the measurement units of regression variables in the literature, it is imperative that we re-compute the individual estimates (reported coefficient β) to a common metric. We transform the reported estimates into partial correlation coefficients (PCCs) as follow:

$$PCC_{ij} = \frac{t_{ij}}{\sqrt{t_{ij}^2 + df_{ij}}} \qquad (2)$$

where t_{ij} and df_{ij} are t-statistic and degree of freedom of the reported estimates jth in study ith, respectively. PCC represents the statistical strength of the relationship between bank capital and risk (Since ZSCORE has reverse interpretation with other risk measurements. That is, higher ZSCORE implies lower risk. Thus, all betas and t-statistics in studies using ZSCORE are multiplied with (−1) before calculating PCC to be consistent with other measurements).

For cases that standard errors (se) of estimates β are reported instead of t-statistics, we derive t-statistics from the following equation:

$$t = \frac{\hat{\beta}_{ij}}{se(\hat{\beta})_{ij}} \qquad (3)$$

If p-values of estimates β are reported rather than its standard errors, we obtain the t-statistics from estimates β and the number of observations using Excel two-tailed inverse function of the Student's t-distribution (T.INV.2T) with the sign corresponding to the sign of β.

The standard errors of PCCs are denoted as follows:

$$SEPCC = \sqrt{\frac{(1 - PCC_{ij})}{df_{ij}}} \qquad (4)$$

Figure 1 displays the distribution of the effects of bank capital on risk. Before standardizing, the estimates varied greatly from −800 to 200 percentage point (Figure 1a) but distribute more normally and ranged from −1 to 1 after standardizing (Figure 1b).

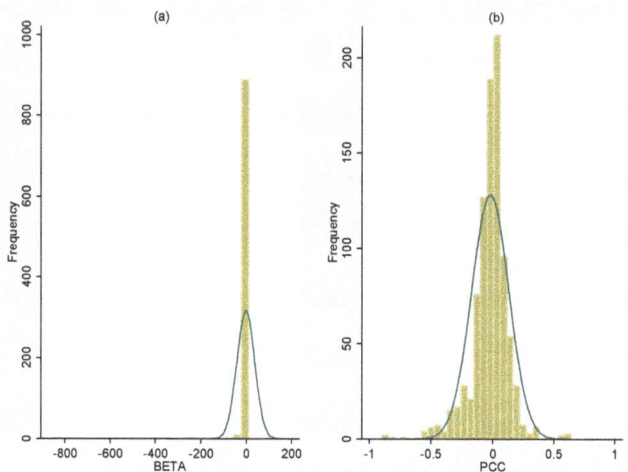

Figure 1. Distribution of the reported (**a**) and standardized effects (**b**) of bank capital on risk.

Table 1 shows that PCC varies substantially across countries. There is both positive and negative evidence on the relationship between bank capital and risk. This explains a large number of studies conducting cross-country analysis. Among the countries, the U.S attracts the most interest of the researchers. Both mean and median of all reported studies are negative and suggest a discipline role of bank capital. That is, higher capital induces banks to operate safely and take less risk.

Table 1. Standardized effects of bank capital on risk (partial correlation coefficient—PCC) across countries.

Country	Observations	Studies	Mean	S.D	Min	Max	Median
Bangladesh	20	3	−0.252	0.087	−0.370	−0.071	−0.284
Brazil	3	1	0.084	0	0.084	0.084	0.084
Canada	7	1	0.100	0.014	0.078	0.120	0.099
China	36	6	−0.122	0.245	−0.803	0.164	−0.073
Egypt	7	1	0.186	0.064	0.112	0.255	0.159
France	4	1	0.066	0.241	−0.181	0.284	0.081
India	35	6	−0.125	0.191	−0.500	0.457	−0.146
Indonesia	4	1	−0.218	0.081	−0.285	−0.100	−0.243
Italy	5	1	−0.010	0.034	−0.054	0.017	0.013
Jamaica	4	1	−0.009	0.071	−0.11.	0.051	0.012
Japan	8	3	0.068	0.121	−0.171	0.218	0.105
Jordan	6	1	0.010	0.144	−0.210	0.203	−0.013
Lebanon	2	1	−0.109	0.019	−0.122	−0.095	−0.109
Luxembourg	4	1	−0.345	0.356	−0.873	−0.130	−0.189
Malaysia	3	2	0.079	0.423	−0.212	0.565	−0.116
Pakistan	12	2	−0.063	0.266	−0.331	0.355	−0.092
Russian Federation	6	1	0.023	0.026	−0.001	0.065	0.016
Switzerland	12	2	0.104	0.05	0.007	0.166	0.128
Tunisia	13	5	−0.075	0.270	−0.488	0.210	0.015
UK	10	1	−0.053	0.025	−0.072	−0.007	−0.066
US	241	20	−0.018	0.106	−0.503	0.213	0
Vietnam	2	1	−0.487	0.296	−0.697	−0.278	−0.487
Cross-country	466	32	0.003	0.127	−0.895	0.646	0.008
Total	**910**	**89**	**−0.021**	**0.154**	**−1.000**	**0.646**	**−0.001**

2.3. Publication Bias

Before further analysis, it is necessary to check for publication bias in our reported estimates. Publication bias refers to the probability of a favoured result to be reported (Rosenthal 1979) and has been detected in many empirical economics studies (Doucouliagos and Stanley 2013). Given the controversies over capital regulation, it is likely in our study that capital regulation supporters tend to report a negative and significant effect of capital on risk, while others, primarily academic researchers, prefer a positive or insignificant result. The bias is non-trivial and can inflate the average estimates (Field and Gillett 2010).

The publication bias can be detected using funnel plot (Light and Pillemer 1984). The funnel plot graphs the estimated effects on the x-axis and their precision on the y-axis. The top of the funnel contains the most precise estimates that are close to the true effect. Without publication bias, the estimates should be randomly distributed, and the funnel is symmetric. In contrast, asymmetrical or hollow funnel indicates the presence of publication bias (Egger et al. 1997). Figure 2 depicts the funnel plot of standardized effects of capital on risk (PCC) against its precision. The funnel is not symmetric and suggests the existence of publication bias in the reported estimates. In addition, there are more negative than positive estimates. This either implies a discipline effect of capital on bank risk-taking, or in other words, there is more evidence supporting capital regulation to be reported.

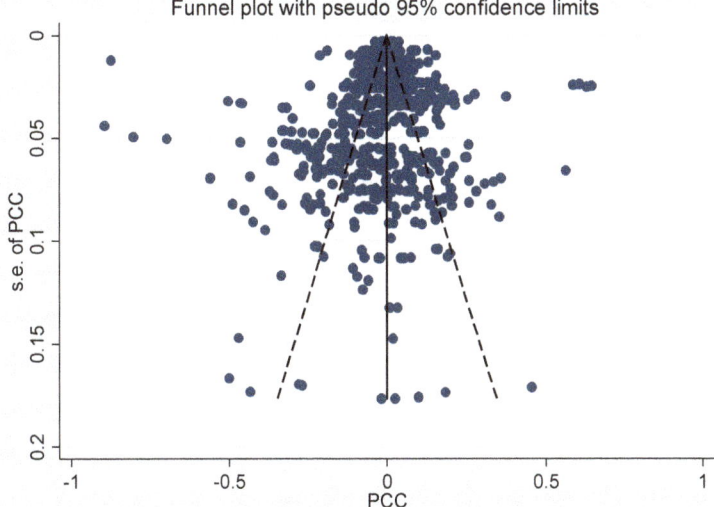

Figure 2. Funnel plot of standardized effects of capital on risk (PCC). Note: The vertical line shows the estimation of the population effect size. The two diagonal lines are the 95% confidence interval of the estimation.

Since the interpretation of funnel plot is subjective, we statistically test for publication bias using funnel asymmetry test. Two common methods for funnel asymmetry test are Begg and Mazumdar's rank correlation test (hereafter, Begg test), and Egger's regression test (hereafter, Egger test). Begg test reports the rank correlation (Kendall's tau) between the standardized effect size and its precision. A Tau statistic deviating from zero will suggest the presence of publication bias (Sterne et al. 2000). On the other hand, Egger test regresses the standardized effect size against its precision, as follows:

$$t_{ij} = \frac{PCC_{ij}}{SEPCC_{ij}} = \beta_0 + \beta_1 \frac{1}{SEPCC_{ij}} + \vartheta_{ij} \qquad (5)$$

where, t_{ij} is the standardized effect size, $\frac{1}{SEPCC_{ij}}$ is the precision of effect size, β_0 measures the asymmetry, β_1 is the true effect of the population, and ϑ_{ij} is the error term. The larger the deviation of β_0 from zero, the more pronounced the asymmetry, and more severe the bias (Egger et al. 1997).

Both the Begg and Egger tests in Table 2 confirms the presence of publication bias as suggested in the funnel plot in Figure 2.

Table 2. Funnel asymmetry test for publication bias.

	Begg Test		Egger Test	
	z	p-Value	β_0	p-Value
Bias	−3.48	<0.0001	−0.454	0.039
Observation	910		910	

However, there are factors other than publication bias that can cause asymmetry, such as true heterogeneity, data irregularities, poor study design (Egger et al. 1997). Peters et al. (2008) suggest the use of a contour-enhanced funnel plot to differentiate asymmetry due to publication bias from other factors. It displays areas of statistical significance, which is derived from the estimated effect sizes and their standard errors, on a funnel plot. If there are missing studies in areas of statistical non-significance (for example, p-value > 0.1), the publication bias causes the asymmetry. Conversely, it might be due to other factors. The contour-enhanced funnel plot in Figure 3 shows that published studies are found not only in the areas of statistical significance (shaded area) but also in areas of statistical non-significance (white area). Thus, publication bias is not the only cause of asymmetry.

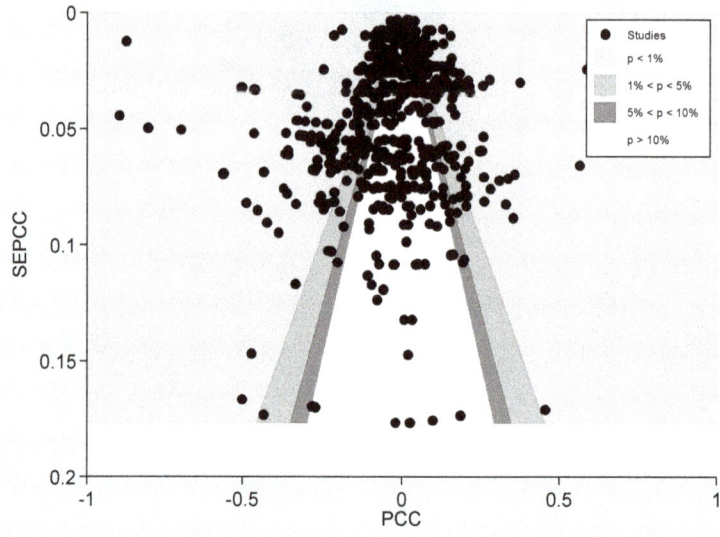

Figure 3. Contour-enhanced funnel plot of standardized effects of capital on risk (PCC).

2.4. Meta-Regression Analysis

To investigate whether the effect of capital on risk is affected by study characteristics, we employ a multivariate meta-regression analysis. It is a powerful method to assess and explore the variability of reported results by the synthesizing of empirical evidence (Stanley and Jarrell 1989). Our meta-regression model is as follows:

$$PCC_{ij} = \gamma_0 + \sum_{k=1}^{K} \gamma_k D_{kij} + u_{kij} \qquad (6)$$

where, D_{kij} are independent variables kth describing study characteristics; γ are coefficients to be estimated; u_{kij} is error term. We codify the study characteristics that potentially affect PCC variation into seven groups. These groups include measurement of risk variable, measurement of capital variable, study model, estimation method, sample characteristics, and publication quality.

The summary of these variables in Table 3 shows that the effect of bank capital on risk (PCC) varies across risk measurements. An average negative effect of bank capital on risk is reported in studies using RWATA, MARKET, and PROFIT_VOL as risk measurement. Whereas, when risk is referred to as CREDIT and Z-SCORE, the effect is positive. Among risk measurements, credit (CREDIT) and market risks measurements (MARKET) are the most frequently used. Similarly, the effect of bank capital on risk also varies across measurements and transformation of capital. Regulatory total capital (CAP) and Equity (EQUITY) are popular measurements of capital. Except for studies using Tier 1 ratio (TIER1) as capital measurement, all other studies report a negative effect of bank capital on risk. Almost half of estimations consider the endogeneity of capital (ENDO) and unobserved time fixed effects (TIME_EFFECT). These models are estimated with different methods, varying from the simple Ordinary Least Square (EST_OLS) to Instrumental Variables estimation (EST_IV) or dynamic model estimation (EST_DYN). Despite different models and methods used, there is a persistent average negative effect of capital on risk. Annual data (ANNUAL_DATA) are mostly used. Most studies are conducted in high-income countries (HIGH). In addition, a negative PCC, on average, is reported in most countries. Noteworthy, journal articles (JNAL), especially those published in high quality journals (PUB_QUAL), tend to report negative estimates.

Table 3. Main variables in meta-regression analysis.

Variable	Label	Description	N	Mean PCC	S.D
Dependent variable	PCC	Standardized effect of bank capital on risk	910	−0.019	0.151
Measurement of RISK variable	RWATA	Dummy variable, equal 1 if risk is measured as Risk-weighted assets over Total assets	132	−0.003	0.163
	CREDIT	Dummy variable, equal 1 if risk is measured as Non-performing loan ratio, loan loss reserve/provision ratio, Risk-weighted loans over assets, Distance to Default	325	0.012	0.146
	MARKET	Dummy variable, equal 1 if risk is measured as total market risk, idiosyncratic risk, specific risk, systematic risk, market risk	226	−0.034	0.110
	ZSCORE	Dummy variable, equal 1 if risk is measured as Z-score	105	0.125	0.200
	PROFIT_VOL	Dummy variable, equal 1 if risk is measured as standard deviation of bank profitability (ROA, ROE)	95	−0.031	0.119
	RISK_OTHER	Dummy variable, equal 1 if less frequent measurements of risk are used (Reference Group)	43	0.066	0.126
	RISK_DIF	Dummy variable, equal 1 if RISK is measured in first differences	202	0.007	0.127

Table 3. *Cont.*

Variable	Label	Description	N	Mean PCC	S.D
Measurement of CAPITAL variable	CAP	Dummy variable, equal 1 if the numerator in capital measurement is Total Regulatory Capital	324	−0.022	0.153
	TIER1	Dummy variable, equal 1 if the numerator in capital measurement is Tier 1 Regulatory Capital	190	0.006	0.129
	EQUITY	Dummy variable, equal 1 if the numerator in capital measurement is Equity	341	−0.029	0.156
	CAP_TA	Dummy variable, equal 1 if the denominator in capital measurement is Total Assets	507	−0.003	0.157
	CAP_RWA	Dummy variable, equal 1 if the numerator in capital measurement is Risk-weighted Assets (Reference group)	383	−0.037	0.137
	CAP_OTHER	Dummy variable, equal 1 if less frequent measurements of capital are used (Reference Group)	64	−0.014	0.159
Model	NONLN	Dummy variable, equal 1 if capital is quadratic or interacted with other variables	133	0.008	0.105
	DYN	Dummy variable, equal 1 if the dynamic of risk is considered	301	−0.033	0.154
	ENDO	Dummy variable, equal 1 if the endogeneity of capital is considered	410	−0.019	0.143
	TIME_EFFECT	Dummy variable, equal 1 if Time effect is considered	449	−0.024	0.121
	VAR_NO [a]	Number of explanatory variables in the model	910	9.841	4.413
Estimation Method	EST_OLS	Dummy variable, equal 1 if estimation method is pooled OLS	218	−0.017	0.156
	EST_PANEL	Dummy variable, equal 1 if estimation method is Fixed Effects, Random Effects, Least Square Dummy Variables	230	−0.013	0.156
	EST_IV	Dummy variable, equal 1 if estimation method is Instrumental Variables estimation	214	−0.004	0.155
	EST_DYN	Dummy variable, equal 1 if estimation method is Dynamic Panel Data estimation	201	−0.049	0.139
	EST_OTHER	Dummy variable, equal 1 if less frequently method is used (Reference Group)	81	0.0004	0.113
Sample Characteristics	SAMPLE [a]	The logarithm of the total number of observations used	910	6.981	1.639
	DATA_ANNUAL	Dummy variable, equal 1 if annual data is used, 0 if higher frequency data is used	780	−0.021	0.157
	BHC	Dummy variable, equal 1 if only bank holding companies are examined	204	−0.032	0.104
	COM	Dummy variable, equal 1 if only commercial banks are examined	246	−0.042	0.16
	TYPE_OTHER	Dummy variable, equal 1 if other bank types or a mix of banks are examined (Reference Group)	664	−0.011	0.146
	HIGH	Dummy variable, equal 1 if the study is conducted in high income countries	445	−0.014	0.121
	UPPER	Dummy variable, equal 1 if the study is conducted in upper income countries	59	−0.072	0.225
	LOW	Dummy variable, equal 1 if the study is conducted in lower and low-income countries	102	−0.117	0.217
Publication Characteristics	JNAL	Dummy variable, equal 1 if the study was published as a journal article, 0 if the study is a working paper	815	−0.016	0.154
	PUB_QUAL	Dummy variable, equal 1 if the study was published in a journal indexed in ISI, SSCI, or ranked in ABDC list, 0 otherwise	629	−0.01	0.152
	CITE [a]	The logarithm of the number of Google Scholar citations normalized by the difference between 2018 and the year the study first appeared in Google Scholar	910	0.573	0.484

Notes: [a] For continuous variables, their means and standard deviations are reported instead.

There are a large number of potential factors of PCC variation. This causes model uncertainty problem and affects the study inference. Therefore, we apply Bayesian model-averaging techniques, specifically the Bayesian model-averaging (BMA) and the weighted-average least-squares (WALS) estimators to address the model uncertainty and identify potential factors of PCC. Both estimators consider all possible combinations of explanatory variables and estimate the parameters of interest as a weighted average of conditional estimates of each model. The BMA approach combines prior beliefs on the uncertain variables of the model with the additional information from the data and weights these individual regressions using the posterior model probabilities (PMP). The relevance important of a variable is reflected in the posterior inclusion probability (PIP), which is calculated by summing PMP of all models consisting the variable (Leamer 1978). A variable is robust if it has a PIP value at least 0.50 (Raftery 1995).

However, the BMA estimator encounters the computational burden proportional to the dimension of the model space, the difficulty in choosing the prior distribution where no prior information is available, as well as the unbounded risk related to the chosen priors (Magnus et al. 2010). Therefore, the WALS estimator is an alternative to the BMA since it relies on preliminary orthogonal transformations of the uncertain regressors and their parameters. WALS has proved useful with equivalent estimations to BMA (De Luca et al. 2018, Magnus et al. 2010). A variable is robustly correlated with the dependent variable if the absolute t-ratio is greater than 1 (Magnus et al. 2010).

3. Results

Table 4 reports the estimations of Equation (6) employing both BMA and WALS estimators. Our model comprises 29 explanatory variables and result a model space of 2^{29} models. With a small to moderate (less than 20) number of variables, the BMA calculation can be completed within one hour. However, when the number of explanatory variables is large (more than 20), it can take up to thousand years (Luca and Magnus 2011). Therefore, we use the Markov chain Monte Carlo (MCMC) samplers, which gather results on the most important part of the posterior model distribution and approximate it as closely to the actual posterior distribution as possible. The quality of the MCMC approximation depends on the number of draws of the MCMC samplers. We set this number at 1 million. Figure A1 in the Appendix B shows that the correlation between iteration counts and analytical PMPs for the 5000 best models is 0.997. This indicates a good convergence of MCMC samplers. For the WALS estimator, we follow (Einmahl et al. 2011) to use Subbotin prior instead of the Gaussian and Laplace due to its less fat and thicker tails distribution. For robustness, we also report the Ordinary Least Square (OLS) estimation to see how the estimations without model uncertainty consideration differ.

Table 4 shows that the most robust determinants in BMA estimator are risk measurements (MARKET, ZSCORE, and RISK_DIF), capital measurements (EQUITY and CAP_TA), model setting (DYN and TIME_EFFECT), data characteristics (SAMPLE), and publication characteristics (PUB_QUAL and CITE). The WALS estimator confirms the importance of these variables except for TIME_EFFECT and PUB_QUAL. It also emphasizes the importance of risk and capital measurements by suggesting the robustness of PROF_VOL, CAP and TIER1. In addition, the endogeneity in the empirical model (ENDO), the larger number of explanatory variables (VAR_NO), the sample for bank-holding companies (BHC), high-income countries (HIGH) and the publication in journals (JNAL) are also important determinants. The estimations in BMA and WALS are quite similar. Disregarding the model uncertainty, the OLS regression comprises a larger set of variables than BMA estimator but quite different from the WALS. This suggests the superior and necessary of model uncertainty consideration.

The effect of capital on risk (PCC) will be negative if the dependent variable uses market measures of risk (MARKET) or profit volatility (PROF_VOL), but positive if the risk is referred to as the bank insolvency (ZSCORE). In addition, the effect is positive if risk is measured in first differences (RISK_DIF). This suggests that the risk measurement is important for the result inference. The capital measurement also affects the conclusion. If the capital is measured as total regulatory capital (CAP) or equity (EQUITY), the effect will be negative. Conversely, if the capital is measured as Tier capital (TIER1) or standardized by the total assets (CAP_TA), instead of the risk-weighted assets, the effect will be positive. Among 15 potential factors affecting PCC, half of them are from the risk and capital measurements. The effects of these factors are also large compared to other explanatory variables.

Table 4. Bayesian model averaging regression.

Variables	BMA				WALS				OLS		
	Coef.	SE	PIP	Coef.	SE		t		Coef.	SE	P > t
RWATA	−0.0228	0.0267	0.4798	−0.0673	0.0218	0.22	−0.0213	0.0337	0.5280
CREDIT	0.0034	0.0105	0.1275	−0.0274	0.0187	0.46	−0.0082	0.0261	0.7530
MARKET	−0.0427 [a]	0.0234	0.8428	−0.0590 [b]	0.0187	1.29	−0.0376	0.0262	0.1510
ZSCORE	0.1362 [a]	0.0185	1.0000	0.0954 [b]	0.0209	4.55	−0.1287 ***	0.0349	0.0000
PROFIT_VOL	−0.0012	0.0067	0.0539	−0.0556 [b]	0.0214	1.61	−0.0404	0.0273	0.1390
RISK_DIF	0.0605 [a]	0.0241	0.9344	0.0692 [b]	0.0184	2.62	0.0653***	0.0196	0.0010
CAP	−0.0070	0.0140	0.2427	−0.0117 [b]	0.0201	1.16	0.0315	0.0203	0.1200
TIER1	0.0020	0.0079	0.0883	0.0098 [b]	0.0213	1.19	0.0336 *	0.0200	0.0940
EQUITY	−0.0656 [a]	0.0165	0.9970	−0.0587 [b]	0.0221	1.55	−0.0428 **	0.0204	0.0360
CAP_TA	0.0991 [a]	0.0149	1.0000	0.0760 [b]	0.0138	5.28	0.1018 ***	0.0180	0.0000
NONLN	−0.0008	0.0048	0.0443	−0.0325	0.0145	0.78	−0.0122	0.0153	0.4250
DYN	−0.0769 [a]	0.0135	1.0000	−0.0664 [b]	0.0134	3.31	−0.0535 ***	0.0156	0.0010
ENDO	−0.0002	0.0025	0.0266	−0.0058 [b]	0.0133	1.15	−0.0260 *	0.0153	0.0890
TIME_EFFECT	−0.0391 [a]	0.0147	0.9543	−0.0400	0.0113	0.34	−0.0102	0.0157	0.5170
EST_OLS	−0.0004	0.0032	0.0308	0.0207	0.0198	0.68	0.0158	0.0212	0.4560
EST_PANEL	0.0005	0.0035	0.0401	0.0379 [b]	0.0169	2.09	0.0450 **	0.0177	0.0110
EST_IV	0.0078	0.0157	0.2430	0.0433	0.0214	0.76	0.0245	0.0207	0.2380
EST_DYN	0.0001	0.0025	0.0226	0.0406	0.0220	0.13	0.0168	0.0256	0.5120
VAR_NO	0.0000	0.0002	0.0230	0.0019 [b]	0.0011	1.11	0.0016	0.0013	0.2200
SAMPLE	0.0057 [a]	0.0052	0.6172	0.0119 [b]	0.0036	3.05	0.0129 ***	0.0049	0.0080
DATA_ANNUAL	−0.0001	0.0030	0.0247	−0.0052	0.0161	0.42	0.0025	0.0172	0.8840
BHC	−0.0085	0.0158	0.2699	−0.0316 [b]	0.0173	1.99	−0.0319	0.0211	0.1300
COM	−0.0015	0.0064	0.0756	−0.0178	0.0117	0.65	−0.0044	0.0164	0.7890
HIGH	−0.0005	0.0036	0.0417	0.0057 [b]	0.0118	2.28	0.0287 **	0.0133	0.0310
UPPER	0.0157	0.0251	0.3312	0.0587	0.0180	0.11	0.0080	0.0296	0.7870
LOW	0.0007	0.0122	0.0195	0.0866	0.0753	0.49	0.0391	0.0954	0.6820
JNAL	−0.0001	0.0033	0.0230	0.0042 [b]	0.0162	1.95	0.0360 *	0.0209	0.0850
PUB_QUAL	0.0310 [a]	0.0193	0.7940	0.0349	0.0108	0.89	−0.0188	0.0172	0.2740
CITE	0.0191 [a]	0.0199	0.5489	0.0245 [b]	0.0119	6.00	0.0838 ***	0.0159	0.0000

Notes: BMA estimation uses the MCMC samplers. WALS estimation employs the Subbotin prior ($q = 0.5$). [a] denotes a PIP larger than 0.5. [b] denotes a t absolute value larger than 1. *, **, and *** denote significance at the 10%, 5%, and 1% level, respectively. Robust standard errors in OLS regression.

Another source of PCC variation is the model setting. If the model is concerned about the dynamic of bank risk behaviors (DYN), the endogeneity of the capital (ENDO) and unobserved time fixed effects (TIME_EFFECT), the reported coefficients will be negative. Against our expectation, the estimation method does not alter the effect of capital on risk, except for the panel data estimation (EST_PANEL). The sample and publication characteristics affect PCC in the same way that the reported effects are positive. However, studies on bank-holding companies (BHC) will report a negative PCC.

4. Further Analysis

4.1. Different Risk Measurements

Results in Table 4 suggest that the effect of capital on risk varies with the risk measurements. Figure 4 displays the distribution of PCC across different risk measurements. Even using the same measurement, PCCs still vary. There is evidence of both positive and negative effects of capital on risk. Therefore, we re-estimate Equation (6) on different risk measurements to examine the underlying factors of these variations.

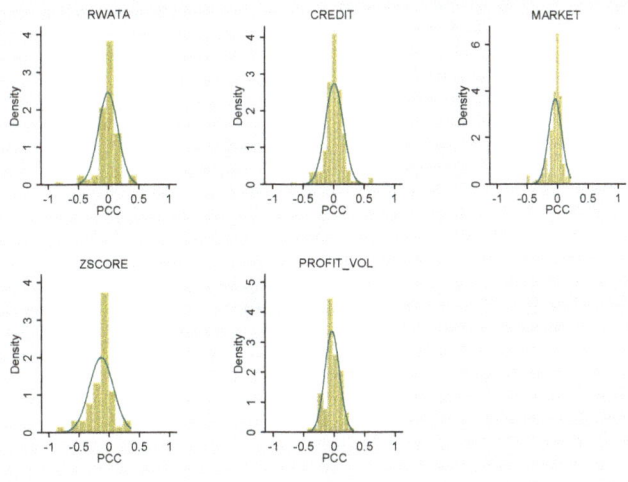

Figure 4. The PCC distribution by risk measurements.

Table 5 reports the WALS estimation on different risk measurements. EQUITY and LOW are omitted in the RWATA estimation to avoid the multicollinearity since there are few studies employing the EQUITY measurement and no studies are carried out in low and lower-income countries. Similarly, LOW is omitted in MARKET and ZSCORE estimations. In addition, most ZSCORE studies are journals, thus, JNAL is omitted in the ZSCORE estimation.

Table 5 shows that the determinants of PCC variations and their effects across risk measurements are similar to the total sample in Table 4 despite some slight differences. Specifically, measurement by regulatory capital (CAP) and Tier 1 capital (TIER1) will have positive effect on the reported PCC of credit risk (CREDIT) and market risk (MARKET), while exert negative influences on other risk measurements. The consideration of endogeneity (ENDO) and time fixed effects (TIME_EFFECT) will lead to positive reported PCC for RWATA and ZSCORE. When risk is regarded as market risk (MARKET), a panel model setting will result a negative PCC. Whereas, when risk is referred as ZSCORE, the larger the sample, the more negative the PCC is. Studies in high income countries will have a negative effect on PCC of credit risk (CREDIT) and ZSCORE. In addition, the effect of publication characteristics also varies across risk measurements.

Table 5. WALS Estimations on Different Risk Measurements.

	RWATA		CREDIT		MARKET		ZSCORE		PROFIT_VOL	
	Coef.	|t|	Coef.	|t|	Coef.	|t|	Coef.	|t|	Coef.	|t|
RISK_DIF	−0.0440	0.57	0.1090 *	3.89	−0.1180 *	1.09	0.1270 *	1.63	0.0730	0.60
CAP	−0.0410	0.67	0.0210	0.84	0.1430 *	4.57	−0.0900 *	1.20	−0.1200 *	1.38
TIER1	−0.0300	0.45	0.0370 *	1.34	0.1300 *	4.27	−0.0270	0.34	−0.1890	0.79
EQUITY			−0.0500 *	1.93	0.0390	0.65	−0.1500 *	1.83	−0.1890 *	2.00
CAP_TA	0.1130 *	2.51	0.0940 *	4.40	−0.0230	0.35	0.0730 *	1.22	0.0750 *	1.49
NONLN	0.0400 *	1.03	−0.0110	0.45	−0.1120 *	3.57	−0.1130 *	1.89	0.1670 *	1.65
DYN	−0.1630 *	2.79	−0.0740 *	4.20	0.0440	0.58	−0.0820 *	1.31	−0.0910 *	1.06
ENDO	0.1300 *	1.47	−0.0440 *	1.99	−0.0280 *	1.05	0.1910 *	2.91	−0.1570 *	1.97
TIME_EFFECT	0.0470 *	1.00	−0.0470 *	2.81	0.0040	0.19	0.0100	0.25	−0.1160 *	1.03
EST_OLS	0.1020	0.98	−0.0150	0.55	−0.0270	0.53	−0.0430	0.50	−0.0640	0.34
EST_PANEL	0.0440	0.47	0.0420 *	1.84	−0.0650 *	1.28	0.0310	0.41	0.0790	0.41
EST_IV	−0.0540	0.62	0.0220	0.79	0.0580 *	1.16	−0.1080 *	1.36	0.1540 *	1.04
EST_DYN	−0.0140	0.17	0.0160	0.51	−0.0210	0.37	−0.1980 *	2.20	0.1440 *	1.05
VAR_NO	−0.0030	0.54	0.0050 *	2.66	−0.0030 *	1.79	0.0220 *	3.26	0.0110 *	1.76
SAMPLE	0.0010	0.08	0.0290 *	4.87	−0.0040	0.64	−0.0190 *	1.22	0.0080	0.63
DATA_ANNUAL	−0.2740 *	3.06	0.0370	0.81	−0.1430 *	3.66	−0.0030	0.05	0.0300	0.19
BHC	−0.2450 *	2.50	−0.0010	0.03	−0.1180 *	4.06	−0.0510	0.73	0.1700	0.71
COM	0.1320 *	2.35	−0.0590 *	3.25	0.1440 *	3.00	−0.0970 *	1.85	0.0110	0.23
HIGH	0.0190	0.39	−0.0330 *	1.74	0.0500 *	1.44	−0.1050 *	1.86	0.0020	0.04
UPPER	−0.1170 *	1.04	0.0390 *	1.42	−0.0380	0.54	0.0880 *	1.80	0.0030	0.06
LOW			0.1990 *	1.69					0.0420	0.74
JNAL	0.0550	0.47	0.0030	0.13	0.2310 *	2.06			−0.0870	0.29
PUB_QUAL	0.1910 *	2.25	−0.0280 *	1.36	−0.1530 *	5.17	0.2390 *	4.83	−0.0420	0.61
CITE	−0.1550 *	1.40	0.0670 *	3.77	0.0240	0.49	−0.3370 *	5.56	0.1920	0.61
Constant	0.0700	0.40	−0.2990 *	3.52	−0.0020	0.02	0.1910 *	1.28	−0.1540	0.84
N	132		325		226		105		95	

Notes: WALS estimation employs the Subbotin prior ($q = 0.5$). * denotes an absolute t value larger than 1.

Apart from these factors, the variation in the estimation of risk measurements is further affected by the non-linearity of model (NONLN), the instrumental variable estimation (EST_IV), the sample characteristics such as whether data is annual, whether banks are bank-holding companies or commercial banks, as well as whether banks are located in upper income countries (UPPER).

4.2. Benchmark and Best-Practice Results

To gain further insights into how the effects of capital on bank risk should be regarding different determinants of the total sample and risk measurements, we calculate the "benchmark" and "best-practice" results from these estimations. The "benchmark" results are computed from the coefficients of non-robust determinants and their sample means and thus, it implies the average study in the field (Feld et al. 2013). Whereas, the "best-practice" results are derived from the robust determinants and represents the best practice in the field. Its purpose is to correct the potential effect of wrongly specified studies (DouCouliagos 2016).

Table 6 presents the "benchmark" and "best-practice" estimates for different risk measurements and samples. The "benchmark" effect of the capital on the bank's risk-weighted assets (RWATA) is approximately 0.095. This effect is higher for bank-holding companies (BHC), but lower for commercial banks (COM), and banks in high- and upper-income countries. However, considering the scale of the capital measurement (CAPTA), the model specification (NONLN, DYN, ENDO, TIME_EFFECT), data characteristics (DATA_ANNUAL), bank types (BHC, COM), country development (UPPER), and publication characteristics (PUB_QUAL, CITE) (see Table 5), the "best practice" effect turns negative at −0.0518. Nevertheless, the positive effect is persistent across BHC and UPPER samples. Similarly, we also found a substantial difference in the effect of capital on the market risk (MARKET) between the benchmark and best-practice estimates. In addition, this effect also varies across sub-samples (Table 6). Therefore, careful treatments for the capital measurements (CAP, TIER1), model design (NONLN, ENDO), estimation techniques (EST_PANEL, EST_IV), the control variables (VAR_NO), data characteristics (DATA_ANNUAL), bank types (BHC, COM) and country development (HIGH) should be considered in estimating the effect of capital on the bank's market risk.

The effects of capital on the credit risk (CREDIT), insolvency risk (ZSCORE) and profit volatility (PROFIT_VOL) in the benchmark and best-practice estimates are of the same sign. This suggests that the studies on these risks are quite consistent. The estimates for PROFIT_VOL change greatly across samples in both benchmark and best practice results and suggests the importance of the selected sample. That is, the bank-holding companies or commercial banks, banks in high-income countries or upper income (see Table 6).

Table 6. Predicted Benchmark and Best Practice Results across Risk Measurements and Samples.

	Benchmark Results					Best Practice				
	Total	BHC	COM	HIGH	UPPER	Total	BHC	COM	HIGH	UPPER
RWATA	0.095145	0.12521	0.062582	0.089907	0.057983	−0.05177	0.141112	−0.09247	−0.04699	0.031717
CREDIT	−0.25384	−0.26528	−0.24567	−0.25831	−0.24554	−0.04857	−0.04393	−0.03629	−0.02123	−0.09672
MARKET	−0.01142	−0.02494	−0.01238	−0.01647	0.001743	0.004052	0.088588	−0.03307	−0.04116	0.034949
ZSCORE	0.173826	0.191152	0.188451	0.162209	0.190169	0.129122	0.295267	0.171561	0.275456	0.167132
PROFIT_VOL	−0.04567	−0.12419	−0.09766	−0.02968	−0.0726	−0.18316	−0.24249	−0.17905	−0.20342	−0.16056

Notes: Benchmark results are computed from the intercept, the coefficients of variables with absolute t-values less than 1 from Table 5, and their sample means.

5. Conclusions

This paper examines the effect of capital on bank risk using a meta-analysis approach. From a wide range of empirical papers from 1990 to 2018, we found that there is both positive and negative evidence on the relationship between bank capital and risk. Nevertheless, there are more negative effect to be reported. This suggests the discipline role of the capital on the bank risk.

Both funnel plots and formal funnel tests indicate the existence of the publication bias, which the significant and negative effects are more likely to be reported. This finding is not surprising since the capital regulation has gained an increasing importance recently and these negative reported effects give support to the regulation.

Nevertheless, the publication bias is not the only source of the variation. Our Bayesian Model Averaging estimations show that the reported effect of capital on bank risk is affected by the risk measurements, capital measurements, the model specification, and the sample characteristics. Even using the same risk measurements, the effect may also vary due to the different model setting and samples.

These results have significant academic and practice implications. Specifically, the researchers should consider various risk and capital measurements for the most precise estimations of the capital effect. In addition, they should carefully design the model by taking into account the non-linear effect of the capital, the dynamic of bank risk, the potential endogeneity of the capital, and the unobserved time effects since the results are sensitive to these specifications. It is preferable to have a large dataset and control for as most variables as possible. However, in such case, the attention should be paid to the sample characteristics since the risk behavior may not be homogeneous across samples.

These empirical results act as a guideline for the capital regulation in addition to the considerations for the macro-impacts. Our results also indicate that the effect of capital varies with risk types. Therefore, the regulators should consider the risk of interest, for example, the bank-specific risk or the systemic risk in designing the capital regulation. In addition, the effect of capital on risk is different across countries given their different contexts. Therefore, it is important for the regulators to consider their national markets and condition to have proper policies. In this regard, the common minimum requirements under the current Basel III framework would not be appropriate.

We acknowledge the limitations of meta-analysis in terms of the overreliance on statistics and potential sampling bias. However, there is no perfect method and meta-analysis using statistics are still superior comparing to qualitative methods such as narrative review and descriptive review. In our study, we tried to minimize these limitations' effect by including the most papers as possible by searching wide and various databases and considering working papers in addition to published articles. We are also concerned about the quality of these papers by considering the quality of journals and number of citations. The study focuses on the quantitative review of research only while theoretical papers on mathematical models, qualitative research, secondary data analysis, interviews, and case studies are omitted. Therefore, in the future, a narrative review of these articles will be a perfect complement for the current study to provide a full overview of the impact of bank capital on bank risk.

Author Contributions: Conceptualization, methodology, formal analysis, writing—original draft preparation, Q.T.T.N.; data collection and preparation, S.T.B.N.; writing—review and editing, Q.V.N.

Funding: This research received no external funding.

Conflicts of Interest: The authors declare no conflicts of interest.

Appendix A. List of Surveyed Studies

1. Abou-El-Sood, Heba. 2017. Corporate governance structure and capital adequacy: implications to bank risk taking. *International Journal of Managerial Finance* 13: 165–85.
2. Aggarwal, Raj, and Kevin T. Jacques. 2001. The impact of FDICIA and prompt corrective action on bank capital and risk: Estimates using a simultaneous equations model. *Journal of Banking & Finance* 25: 1139–60.

3. Akinsoyinu, Clements Adeyinka. 2015. The Impact of Capital Regulation on Bank Capital and Risk Decision. Evidence for European Global Systemically Important Banks.
4. Alkadamani, Khaled. 2015. Capital adequacy, bank behavior and crisis: evidence from emergent economies. *European Journal of Sustainable Development* 4: 329–38.
5. Altunbas, Yener, Santiago Carbo, P. M. Gardener Edward, and Philip Molyneux. 2007. Examining the Relationships between Capital, Risk and Efficiency in European Banking. *European Financial Management* 13: 49–70. doi:10.1111/j.1468-036X.2006.00285.x.
6. Al-Zubi, Khaled, Mohammad Al-Abadi, and Hanadi Afaneh. 2008. Capital adequacy, risk profiles and bank behaviour: Empirical evidence from Jordan. *Jordan Journal of Business Administration* 4: 89–106.
7. Angkinand, Apanard Penny, James R. Barth, John S. Jahera, Jr., Triphon Phumiwasana, and Clas Wihlborg. 2013. Regulatory and market forces in controlling bank risk-taking: a cross-country analysis. *Journal of Current Issues in Finance, Business and Economics* 6: 271–86.
8. Ashraf, Badar, Sidra Arshad, and Yuancheng Hu. 2016. Capital Regulation and Bank Risk-Taking Behavior: Evidence from Pakistan. *International Journal of Financial Studies* 4: 16.
9. Athanasoglou, Panayiotis. 2011. "Bank capital and risk in the South Eastern European region." Working paper No.137. Bank of Greece.
10. Awdeh, Ali, C El-Moussawi, and Fouad Machrouh. 2011. The effect of capital requirements on banking risk. *International Research Journal of Finance and Economics* 66: 133–46.
11. Banerjee, Gaurango, Abhiman Das, Kalidas Jana, and Shekar Shetty. 2017. Effects of derivatives usage and financial statement items on capital market risk measures of Bank stocks: evidence from India. *Journal of Economics and Finance* 41: 487–504. doi:10.1007/s12197-016-9366-6.
12. Barrell, Ray, E Philip Davis, Tatiana Fic, and Dilruba Karim. 2011. Bank capital composition, regulation and risk taking. Working paper. NIESR and Brunel University, London.
13. Basher, Syed Abul, Lawrence M. Kessler, and Murat K. Munkin. 2017. Bank capital and portfolio risk among Islamic banks. *Review of Financial Economics* 34: 1–9. doi:10.1016/j.rfe.2017.03.004.
14. Beatty, Anne, and Anne Gron. 2001. Capital, portfolio, and growth: Bank behavior under risk-based capital guidelines. *Journal of Financial Services Research* 20: 5–31. doi:10.1023/A:1011146725028.
15. Berger, Allen N. 1995. The relationship between capital and earnings in banking. *Journal of Money, Credit and Banking* 27: 432–56.
16. Bichsel, Robert, and Jürg Blum. 2004. The relationship between risk and capital in Swiss commercial banks: a panel study. *Applied Financial Economics* 14: 591–97. doi:10.1080/0960310042000233881.
17. Bitar, Mohammad, Wadad Saad, and Mohammed Benlemlih. 2016. Bank risk and performance in the MENA region: The importance of capital requirements. *Economic Systems* 40: 398–421. doi:10.1016/j.ecosys.2015.12.001.
18. Blundell-Wignall, Adrian, and Caroline Roulet. 2013. Macro-prudential policy, bank systemic risk and capital controls. *OECD Journal. Financial Market Trends* 2013: 7–28. doi:10.1787/19952872.
19. Bougatef, Khemaies, and Nidhal Mgadmi. 2016. The impact of prudential regulation on bank capital and risk-taking: The case of MENA countries. *The Spanish Review of Financial Economics* 14: 51–56. doi:10.1016/j.srfe.2015.11.001.
20. Bouheni, Faten Ben, Hachmi Ben Ameur, Abdoulkarim Idi Cheffou, and Fredj Jawadi. 2014. The Effects of Regulation and Supervision on European Banking Profitability and Risk: A Panel Data Investigation. *Journal of Applied Business Research* 30: 16–65.
21. Bouheni, Faten Ben, and Houssem Rachdi. 2015. Bank Capital Adequacy Requirements And Risk-Taking Behavior In Tunisia: A Simultaneous Equations Framework. *Journal of Applied Business Research* 31: 231.
22. Camara, Boubacar, Laetitia Lepetit, and Amine Tarazi. 2013. Ex ante capital position, changes in the different components of regulatory capital and bank risk. *Applied Economics* 45: 4831–56.

23. Cannata, Francesco, and Mario Quagliariello. 2006. Capital and risk in Italian banks: A simultaneous equation approach. *Journal of Banking Regulation* 7: 283–97.
24. Carey, Mark. 1995. Partial market value accounting, bank capital volatility, and bank risk. *Journal of Banking & Finance* 19: 607–22. doi:10.1016/0378-4266(94)00142-P.
25. Cebenoyan, A. Sinan, and Philip E. Strahan. 2004. Risk management, capital structure and lending at banks. *Journal of Banking & Finance* 28: 19–43. doi:10.1016/S0378-4266(02)00391-6.
26. Coote, Howard. 2004. Bank Default Risk and Capital Regulation: Evidence from Jamaica. Paper presented at the XXXVI Annual Monetary Studies Conference, Bank of Jamaica.
27. Nachane, D. M., and Ghosh Saibal. 2001. Risk-Based Standards, Portfolio Risk and Bank Capital: An Econometric Study. *Economic and Political Weekly* 36: 871–76.
28. Das, Nupur Moni, and Joyeeta Deb. 2017. Regulatory Capital and Its Impact on Credit Risk: The Case of Indian Commercial Banks. *IUP Journal of Bank Management* 16: 7–22.
29. Deelchand, Tara, and Carol Padgett. 2009. The relationship between risk, capital and efficiency: Evidence from Japanese cooperative banks. Working paper
30. Delis, Manthos D., Kien C. Tran, and Efthymios G. Tsionas. 2012. Quantifying and explaining parameter heterogeneity in the capital regulation-bank risk nexus. *Journal of Financial Stability* 8: 57–68. doi:10.1016/j.jfs.2011.04.002.
31. Demsetz, Rebecca S., and Philip E. Strahan. 1997. Diversification, Size, and Risk at Bank Holding Companies. *Journal of Money, Credit and Banking* 29: 300–13. doi:10.2307/2953695.
32. Deng, Saiying, and Elyas Elyasiani. 2008. Geographic Diversification, Bank Holding Company Value, and Risk. *Journal of Money, Credit and Banking* 40: 1217–38.
33. Dionne, Georges, and Tarek M. Harchaoui. 2008. Bank Capital, Securitization and Credit Risk: an Empirical Evidence. *Assurances et Gestion des Risques* 75: 459–84.
34. Dong, Xianlei, Jia Liu, and Beibei Hu. 2012. Research on the relationship of commercial bank's loan loss provision and earning management and capital management. *Journal of Service Science and Management* 5: 171.
35. ElBannan, Mona A. 2015. Do consolidation and foreign ownership affect bank risk taking in an emerging economy? An empirical investigation. *Managerial Finance* 41: 874–907.
36. Gaston, Giordana, and Ingmar Schumacher. 2012. An Empirical Study on the Impact of Basel III Standards on Banks? Default Risk: The Case of Luxembourg. Working paper No. 37. St. Louis: Federal Reserve Bank of St Louis.
37. Gatev, Evan, Til Schuermann, and Philip E. Strahan. 2009. Managing Bank Liquidity Risk: How Deposit-Loan Synergies Vary with Market Conditions. *The Review of Financial Studies* 22: 995–1020.
38. Godlewski, Christophe J. 2005. Bank capital and credit risk taking in emerging market economies. *Journal of Banking Regulation* 6: 128–45.
39. Gregory, Katina, and Gerhard Hambusch. 2015. Factors driving risk in the US banking industry. *International Journal of Managerial Finance* 11: 388–410.
40. Grossman, Richard S., and Masami Imai. 2013. Contingent capital and bank risk-taking among British banks before the First World War. *The Economic History Review* 66: 132.
41. Hao, Jia, and Kuncheng KC Zheng. 2016. Bank Equity Capital and Risk-Taking Behavior: The Effect of Competition. Working paper.
42. Haq, Mamiza, Robert Faff, Rama Seth, and Sunil Mohanty. 2014. Disciplinary tools and bank risk exposure. *Pacific-Basin Finance Journal* 26: 37–64. doi:10.1016/j.pacfin.2013.10.005.
43. Hogan, Thomas L. 2015. Capital and risk in commercial banking: A comparison of capital and risk-based capital ratios. *The Quarterly Review of Economics and Finance* 57: 32–45. doi:10.1016/j.qref.2014.11.003.
44. Hogan, Thomas L., and Neil R. Meredith. 2016. Risk and risk-based capital of U.S. bank holding companies. *Journal of Regulatory Economics* 49: 86–112. doi:10.1007/s11149-015-9289-8.

45. Holod, Dmytro, Yuriy Kitsul, and Gökhan Torna. 2017. Market risk-based capital requirements, trading activity, and bank risk. *Journal of Banking and Finance*. doi:10.1016/j.jbankfin.2017.08.019.
46. Hoque, Hafiz, Dimitris Andriosopoulos, Kostas Andriosopoulos, and Raphael Douady. 2015. Bank regulation, risk and return: Evidence from the credit and sovereign debt crises. *Journal of Banking & Finance* 50: 455–74. doi:10.1016/j.jbankfin.2014.06.003.
47. How, Janice C. Y., Karim Melina Abdul, and Peter Verhoeven. 2005. Islamic financing and bank risks: The case of Malaysia. *Thunderbird International Business Review* 47: 75–94.
48. Hussain, M Ershad, and M Kabir Hassan. 2005. Basel capital requirements and bank credit risk taking in developing countries. Working paper.
49. Jabra, Wiem Ben, Zouheir Mighri, and Faysal Mansouri. 2017. Bank capital, profitability and risk in BRICS banking industry. *Global Business and Economics Review* 19: 89–119
50. Jacques, Kevin, and Peter Nigro. 1997. Risk-based capital, portfolio risk, and bank capital: A simultaneous equations approach. *Journal of Economics and Business* 49: 533–47. doi:10.1016/s0148-6195(97)00038-6.
51. Kalluru, Siva Reddy. 2009. Ownership Structure, Performance and Risk in Indian Commercial Banks. *IUP Journal of Applied Finance* 15: 31–45.
52. Kasman, Adnan, and Oscar Carvallo. 2013. Efficiency and Risk in Latin American Banking: Explaining Resilience. *Emerging Markets Finance and Trade* 49: 105–30. doi:10.2753/REE1540-496X490207.
53. Kouretas, Georgios, Chris Tsoumas, and Anastasios A. Drakos. 2013. Ownership, institutions and bank risk-taking in Central and Eastern European countries. Working paper. St. Louis: Federal Reserve Bank of St Louis.
54. Kumar, Vijay, Abdur Rahman Aleemi, and Akhtiar Ali. 2015. The Determinants of Systematic Risk: Empirical Evidence from Pakistan's Banking Sector. *Global Management Journal for Academic & Corporate Studies* 5: 146–54.
55. Laeven, Luc, Lev Ratnovski, and Hui Tong. 2016. Bank size, capital, and systemic risk: Some international evidence. *Journal of Banking & Finance* 69: S25–S34. doi:10.1016/j.jbankfin.2015.06.022.
56. Lee, Chien-Chiang, and Meng-Fen Hsieh. 2013. The impact of bank capital on profitability and risk in Asian banking. *Journal of International Money and Finance* 32: 251–81. doi:10.1016/j.jimonfin.2012.04.013.
57. Lee, Chien-Chiang, Shao-Lin Ning, and Chi-Chuan Lee. 2015. How does Bank Capital Affect Bank Profitability and Risk? Evidence from China's WTO Accession. *China & World Economy* 23: 19–39, doi:10.1111/cwe.12119.
58. Lee, Tung-Hao, and Shu-Hwa Chih. 2013. Does financial regulation affect the profit efficiency and risk of banks? Evidence from China's commercial banks. *North American Journal of Economics and Finance* 26: 705.
59. Lin, Shu Ling, Dar-Yeh Hwang, Keh Luh Wang, and Zhe Wen Xie. 2013. Banking Capital and Risk-taking Adjustment under Capital Regulation: The Role of Financial Freedom, Concentration and Governance Control. *International Journal of Management, Economics and Social Sciences* 2: 99–128.
60. Lin, Shu Ling. 2011. Do supervisory mechanisms or market discipline relate to bank capital requirements and risk-taking adjustment? International evidence. *African Journal of Business Management* 5: 2766–85. doi:10.5897/AJBM10.1108.
61. Lucia Dalla, Pellegrina. 2012. Does capitalization enhance efficient risk undertaking? *Accounting Research Journal* 25: 185–207. doi:10.1108/10309611211290167.
62. Maji, Santi Gopal, and Utpal Kumar De. 2015. Regulatory capital and risk of Indian banks: a simultaneous equation approach. *Journal of Financial Economic Policy* 7: 140–56.
63. Makri, Vasiliki. 2016. Towards an investigation of credit risk determinants in Eurozone countries. *Accounting and Management Information Systems* 15: 27–57.

64. Maraghni, Hichem. 2016. Bank Regulation, Capital Ratio Behaviour and Risk Taking in a Simultanious Approach. *International Journal of Financial Research* 8: 43.
65. Michalak, Tobias C., and André Uhde. 2012. Credit risk securitization and bank soundness in Europe. *Quarterly Review of Economics and Finance* 52: 272.
66. Mohammad, M. Rahman, Zheng Changjun, and N. Ashraf Badar. 2015. Bank Size, Risk-taking and Capital Regulation in Bangladesh. *Eurasian Journal of Business and Economics* 8: 95–114. doi:10.17015/ejbe.2015.015.05.
67. Moussa, Mohamed. 2015. The Relationship between Capital and Bank Risk: Evidence from Tunisia. *International Journal of Economics and Finance* 7: 223–32.
68. Pereira, João André Marques, and Richard Saito. 2015. Coordination of capital buffer and risk profile under supervision of Central Bank (Coordenação entre capital buffer e perfil de risco sob supervisão do Banco Central). *Revista Brasileira de Finanças* 13: 73–101.
69. Pham Thien Nguyen, Thanh, and Son Hong Nghiem. 2015. The interrelationships among default risk, capital ratio and efficiency. *Managerial Finance* 41: 507–25.
70. Rachdi, Houssem, Mohamed Ali Trabelsi, and Naama Trad. 2013. Banking Governance and Risk: The Case of Tunisian Conventional Banks. Working paper. St. Louis: Federal Reserve Bank of St Louis.
71. Rahman, Mohammed Mizanur, Changjun Zheng, Badar Nadeem Ashraf, and Mohammad Morshedur Rahman. 2018. Capital requirements, the cost of financial intermediation and bank risk-taking: Empirical evidence from Bangladesh. *Research in International Business and Finance* 44: 488–503. doi:10.1016/j.ribaf.2017.07.119.
72. Rahman, Nora Azureen Abdul, Nor Hayati Ahmad, and Nur Adiana Hiau Abdullah. 2012. Ownership structure, capital regulation and bank risk taking. *Journal of Business and Economics* 176.
73. Raj, Aggarwal, and T. Jacques Kevin. 1998. Assessing the impact of prompt corrective action on bank capital and risk. *Economic Policy Review—Federal Reserve Bank of New York* 4: 23–32.
74. Rajhi, Mohamed, and Wiem Hmadi. 2011. Examining the determinants of risk-taking in European banks. *Journal of Business Studies Quarterly* 3: 98–111
75. Rajhi, Mohamed Tahar, and Wiem Hmadi. 2011. Governance and bank risk-taking: a comparison analysis between commercial and cooperative French banks. *Journal of Business Studies Quarterly* 3: 260–73.
76. Rime, Bertrand. 2001. Capital requirements and bank behaviour: Empirical evidence for Switzerland. *Journal of Banking & Finance* 25: 789–805. doi:1016/S0378-4266(00)00105-9.
77. Saadaoui, Zied. 2011. Risk-based capital standards and bank behaviour in emerging and developed countries. *Journal of Banking Regulation* 12: 180–91. doi:10.1057/jbr.2010.26.
78. Sakawa, Hideaki, and Naoki Watanabel. 2016. Bank risk-taking and the board of directors' role: evidence from Japan. *Current Politics and Economics of Northern and Western Asia* 25: 585–600
79. Saunders, Anthony, Elizabeth Strock, and Nickolaos G. Travlos. 1990. Ownership Structure, Deregulation, and Bank Risk Taking. *The Journal of Finance* 45: 643–54. doi:10.2307/2328676
80. Shrieves, Ronald E., and Drew Dahl. 1992. The relationship between risk and capital in commercial banks. *Journal of Banking & Finance* 16: 439–57. doi:10.1016/0378-4266(92)90024-T.
81. Soedarmono, Wahyoe, Philippe Rous, and Amine Tarazi. 2010. Bank capital requirement, managerial self-interest and risk-taking: Evidence from Indonesian banks. Working paper.
82. Sok-Gee, Chan, Eric H. Y. Koh, and Karim Mohd Zaini Abd. 2016. The Chinese banks' directors and their risk-taking behavior. *Chinese Management Studies* 10: 291–311. doi:10.1108/CMS-10-2015-0226.
83. Tan, Yong, and Christos Floros. 2013. Risk, capital and efficiency in Chinese banking. *Journal of International Financial Markets, Institutions and Money* 26: 378–93. doi:10.1016/j.intfin.2013.07.009
84. Trabelsi, Mohamed Ali, and Naama Trad. 2017. Profitability and risk in interest-free banking industries: a dynamic panel data analysis. *International Journal of Islamic and Middle Eastern Finance and Management* 10: 454–69.

85. Van Roy, Patrick. 2008. Capital requirements and bank behavior in the early 1990s: Cross country evidence. *International Journal of Central Banking* 4: 29–60
86. Vinh, Nguyen Thi Hong. 2016. Effects of bank capital on profitability and credit risk: the case of Vietnam's commercial banks. *Journal of Economic Development*: 117–37.
87. Zhang, Zong-yi, Jun Wu, and Qiong-fang Liu. 2008. Impacts of Capital Adequacy Regulation on Risk-taking Behaviors of Banking. *Systems Engineering—Theory & Practice* 28: 183–89. doi:10.1016/S1874-8651(09)60035-1.
88. Zheng, Changjun, Niluthpaul Sarker, and Shamsun Nahar. 2018. Factors affecting bank credit risk: An empirical insight. *Journal of Applied Finance and Banking* 8: 45–67
89. Zribi, Nabila, and Younes Boujelbegrave. 2011. The factors influencing bank credit risk: The case of Tunisia. *Journal of accounting and taxation* 3: 70–78.

Appendix B

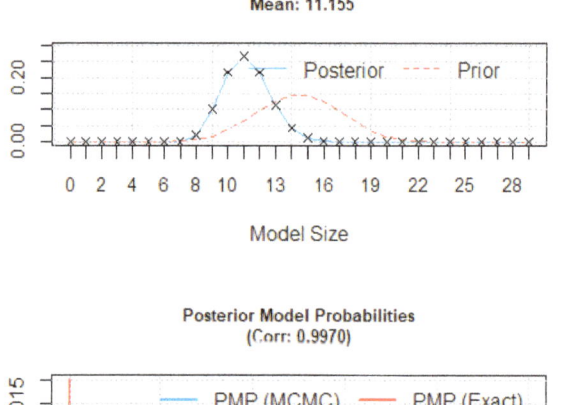

Figure A1. BMA Posterior Model Size Distribution and Probabilities.

References

Admati, Anat R., Peter M. DeMarzo, Martin F. Hellwig, and Paul Pfleiderer. 2013. *Fallacies, Irrelevant Facts, and Myths in the Discussion of Capital Regulation: Why Bank Equity Is Not Socially Expensive*. St. Louis: Federal Reserve Bank of St Louis.

Aiello, Francesco, and Graziella Bonanno. 2016. Efficiency in banking: A meta-regression analysis. *International Review of Applied Economics* 30: 112–49. [CrossRef]

Aiello, Francesco, and Graziella Bonanno. 2018. On the sources of heterogeneity in banking efficiency literature. *Journal of Economic Surveys* 32: 194–225. [CrossRef]

Altunbas, Yener, Santiago Carbo, P. M. Gardener Edward, and Philip Molyneux. 2007. Examining the Relationships between Capital, Risk and Efficiency in European Banking. *European Financial Management* 13: 49–70. [CrossRef]

BIS. 2018. History of the Basel Committee. Available online: https://www.bis.org/bcbs/history.htm?m=3%7C14%7C573%7C76 (accessed on 31 December 2018).

De Luca, Giuseppe, Jan R. Magnus, and Franco Peracchi. 2018. Weighted-average least squares estimation of generalized linear models. *Journal of Econometrics* 204: 1–17. [CrossRef]

DouCouliagos, Chris. 2016. Meta-regression analysis: Producing credible estimates from diverse evidence. *IZA World of Labor* 2016: 320. [CrossRef]

Doucouliagos, Chris, and Tom D. Stanley. 2013. Are all economic facts greatly exaggerated? Theory competition and selectivity. *Journal of Economic Surveys* 27: 316–39. [CrossRef]

Egger, Matthias, George Davey Smith, Martin Schneider, and Christoph Minder. 1997. Bias in meta-analysis detected by a simple, graphical test. *BMJ* 315: 629–34. [CrossRef] [PubMed]

Einmahl, John H. J., Kamlesh Kumar, and Jan R. Magnus. 2011. On the choice of prior in Bayesian model averaging. Discussion Paper 2011-003, Center for Economic Research, Tilburg University, Tilburg, The Netherlands.

Feld, Lars P., Jost H. Heckemeyer, and Michael Overesch. 2013. Capital structure choice and company taxation: A meta-study. *Journal of Banking & Finance* 37: 2850–66.

Fidrmuc, Jarko, and Ronja Lind. 2018. Macroeconomic Impact of Basel III: Evidence from a Meta-Analysis. *Journal of Banking & Finance*. [CrossRef]

Field, Andy P., and Raphael Gillett. 2010. How to do a meta-analysis. *British Journal of Mathematical and Statistical Psychology* 63: 665–94. [CrossRef]

Gale, Douglas. 2010. Capital regulation and risk sharing. *International Journal of Central Banking* 6: 187–204.

Gechert, Sebastian. 2015. What fiscal policy is most effective? A meta-regression analysis. *Oxford Economic Papers* 67: 553–80. [CrossRef]

Glass, Gene V. 1976. Primary, secondary, and meta-analysis of research. *Educational Researcher* 5: 3–8. [CrossRef]

King, William R, and Jun He. 2005. Understanding the role and methods of meta-analysis in IS research. *Communications of the Association for Information Systems* 16: 32. [CrossRef]

Leamer, Edward E. 1978. *Specification Searches: Ad Hoc Inference with Nonexperimental Data*. Hoboken: John Wiley & Sons Incorporated, vol. 53.

Light, Richard J., and David B. Pillemer. 1984. *Summing up; The Science of Reviewing Research*. Cambridge: Harvard University Press.

Luca, Giuseppe De, and Jan R Magnus. 2011. Bayesian model averaging and weighted-average least squares: Equivariance, stability, and numerical issues. *The Stata Journal* 11: 518–44. [CrossRef]

Magnus, Jan R., Owen Powell, and Patricia Prüfer. 2010. A comparison of two model averaging techniques with an application to growth empirics. *Journal of Econometrics* 154: 139–53. [CrossRef]

Peters, Jaime L., Alex J. Sutton, David R. Jones, Keith R. Abrams, and Lesley Rushton. 2008. Contour-enhanced meta-analysis funnel plots help distinguish publication bias from other causes of asymmetry. *Journal of Clinical Epidemiology* 61: 991–96. [CrossRef]

Raftery, Adrian E. 1995. Bayesian model selection in social research. *Sociological Methodology* 25: 111–63. [CrossRef]

Rosenthal, Robert. 1979. The file drawer problem and tolerance for null results. *Psychological Bulletin* 86: 638. [CrossRef]

Shrieves, Ronald E., and Drew Dahl. 1992. The relationship between risk and capital in commercial banks. *Journal of Banking & Finance* 16: 439–57. [CrossRef]

Stanley, Tom D., and Stephen B. Jarrell. 1989. Meta-regression analysis: A quantitative method of literature surveys. *Journal of Economic Surveys* 3: 161–70. [CrossRef]

Sterne, Jonathan A. C., David Gavaghan, and Matthias Egger. 2000. Publication and related bias in meta-analysis: Power of statistical tests and prevalence in the literature. *Journal of Clinical Epidemiology* 53: 1119–29. [CrossRef]

Valickova, Petra, Tomas Havranek, and Roman Horvath. 2015. Financial development and economic growth: A meta-analysis. *Journal of Economic Surveys* 29: 506–26. [CrossRef]

World Bank. 2018. *Global Financial Development Database*. Washington: World Bank.

Zigraiova, Diana, and Tomas Havranek. 2016. Bank competition and financial stability: Much ado about nothing? *Journal of Economic Surveys* 30: 944–81. [CrossRef]

© 2019 by the authors. Licensee MDPI, Basel, Switzerland. This article is an open access article distributed under the terms and conditions of the Creative Commons Attribution (CC BY) license (http://creativecommons.org/licenses/by/4.0/).

MDPI
St. Alban-Anlage 66
4052 Basel
Switzerland
Tel. +41 61 683 77 34
Fax +41 61 302 89 18
www.mdpi.com

Journal of Risk and Financial Management Editorial Office
E-mail: jrfm@mdpi.com
www.mdpi.com/journal/jrfm

www.ingramcontent.com/pod-product-compliance
Lightning Source LLC
LaVergne TN
LVHW070602100526
838202LV00012B/544